P9-CKP-296

DISCARDED
Library
Western Wyoming Community College

H. G. WELLS AND THE CULMINATING APE

By the same author

MURIEL SPARK

H. G. Wells and the Culminating Ape

Peter Kemp

823.912
K 32h
1982

St. Martin's Press   New York

© Peter Kemp 1982

All rights reserved. For information, write:
St. Martin's Press, Inc., 175 Fifth Avenue, New York, NY 10010
Printed in Hong Kong
First published in the United States of America in 1982

ISBN 0-312-35592-0

Library of Congress Cataloging in Publication Data

Kemp, Peter.
  H. G. Wells and the culminating ape.

  Bibliography: p.
  Includes index.
  1. Wells, H. G. (Herbert George), 1866–1946—
Knowledge—Biology. 2. Biology in literature. I. Title.
PR5778.B55K4   1982   823′.912   81-13598
ISBN 0-312-35592-0   AACR2

To David Grylls

Contents

Acknowledgements

I should like to thank Professor G. P. Wells for permission to quote from *The Outline of History, A Short History of the World, The Science of Life* and *The Work, Wealth and Happiness of Mankind*; and the Trustees of the Estate of H. G. Wells and Professor G. P. Wells for permission to quote from all other books by Wells.

In addition, I wish to acknowledge my gratitude to all who have helped in the production of this book—particularly David Grylls, Gail Cunningham, David Brown and Judith Stinton.

Introduction:
Wells and Biology

A scientific education saved Wells's life: he assumed it would do the same for the world. Poverty undermined his health from childhood onwards. Drudgery in draperies sapped his energy as a young man. Had he not got away from these conditions, he once said, he could not have survived late into life. What rescued him was the grant he won to study science at South Kensington. Before this, deprivation and frustration dragged at his vitality; after it, he bounded energetically towards affluence and achievement. Not surprisingly, he came to believe that science was—as he affirmed in his college's old students' bulletin—'the light and redemption of the world'. For over fifty years, he cast himself as the evangelist, and sometimes the messiah, of this gospel.

In his *Experiment in Autobiography*, Wells recalls the day he enrolled at the Normal School of Science as 'one of the great days of my life'. It led to what was 'beyond all question, the most educational year of my life'—a year spent studying biology with T. H. Huxley. This veteran campaigner for evolutionary theory and scientific education influenced his student in two ways. His career showed Wells what could be achieved, despite a disadvantaged background, by conviction and pugnacity. His course in biology—'a vivid, sustained attempt to see life clearly and to see it whole, to see into it, to see its inter-connexions, to find out . . . what it was, where it came from, what it was doing and where it was going'—mapped out what Wells would try to establish and convey throughout a prolific writing-life.

'To lay down the main lines of Mr Wells's *Weltanschauung*', F. H. Doughty wrote in 1926, 'necessitates a bird's-eye view of a range of material appalling in its extent.' By the time Wells died, twenty years after this, he had heaped a miscellany of nearly another fifty books onto the vast agglomeration. Understandably, the bulk (well over a hundred works) and the diversity (novels, stories, Utopias, biography and autobiography, history books, scientific text-books, an encyclopaedia of economics, religious polemic, political commentary of all kinds) have tended to discourage overall survey—ironically, perhaps, in view of Wells's own fondness for panorama and generalisation. For all its mass and medley, though, his work does have homogeneity. It is pervaded by responses to life learned in South Kensington.

One of these is a constant stress upon the species rather than the individual. In *God the Invisible King*, Wells says 'the influence of biology upon thought in general consists essentially in diminishing the importance of the individual and developing the realisation of the species'. The 'scientific method', he declares in *An Englishman Looks at the World*, is 'the method of ignoring individualities'. Individual life—even human life, he emphasises— is just an experiment, a slight modification which may, along with other slight modifications, alter a little the future development of the species to which it is utterly subordinate. 'Biologically the species is the accumulation of the experiments of all its successful individuals since the beginning', *A Modern Utopia* explains. And *The Anatomy of Frustration* sternly points out that 'The "biological use" of the individual life is not achievement but experiment, failure and a lesson.' Wells likes to back up this idea by images from the student days when he encountered it. In *The Bulpington of Blup*, Teddy Broxted unconcernedly observes, like the sane biologist he is, that 'Old individuals have to be cleared away, like exercise books that have been filled up'— though Theodore Bulpington, as a cravenly self-centred aesthete, trembles at the thought that 'He was like a test-tube' and will eventually be 'turned over to a sink and swilled away'. *First and Last Things* briskly maintains that death, for the scientist, 'ceases to possess any quality of terror': he regards his dissolution as just a familiar bit of laboratory routine—'The experiment will be over, the rinsed beaker returned to its shelf, the crystals gone dissolving down the waste-pipe.'

The unimportance of the individual is continually preached by Wells. And the doctrine strongly influences his fiction. Arnold Bennett, always one of the most perceptive commentators on Wells, told him, 'You are not really interested in individual humanity. And when you write a "non-scientific" work, you always recur to a variation of the same type of hero, and you always will, because your curiosity about individualities won't lead you any further.' In *The New Machiavelli* Wells attacks Altiora Bailey (a vindictive depiction of Beatrice Webb) on the grounds that it was 'a favourite trick' of hers 'to speak of everybody as a "type"; she saw men as samples moving'. Yet, in his novels, this is what he repeatedly does. In his first published fiction, *The Time Machine*, most of the characters are not even named but are given labels underlining their generalised nature: 'the Very Young Man', 'the Provincial Mayor', 'the Medical Man', and so on. Even a book like *Kipps*, concentrating on a single character whose life is presented in great detail, was not intended as the portrait of an individual, Wells explained to Frederick Macmillan, but as a representative picture of 'a typical member of the English lower middle class' surrounded by a 'study of living types'. In his autobiography he cheerily admits, with regard to James's convoluted dismay about the presentation of Trafford and Marjorie in *Marriage*, 'I had not thought out the individualities concerned with sufficient care and thoroughness. I had not cared enough about these individualities.' Types are what he deals in, as he keeps declaring. Glancing back at *Marriage*, *The Passionate Friends* and *The Wife of Sir Isaac Harman* in his autobiography, he stresses that 'The actors in them are types . . . rather than acutely individualized persons'; in *The Camford Visitation*, 'My characters are types'; and *The Autocracy of Mr Parham* is about 'a modern British imperialist of the university type'. Even *Apropos of Dolores*, an extremely personal attack on the idiosyncrasies of a woman Wells had lived with, claims to be a diagnosis of 'The Dolores type', of 'Dolores nations, races and peoples'.

The quality Wells most castigates Dolores for is egotism. Opposed to self-centredness—at least, in theory—he frequently attacks it in his books, and tries to counter it, not only by playing up the importance of the species but by casting doubts on the existence of individuality. His later books, in fact, proclaim that it is an illusion. *After Democracy* seeks to dismantle 'this idea of the complete integrity of individuals' by a pincer-movement employing both 'descriptive biology' and 'modern psychology'. Physiologically, it claims, 'Our particular individuality . . . does not penetrate to our interiors', since corpuscles 'have minute individualities of their own'; while psychological investigation brings to light 'minds split and divided against themselves', bizarre cases of 'divided personality'. The idea of the fragmented, incoherent personality much appeals to Wells—himself quite often given to contradictory patterns of behaviour—and he spells it out in the thesis he submitted to London University, *On the Quality of Illusion in the Continuity of the Individual Life in the Higher Metazoa, with Particular Reference to the Species Homo Sapiens*. Here, he maintains that each person is '*a collection of mutually replaceable individual systems held together in a common habitation*'; any apparent consistency derives from 'a *persona*, a behaviour mask'.

The *persona*—a concept Wells took from Jung—is, he explains in his autobiography, 'the private conception a man has of himself, his idea of what he wants to be and of how he wants other people to take him'. His own *persona* was, in many ways, that of science-teacher to the human race. His mission in life, he felt, was to make man aware of his place in nature. In keeping with this, he likes to regard himself as a biologically trained observer of the human species—'seeing human life in the light of ecological science', as he puts it in *The Outlook for Homo Sapiens*. Ecology, a very elastic term in Wells's hands, is often stretched to cover his different undertakings. *The Work, Wealth and Happiness of Mankind*, a book about economics, is described as offering 'the ecology of the human species'; *Guide to the New World* confidently talks of 'human ecology, erstwhile called history'; *Phoenix* refers to 'professors of human ecology or . . . of Foresight'.

There is, in Wells's writings, a continuing stress on the fact that men consist of 'matter with minds growing out of ourselves', as *The Sea Lady* has it. He writes in his autobiography of 'the organized mass of phosphorized fat and connective tissue which is, so to speak, the hero of the piece'. And the deliberate jolt caused by throwing a heavy emphasis on to human physicality is typical. In both *The Time Machine* and *The Island of Doctor Moreau*, there is a particularly creepy moment when a character, hunted by carnivores, hears the blood-vessels throbbing in his ears, and so catches, as it were, the sound of his own substance, what the predators are closing in to eat. The latter of these books, Wells said in his preface to the Atlantic edition, 'was written to give the utmost possible vividness' to the 'conception of men as hewn and confused and tormented beasts'. This same idea, he goes on, appears in his later works 'no longer in flaming caricature, but as a weighed and settled conviction'. The belief that 'humanity is but animal rough-hewn to a reasonable shape' is fundamental to his books, and very often voiced inside them. Stroking her slightly hairy arm, Ann Veronica affectionately murmurs, 'Etherealized monkey.' Putting things less cosily, *The Secret Places of the Heart* urgently snaps, 'Face the accepted facts. Here is a creature not ten thousand generations from the ape his ancestor.' What is said of Oswald Sydenham in *Joan and Peter*—'The view he had developed of human nature and human conditions was saturated with the idea of the ancestral ape'—applies crucially to Wells. In a very early essay on 'Human Evolution', he describes man as 'the culminating ape'. Later, his books become obsessively concerned with the possibility that man may also turn out to be a terminating ape—destroying his own species, unless he can adapt his animal nature to rapidly changing circumstances. *The Outline of History* reminds us of the 'millions of simian generations' that preceded man's existence, and the fact that he is 'still only shambling towards the light'. *'42 to '44* comments disapprovingly on the way what was once 'a swift-running ground ape' pats itself on the back with descriptions like 'Homo Sapiens' and 'Primates'. Despite this self-satisfaction, *The Outlook for Homo Sapiens* observes, man 'is no privileged exception to the general conditions that determine the destinies of other living species'. He needs to eat, mate, find a congenial habitat, and survive danger— by fighting, escaping, or co-operating with the other members of his species.

All of these activities are the subject of voluminous attention in Wells's books. They are what he is most concerned with writing about. True to his scientific training, his books concentrate on biological imperatives. But there is nothing clinically neutral about the way they do so. Wells writes not just as a biologist, but as a highly idiosyncratic personality whose very individual menagerie of hobby-horses and *bêtes noires* is unleashed at every opportunity. Food, sex, habitat, survival-mechanisms were staked out by his training as fields of investigation. His imagination piles them high with a bizarre miscellany of such things as tentacles, blood-drinkers, battling puddings, statue-women, suffragettes with squeaky voices, basements turned inside out, sex-starved dons, murderous pacifists, bicycles and bishops. Biological themes run through Wells's books as common factors. What makes them worth tracing is the fact that, where they connect with powerful obsessions, they generate uncommon excitements.

1 The Edible Predator: Wells and Food

Eating is a creature's basic need: avoiding being eaten, an accompanying necessity. 'Hunger or the hunter is the common alternative of life', Wells states in *The Work, Wealth and Happiness of Mankind*. His other books recurrently and zestfully serve up this fact with lavish helpings of documentation and dramatisation. Food obsesses him—the forms it takes, the ways it is obtained, how it is consumed, and what it does to those who are absorbing it. Larded with gastronomic metaphor, stuffed with piquant culinary tit-bits, his writing caters for all appetites, from the qualmishly vegetarian to the most raveningly cannibal. There is even, in *Bealby*, a recipe for the way he himself would prefer to be cooked, should the eventuality arise: 'If it should ever fall to my lot to be cooked, may I be fried in potatoes and butter. May I be fried with potatoes and good butter made from the milk of the cow. God send I am spared boiling; the prison of the pot, the rattling lid, the evil darkness, the greasy water.'

Memorable meals and toothsome moments garnished with odd eatables turn up constantly in Wells. His characters consume a whole spread of bizarre comestibles, from lynx-soup with brandy to exotic fruit such as hypertrophied raspberries or the 'floury thing in a three-sided husk' which becomes the Time Traveller's staple diet. 'Every day upon this planet about 1,900,000,000 people eat', we are reminded in *The Work, Wealth and Happiness of Mankind*. As a writer, Wells spends a great deal of time depicting a great many of them doing it. Continually, too, he is concerned to chart the differing effects of food and drink on his characters' appearance and morale. Malnutrition keeps some cowed and skinny; timely meals put fibre into others. Indigestion rages through his fiction like an epidemic: liverish malcontents and yellow-tinged dyspeptics grumble sourly in novel after novel as inferior cooking and low-grade ingredients take their bilious toll.

Consumption of more arcane commodities—bits of moon-plant, stimulating syrups, potent fungi—can send his protagonists into euphoria, hallucination, or off on the rampage. What and how man eats, and what this does to him, engage Wells's keenest interest and excite him into his most vivid and imaginative writing: as does the accompanying thought that man is edible, a succulent temptation to a range of predators. Eloquently testifying to this fact, human scraps regularly litter Wells's narratives. Many of his characters are eaten, falling prey to what a shark in *Mr Blettsworthy on Rampole Island* calls 'the gullet of Reality'. A large number of others narrowly escape this fate but are bitten, nibbled, mouthed, assailed by peckish bird life, leeched on by bloodthirsty orchids, or in other graphically rendered ways subjected to pre-masticatory assault. The means by which live provender, including *homo sapiens*, is captured fascinate Wells. The slithering of a tentacle towards its nutriment, bloodstained teeth, extending claws: these things seize his attention fiercely. His writing, fiction and non-fiction, offers a burstingly-stocked anthology of reference to ingestion and digestion, gluttony and near-starvation, knives and forks and teeth and claws, saliva, alimentary tracts, gastric disturbance, hearty meals, crank diets, steaks and carnivores. From the mildly helpful early pages of his first publication, *A Text Book of Biology*—'We find the rabbit occupies a considerable amount of its time in taking in vegetable matter. . . . It is a pure vegetarian, and a remarkably moderate drinker'—to the terminal exasperations of *Mind at the End of Its Tether*—'There is an internecine struggle for existence. The bigger aggregations or individuals eliminate the smaller and consume more and more. The distinctive pabulum of the type runs short'—this devouring interest holds.

Writing and food were, in fact, brought together as early as possible in Wells's career. 'Butter' was the first word he wrote, tracing it over his mother's handwriting against a window-pane, as he recalls on a couple of occasions—one of them in his *Experiment in Autobiography*, a book which also recounts the dietary deprivations of his formative years. Rather oddly in view of her choice of illustration when it came to writing-lessons, Mrs Wells's attitude to food, it emerges from this memoir, was markedly unenthusiastic. In her younger days, as a lady's maid, she recorded disapprovingly in her diary that at Christmas 'Up Park just did nothing but eat.' Years later, in Bromley, when her daughter Fanny died after the onset of appendicitis at a local children's party, she immediately concluded it must be because she 'had been given something unsuitable to eat', and never forgave the hosts. She was, Wells stresses, 'that sort of woman who is an incorrigibly bad cook'. In this, as in so many things, she differed from her husband. Left alone in the shop at Atlas House after Mrs Wells had returned to Up Park to work as housekeeper, 'He cooked very well, far better than my mother had ever done.' And a responsiveness to food seems to have stayed with him to the very end. Mr Wells's last words, in his son's account, are a recipe; he drops dead after explaining carefully the proper way to make suet pudding (it should be chopped very small, as he disliked finding in it 'lumps the size of my thumb').

Still, whatever their differing attitudes to food, the members of the family were united, during Wells's childhood, in not getting enough of it. Two of the children, he remembers, suffered badly from malnutrition. Vitamin insufficiency gave his brother Frank 'a pigeon breast and a retarded growth' while his sister Fanny developed an unnatural piety—'Such early goodness, says Dr W. R. Ackroyd (in *Vitamins and Other Dietary Essentials*) is generally a sign of some dietary deficiency, and that, I fear, is how things were with her.' Cod-liver oil, in which his mother had 'acquired a fanatical belief', saved Wells from the piety and the pigeon breast. But, though he was getting his vitamin D, other desirables were scarce: 'Sometimes there was not much to eat . . . and sometimes the cooking had been unfortunate. . . . frequently I would have headaches and bad bilious attacks in the afternoon.' This scamped and skimpy regimen continued through his childhood and youth. With the exception of a cheering interlude when his leg was accidentally broken by an older boy whose mother then plied the couch-bound invalid with placatory jellies, fruit, chicken, and brawn, Wells's account of his early eating is an unalluring retrospect of 'meagre feeding' and unpalatable fare. As the floundering little shop in Atlas House sank towards its final dissolution, 'An increasing skimpiness distinguished our catering. Bread and cheese for supper and half a herring each with our bread and butter at breakfast and a growing tendency for potatoes to dominate the stew at midday in place of meat, intimated retrenchment.' Insufficient food, Wells felt, was sapping both his body—'I was growing fast and growing very thin'— and his character—'Like most undernourished growing boys

I was cowardly.' Once the shop collapsed, however, things became a little healthier. Trying out various jobs and putting in quite lengthy visits at Up Park, he encountered 'a more varied and better dietary'. And when at last he got the opportunity he wanted and began to work as a pupil-teacher at Midhurst, Wells found life improved gastronomically as well as psychologically. His landlady there

> was a dear little energetic woman with a round friendly face, brown eyes and spectacles. I owe her incalculable things. I paid her twelve shillings a week and she fed me well. She liked cooking and she liked her food to be eaten. My meals at Midhurst are the first in my life that I remember with pleasure. Her stews were marvellously honest and she was great at junket, custard and whortleberry and blackberry jam. Bless her memory.

It must have been an interlude looked back on hungrily during the next few years, for, leaving Midhurst in triumph to become a scholarship student at South Kensington, Wells soon found he had dropped down to near-subsistence fare again. Trying hard to survive on his maintenance allowance of a guinea a week—it left him 'with only a shilling or two for a week of midday meals'— he rapidly reverted to a physically depleted state: 'underfed . . . getting perceptibly thinner and flimsier'. He recalls with gratitude the generosity of a fellow-student who 'almost by force' carried him off to a chop-house for a proper meal, kindly insisting, 'This makes competition fairer'; and points out that he was far from alone in his plight: 'I fainted only mentally, but twice in my time undernourished men fainted altogether in the laboratories.' Bitterness at what he had endured at home and as a student breaks out as late as 1942 in *The Outlook for Homo Sapiens*, when reflections on the pantomime proletariat of the Oxford 'thirties provoke him to exclaim,

> It has been my absurd experience to encounter noisy meetings of expensive young men at Oxford, not one of them stunted physically as I was by twenty years of under-nourishment and devitalised upbringing, all pretending to be rough-hewn collarless proletarians in shocked revolt against my bourgeois tyranny.

In his autobiography he insists, 'I paid in health for South Kensington all my life.' The details he supplies would certainly support this. Glumly taking stock of his physique, he had to face the fact that

> By 1887, it had become a scandalously skinny body. I was five foot five and always I weighed less than eight stone. . . . I was as light and thin as I have said because I was undernourished. . . . I would survey my naked body so far as my bedroom looking-glass permitted, with extreme distaste, and compare it with the Apollos and Mercuries in the Art Museum. There were hollows under the clavicles, the ribs showed and the muscles of the arms and legs were contemptible.

What was driving him to this gloomy scrutiny, he recognises, was increasing sexual consciousness—'To me, in my hidden thoughts, the realization that my own body was thin and ugly was almost insupportable. . . . In the secret places of my heart I wanted a beautiful body and I wanted it because I wanted to make love with it.' This wincing combination of desire, shame, and honesty is briefly reassembled in *The Wheels of Chance*, when Hoopdriver— a draper's assistant as Wells had been—takes a similar view of himself:

> An expression of distaste crept over his features. 'Looking won't alter it, Hoopdriver,' he remarked. 'You're a weedy customer, my man. Shoulders narrow. Skimpy, somehow.' . . .
> He sat down on the bed, his eye still on the glass. 'If I'd been exercised properly, if I'd been fed reasonable, if I hadn't been shoved out of a silly school into a silly shop—But there! the old folks didn't know no better. . . . Still, when it comes to meeting a girl like this—it's 'ard.'

By the time Wells came to write this, of course, things were not quite so hard. He had left South Kensington and, after weathering a period of particular rigour in Wales (where his health broke down frighteningly), had started his climb towards comfort. A teaching post in a school run by A. A. Milne's father brought some benefits, including the fact that 'The midday meal was an excellent one. . . . And at the end of the table, facing me, sat Mrs Milne, rather concerned if I did not eat enough, because I was still, she thought, scandalously thin.' There was no longer the need to do 'very fine computations' outside fried-fish shops or feel grateful that a 'halfpenny' in his pocket turned out to be a discoloured shilling, meaning he could eat. Marriage and employment at a university correspondence college brought further improvements, so that 'he was beginning to look more compact and substantial'. And, moving through literary journalism to a full-time writing career, Wells soon became set on a course of increasing prosperity—to such an extent that, by 1894, he and his second wife were confronting the luxury of social embarrassment over food rather than worrying about where the next meal was coming from:

> People, often strange people, were beginning to ask us out. All sorts of unfamiliar food and drink might be sprung upon us, for the dietary Jane had been brought up upon was scarcely less restricted than my own. . . . Accordingly we decided to experiment with food and drink so far as the resources of the Camden Town and Tottenham Court Road luxury trade permitted. . . . we discussed whether we should go out to a dinner or so in a restaurant in preparation for our social emergence.

Qualms of this kind are on display in some of Wells's later novels, but the story he was working on in 1894, *The Time Machine*, concerns itself with activating far more basic fears about eating. Like much of his early work, it is designed to discredit what he called 'Bio-Optimism' or 'Excelsior Biology', the hopeful belief that life must steadily improve, move ever upwards from the slime towards nobility. This complacent equation of evolution with amelioration offered a comfortable resting place for the conviction that man now occupied a position of unassailable supremacy. In his early narratives, Wells often seeks to overturn this smugness by shock tactics—disturbing depictions of regression or extinction; menacing accounts of the arrival of ferociously competitive new species; startling reminders of the fact that man is still very much subject to biological constraints and pressures. Thus, in *The Time Machine*, the Traveller learns that the future holds in store for man degeneration, loss of control, and annihilation; he is shown that aspects of human life which could be thought of as a long way from the natural impulses—

matters of class, social structure, economics—are violently affected by them; and he is continually brought up against the primacy of physical appetites.

Basically, the story is a parable of evolutionary nemesis. Journeying to the remote future, the Traveller discovers that social distinctions have become biological ones. The property class and the proletariat have split further and further apart; the wealthy have taken over the surface of the earth, the working classes have been pushed beneath it; modified by vastly differing habitats and habits, these two sections of humanity have then evolved into separate species, the Eloi and the Morlocks. Erroneously, though, the Traveller at first assumes that the Eloi, descendants of the old dominant class, are still in control. Much taken by the resemblance of this world to a Golden Age, he misinterprets the role played by the figures in its landscape. The scene—lush vegetation and picturesque ruins bathed in an amber glow—is pastoral: against its background, the Eloi frolic like the heedless beatifics of mythology. Repeatedly, this is highlighted: 'the whole earth had become a garden', 'It was natural on that golden evening that I should jump at the idea of a social paradise', 'how wide the interval between myself and these of the Golden Age', 'They spent all their time in playing gently, in bathing in the river, in making love in a half-playful fashion, in eating fruit and sleeping.' The foreground of the picture is so classically Arcadian—'The male pursued the female, flinging flowers at her as he ran'—that it is some time before the Traveller perceives its other elements, discovers that this is a pastoral that includes the abattoir. The Eloi are not nymphs and shepherds but the grazing flock, 'fatted cattle': 'Very pleasant was their day, as pleasant as the day of the cattle in the field. Like the cattle they knew no enemies and provided against no needs. And their end was the same.' Thoughts which have indolently drifted through the Traveller's mind as he viewed the golden scene and its 'delicious' people suddenly, in retrospect, jump to grim attention: 'The harvest was what I saw!', 'We improve our favourite plants and animals . . . by selective breeding . . . now a sweeter and larger flower, now a more convenient breed of cattle.' Treated as a separate species by the Eloi-section of humanity, the Morlock-class has gradually evolved into one; the taboo on eating the flesh of one's own species no longer holds; and biological retribution enables a class which was economically preyed upon to get its revenge by carnivorous preying.

To this extent, the book could be seen as a blend of Marx and Darwin: a cautionary tale about expropriators becoming expropriated. But eating, in this story, is not simply used as an instance of ironic nemesis. It is depicted with both relish and ferocity, the book warming to its theme with a responsiveness well beyond the mere requirements of didacticism. Though the Traveller piously enlists on the side of the Eloi, Wells's imagination enters most excitedly into the world of the Morlocks. They live, it is noticeable, in an environment shadowily resembling some that he had known: it seems fabricated from memories of the underground servant-tunnels at Up Park (there are similar ventilation shafts) and the underground kitchen in Atlas House where he spent much of his childhood. The scene where they are glimpsed in this subterranean setting, gathered round a table 'laid with what seemed a meal', is presented with especial pungency—the Traveller scenting 'the faint halitus of freshly shed blood' and wondering 'what large animal could have survived to furnish the red joint I saw'. The sinister suggestiveness breathed out by 'halitus' and the queasy serving-up of the domestic 'joint' with the factually brutal daub of 'red' make the moment—though a brief one—sickeningly memorable.

This grisly little tableau (which has been seen, incidentally, after the Traveller has clambered into 'the mouth' and down 'the throat' of a well) is not the only lurid depiction of carnivorous appetite in the book. The Traveller himself is almost eaten—'I felt little teeth nipping at my neck'—by the Morlocks, just escaping by leaping rapidly forward in time. And the first—in fact, the only—thing that then happens to him is that something else tries to eat him. A crab 'as large as yonder table' advances on him: 'the many palps of its complicated mouth flickering and feeling as it moved', he notes with horror before taking off again.

In view of all this, it is a little surprising to find that practically his first words on arriving back in his own day are 'Save me some of that mutton. I'm starving for a bit of meat', and that he is soon throwing out such *bon viveur* jocularities as 'What a treat it is to stick a fork into meat again!' or 'I won't say a word until I get some peptone into my arteries.' The fact that he has recently been devoting a great deal of his energy to keeping out of the arteries of others in no way diminishes his own carnivorous cravings. And this is entirely typical of Wells. Eating is presented as a gruesome threat and entered into with considerable gusto. The nibbled Traveller, after he has 'sniffed good wholesome meat', settles down with unaffected relish to his first meal back.

One of the reasons for this eagerness is the diet he has been forced to live upon while with the Eloi. Like the exemplary rabbit in the *Text Book of Biology*, they are vegetarian—a sure sign that Wells's sympathy for them is less than wholehearted. Vegetarians turn up fairly regularly in Wells and are received with increasing impatience. A very early piece of joky journalism, 'Thoughts on a Bald Head', does suggest that a non-carnal diet has advantages: 'I have noticed that most of your vegetarians are shock-headed, ample-bearded men.' But, after this point, tolerance starts to withdraw. Cavor in *The First Men in the Moon*, for instance, is 'a water-drinker, a vegetarian, and all those logical disciplinary things': he is also suicidally naïve. Utopia is semi-vegetarian, allowing the eating of fish but not meat, in *A Modern Utopia* (1905); but in the later *Men Like Gods* (1923) only 'Eating bacon has gone out of fashion in Utopia.' And, even in the earlier book, some zestfully hostile treatment is handed out to a Nazarite crank who is rather gratuitously pushed into the narrative to babble about 'Simple Foods and Simple Ways' and expound doctrines such as 'No animal substance inside, no vegetable without;—what could be simpler or more logical?' Another nature-fiend appears in the short story 'Little Mother up the Mörderberg', enthusing to unresponsive country-folk about 'plasmon, protose, plobose, digestine, and so forth'. For the most part, vegetarians in Wells tend to seem as nutty as their diet. In *Ann Veronica*, masticating fruit and veg. is one of the few satisfactions available to repressed Miss Miniver. Men, she claims, have been poisoned by 'the juices of meat slain in anger', so that 'they are swollen up and inflamed. . . . they look at life with bloodshot eyes and dilated nostrils.' Her own non-carnal existence is very different, as she reflects: 'When I am leading a true life, a pure and simple life, free of all stimulants and excitement, I think—I think—oh! with *pellucid* clearness; but if I so much as take a mouthful of meat—or anything—the mirror is all blurred.' A social highlight of her week is a visit to the Goopeses, 'the oddest little couple conceivable, following a fruitarian career upon an upper floor in Theobald's Road'. There, while characters ingesting 'chestnut sandwiches buttered with nutter' wander round in purple djibbahs or suits of canvas-sacking tied with brown ribbons, conversation turns excitedly to such matters as 'a new substitute for dripping in vegetarian cookery'. The contempt Wells obviously feels for these etiolated goings-on bursts out again in *The New Machiavelli*. One of the various horrors Remington encounters when holding receptions at his home is the sight of 'an unbleached young gentleman before the oval mirror on the landing engaged in removing the remains of an anchovy sandwich from his protruded tongue—visible ends of cress having misled him into the belief that he was dealing with doctrinally permissible food'. In *The Research Magnificent*, the pretentiously 'advanced' nature of Amanda's female relatives is established by the fact that they surround themselves with such despicable decor as 'A photographic enlargement of somebody with a vegetarian expression of face'.

Lurking behind Wells's contemptuous exasperation at the thought of people denying themselves meat is a fairly obvious suspicion that they're probably perverse—or pathetic—enough to be denying themselves sex as well. Miss Miniver isn't the only celibate herbivore on display in his fiction. Miss Summersley Satchel, the sneaky companion-spy in *The Passionate Friends*, 'marches, I understand, like the British infantry but on a vegetarian "basis"—fancy calling your nourishment a "basis"!' In *Joan and Peter*, two more spinster faddists, Aunts Phyllis and Phoebe, join the woolly flock, showing all the usual markings—droopily arty clothing, tremulous enthusiasm for vague causes, and a tendency to get mildly belligerent about the peace-inducing properties of a vegetarian diet: '"Never let him touch butcher's meat in any shape or form," said Aunt Phoebe. "Once a human child tastes blood the mischief is done."' The connection between abstention from meat and a deprived sex life is finally brought into the open in *The Research Magnificent* when Prothero, a sexually frustrated don, rages against his enforced celibacy, 'Why am I troubled by a way of life that is convenient for Rigdon the vegetarian?'

As might be expected, dietary crankiness—'digest *consciously*, waggle your abdomen this way and that, never touch meat, never touch *tinned* food, eat the *peel* of your fruit'—is one of the unlovely appurtenances of affected Mrs Bunnington, a voraciously soulful widow in *Apropos of Dolores*; and it is characteristic, too, that the exacerbated narrator of that novel should announce with flat candour, 'Manifestly the bare thought of Mrs Bunnington puts me in a vile temper.' Manifestly the bare thought of most vegetarians puts Wells in a vile temper in his later books. Searchers for an escaped lunatic in *Christina Alberta's Father* make what is presented as a very understandable mistake in pursuing, instead, someone who turns out to be 'just a vegetarian in sandals and a beard'. Similar anonymous distastefuls hover on the fringes of other late novels. Attending a New World Summer School in *The Holy Terror*, Rud Whitlow finds 'it included everything from barely cryptic nudists to extremely woolly vegetarians'. In Wells's last novel, *You Can't Be Too Careful*, there is a briefly fatuous appearance from 'an elderly vegetarian who was an expert at book-binding and slightly deaf, who expressed strong views about tinned foods and cancer, and otherwise kept very much to himself'. Keeping very much to themselves is something Wells obviously feels vegetarians would be well advised to do. In a disgruntled aside in his *Guide to the New World*, he remarks that he and his fellow workers have experienced difficulty in getting the Sankey Declaration of the Rights of Man accepted by mankind since 'a considerable number opposed it because it did not assert or impose upon all mankind, some particular fad. Vegetarians, for example, wanted clauses to establish the legal rights of animals (pigs, e.g.)'. The final plosive monosyllable—less an example than a snort of disgust—leaves no doubt about his feelings.

Wells has no patience with vegetarians, and he has little sympathy with vegetables, at least before they reach the plate. Growing vegetables is generally a sign of futility in his fiction. In *The War of the Worlds* an enthusiastic gardener proffers samples of his strawberries, vacuously opining 'This lot'll cost the insurance people a pretty penny', as the Martian missiles crash to earth and Surrey starts to smoulder. One of the enraging attributes of George Ponderevo's father-in-law in *Tono-Bungay* is an obsession with kitchen-garden produce. When he isn't talking about his greenhouse—'I wish I 'ad 'eat. . . . One can do such a lot with 'eat'—he is scattering unwelcome eatables about the Ponderevo home:

> in the summer time he never came in without performing a sort of conjuring trick in the hall, and taking cucumbers and tomatoes from unexpected points of his person. 'All out o' *my* little bit,' he'd say in exemplary tones. He left a trail of

vegetable produce in the most unusual places, on mantel-
boards, sideboards, the tops of pictures. Heavens! how the
sudden unexpected tomato could annoy me!

In *Mr Polly*, curmudgeonly Uncle Pentstemon makes his debut
garnished with home-grown onions and lettuce, full of brooding
resentment against the girl who 'mucked up' his mushroom bed;
and priggish cousin Johnson, 'a steady, successful gardener . . .
particularly good with celery and peas', nourishes his self-esteem
by patrolling 'rows of exceptionally cultivated peas' and boasting
of 'all that he did for the propitiation of that fitful but rewarding
vegetable'.

Propitiation is not what Wells likes vegetables to receive, as the
description of Remington's father losing his patience with the
garden greens in *The New Machiavelli* makes clear:

> At last with the failure of the lettuces came the breaking point.
> . . . He had the hoe in both hands and slogged. Great wipes he
> made, and at each stroke he said, 'Take that!'
> The air was thick with flying fragments of abortive salad. It
> was a fantastic massacre. It was the French Revolution of that
> cold tyranny, the vindictive overthrow of the pampered
> vegetable aristocrats. After he had assuaged his passion upon
> them, he turned for other prey; he kicked holes in two of our
> noblest marrows, flicked off the heads of half a row of arti-
> chokes, and shied the hoe with a splendid smash into the
> cucumber frame. Something of the awe of that moment returns
> to me as I write of it.

What is mainly conveyed here, however, is not awe but relish and
approval. 'There doesn't seem to be rage in the vegetable world',
we are informed in *The Secret Places of the Heart*; but in Wells's
response to it there is a great deal of rage. And, in any case, his
faith in vegetable pacifism did not last: one of his final works, *The
Happy Turning*, finds him inveighing violently against 'the
incredible fierceness, nastiness and brutality of the Vegetable
Kingdom', claiming that 'It feeds greedily upon filth in any form,
and its life is wholly given up to torture and murder.'

Greedy feeding, Wells apparently feels, should be the prerogative of the animal world. Certainly—in the form of subterranean

carnivores, voracious crabs, and hungry late-Victorians—it shows a marked tendency towards this in *The Time Machine*: to such an extent that, when the Traveller fails to come back from his second time-jaunt, the narrator's mind immediately turns to dangers arising from the man's edibility—'Will he ever return? It may be that he swept back into the past, and fell among . . . blood-drinking, hairy savages.' In Wells's next work of science fiction, *The Island of Doctor Moreau*, ravening predators are even more spectacularly unleashed.

The story opens with three famished men adrift in a dinghy, surrounded by sharks and drawing lots as to who should be the first to be eaten by his fellows. A fight sends two toppling overboard, leaving Prendick to survive, rescued on the point of death and resuscitated by 'a dose of some scarlet stuff, iced'. 'It tasted like blood,' he announces with surprising conviction; and, given the amount of gore swilling around in the narrative, it seems quite likely that it is. Wells himself was certainly familiar with the taste of blood. He had tasted his own, in terrified mouthfuls of haemorrhage, when he was dangerously ill in Wales and throughout his convalescence at Up Park: 'Every time I coughed and particularly if I had a bout of coughing, there was the dread of tasting the peculiar tang of blood.' And there was a relapse some years afterwards, when 'I found myself about nine or ten at night hurrying down the slope of Villiers Street to Charing Cross Underground Station, with a heavy bag of specimens. I was seized by a fit of coughing. Once more I tasted blood and felt the dismay that had become associated with it.' Dismay was his reaction, then, but the illness to which this was a prelude marked a crucial stage in Wells's life. It compelled him to abandon teaching and attempt to make a living as a writer; and also—they exchanged sympathetic, joky letters during his con-valescence—it seems to have been one of the things pulling even closer his relationship with Catherine Robbins, who became his second wife. He himself came to feel that 'The last cardinal turning point on the road to fortune had been marked by that mouthful of blood in Villiers Street.' As if in some bizarre tribute to this, only his more sympathetic characters are allowed to share the experience. One of the oddest moments occurs in 'A Story of the Days to Come' when Denton, having refused to eat a cube of bread offered him by a grubby-handed man, is involved in a fight that leaves him with 'the taste of blood . . . in his mouth'. Eager to acquit himself better in future, he takes lessons in pugilism from chirpy Blunt, who is soon

> roaring with laughter at a happy fluke of Denton's that covered his mouth with blood.
>   'I'm always keerless of my mouth,' said Blunt, admitting a weakness. 'Always. It don't seem to matter, like, just getting bashed in the mouth—not if your chin's all right. Tastin' blood does me good. Always.'

Other sharers in this strange prerogative are courageous consumptives like Masterman in *Kipps* or Sirrie Evans in *The World of William Clissold*. George Ponderevo's gliding accident in *Tono-Bungay* gives him a 'mouth . . . full of blood', and after she has nursed him to recovery from this, he becomes Beatrice's lover. Also after an aerial accident, Peter, in *Joan and Peter*, 'found himself . . . being very lively in spite of the strong taste of blood in his mouth'. Mr Blettsworthy not only tastes his own blood but later saves his life, when put to the test on Rampole Island and forced to choose between 'bowls of boga-nut milk and blood', by opting correctly for the blood while 'The vegetarian milk is flung contemptuously away.'

In *The Island of Doctor Moreau*, Prendick, heartened by the scarlet cordial, finds his appetite awakening, and he and his rescuer engage in a lip-smacking exchange:

> 'Am I eligible for solid food?' I asked.
>   'Thanks to me,' he said. 'Even now the mutton is boiling.'
>   'Yes,' I said, with assurance; 'I could eat some mutton.'

And, 'excited by the appetising smell of it', he does, explaining, in this same scene, that he has 'taken to natural history as a relief from the dullness of my comfortable independence'.

What follows is a crash-course in the harsher aspects of biology. To an extent, the novel is about evolution, with Moreau's bloodied laboratory acting as a grisly parody of natural selection (there is a scene in *Joan and Peter* that offers something similar, when God is encountered in a room crawling 'with a buzzing nightmare of horrible and unmeaning life': it is littered with test-tubes, 'returns of nature's waste, sample bones of projected animals', and 'blood was oozing from . . . drawers and little cries came out of them'). Moreau's speculative mutilations, his attempts to turn animals into something different, are intended to emphasise how much of life is painful hypothesis, nature trying out one experiment after another, indifferent to suffering or failure. But, whereas, in the natural realm, change is generally slow so that any pain involved is dispersed throughout a species and over a long period of time, in Moreau's laboratory, where he is attempting to accelerate the process, the suffering is hideously apparent, concentrated in days or weeks of extreme torment and intensified upon one individual. The novel is also searingly insistent upon the pains, needs, and dangers of animal life. Fear and suffering are not confined to Moreau's enclosure. While shrieks and sobs shrill out from the laboratory which acts as an image of evolution, the island around it runs with blood, is increasingly strewn with half-eaten corpses, and pullulates with predatory appetites.

After he has been supplied with further food—something he feels badly in need of, since 'Hunger and lack of blood-corpuscles take all the manhood from a man'—Prendick goes for a walk on the island in order to get out of earshot of the screaming puma that is bearing the brunt of Moreau's ingenuity. Almost the first sight he encounters, though, disturbs him even further: it is 'an unpleasant thing, the dead body of a rabbit, covered with shining flies, but still warm, and with the head torn off'. Then he stumbles on the Beast People and, as 'Their eyes began to sparkle and their ugly faces to brighten with an expression of strange pleasure', he notes with revulsion that 'Saliva dropped from their lipless mouths'. These creatures are, however, as he subsequently learns with some relief, strictly vegetarian: at least, officially— one of their Rules being 'Not to eat Flesh nor Fish; *that* is the Law. Are we not Men?' Men of course, do eat flesh and fish: and it soon transpires that, among the Beast People, a certain amount of dietary truancy has been going on. Although Moreau and Montgomery have tried to keep their creatures from tasting blood, fearing 'the inevitable suggestions of that flavour', they have not succeeded. And soon, blood-stained maws are gaping everywhere: the Hyena-Swine thrusts 'thirsty teeth' into the neck of the Leopard Man; two Swine Men are seen to be 'blood-stained . . . about the mouth'; the jaws of the Beast Man M'ling are marked with 'ominous brown stains'. Prendick has to struggle constantly to keep out of these mouths—'I had my quarrels, of course, and could show some teethmarks still'—and finds that his best defence is, appropriately, 'the bite' of his hatchet. By the end of the book, hungry yearnings for taboo protein are breaking all restraint:

> My St Bernard creature lay on the ground dead, and near his body crouched the Hyena-Swine, gripping the quivering flesh with mis-shapen claws, gnawing at it and snarling with delight. As I approached the monster lifted its glaring eyes to mine, its lips went trembling back from its red-stained teeth, and it growled menacingly.

When Prendick departs, the island has degenerated into one big *al fresco* buffet. Not surprisingly, once back in London, he prefers to skulk behind locked doors rather than brave the streets where 'prowling women would mew after me', or venture into libraries where 'the intent faces over the books seemed but patient creatures waiting for prey'. The natural history lessons he has undergone prove unforgettable. The Beast People have vividly displayed the animal elements from which man is made, with a heavy emphasis on tooth and claw:

> every now and then the beast would flash out upon me beyond doubt or denial. An ugly-looking man, a hunchbacked savage to all appearances, squatting in the aperture of one of the dens, would stretch his arms and yawn, showing with startling suddenness scissor-edge incisors and sabre-like canines, keen and brilliant as knives. Or in some narrow pathway, glancing with a transitory daring into the eyes of some lithe white-swathed female figure, I would suddenly see (with a spasmodic revulsion) that they had slit-like pupils or, glancing down, note the curving nail with which she held her shapeless wrap about her.

Traumatised by what he has learned of biology, Prendick changes his syllabus and opts, instead, to 'spend many of the clear nights in the study of astronomy'.

Not that this would be particularly soothing if *The War of the Worlds* is anything to go by. Setting out, once more, to attack short-sightedness, Wells announces that, for decades, human astronomers have been unable to see just what was going on: 'Had our instruments permitted it, we might have seen the gathering trouble far back in the nineteenth century. Men like Schiaparelli watched the red planet . . . but failed to interpret the fluctuating appearances of the markings they mapped so well. All that time the Martians must have been getting ready.' And so, 'all unsuspected', Martian missiles close in on the earth while the narrator is 'much occupied in learning to ride the bicycle' and 'With infinite complacency' men go 'to and fro over this globe about their little affairs, serene in their assurance of their empire over matter'.

Once again, part of Wells's intention is to disturb man by reminders of his kinship with the natural world. When the novel opens, *Homo sapiens* is on one side of a dividing-line, with the rest of earth-life on the other. With the arrival of the Martians, man is pushed back amongst his fellow terrestrials. Imagery constantly reclaims him for the animal world: in the course of the book, men are compared to infusoria, monkeys, lemurs, sheep, dodos, cows, ants, frogs, bees, wasps, rabbits, rats and oxen. And they are saved not by their intelligence but by the action of 'the humblest things . . . upon this earth', disease bacteria. *The Island of Doctor Moreau* emphasised the sufferings of evolution. *The War of the Worlds* illustrates its benefits: 'directly those invaders arrived, directly they drank and fed, our microscopic allies began to work their overthrow. . . . By the toll of a billion deaths, man has bought his birthright of the earth, and it is his against all comers.' Before this point is reached, however, before they are pecked to shreds by birds and having their gristle gnawed by dogs, the Martians have enthusiastically preyed upon mankind.

They are, in fact, some of the most interesting feeders in Wells's fiction. Their first appearance gives the impression of considerable voracity: 'There was a mouth under the eyes, the brim of which quivered and panted, and dropped saliva.' Fascinated by what he sees, the narrator excitedly heaps up the details:

Those who have never seen a living Martian can scarcely imagine the strange horror of their appearance. The peculiar V-shaped mouth with its pointed upper lip, the absence of brow ridges, the absence of a chin beneath the wedge-like lower lip, the incessant quivering of this mouth, the Gorgon groups of tentacles.

As with the table-sized crab in *The Time Machine*, the Martian countenance is fairly lavishly equipped with mouth, and horrified attention keeps being drawn towards these dribblingly expectant orifices. But this is somewhat misleading, for, as the narrator later explains, despite their chillingly mouthy appearance, the Martians

> were heads, merely heads. Entrails they had none. They did not eat, much less digest. Instead, they took the fresh living blood of other creatures, and *injected* it into their own veins . . . . blood obtained from a still living animal, in most cases from a human being, was run directly by means of a little pipette into the recipient canal.

This seems almost decorously clinical: and Martian calm is emphasised even further—'Men go happy or miserable as they have healthy or unhealthy livers, or sound gastric glands. But the Martians were lifted above all these organic fluctuations of mood and emotion.' Still, though the Martians are theoretically placid, Wells gets so worked up in envisaging them that discrepancies appear. For instance, if it is true that 'all the complex apparatus of digestion . . . did not exist in the Martians', what are they doing dripping saliva across the Home Counties? And if they are merely dispassionate intelligences, why do they respond to 'a stout, ruddy, middle-aged man' who has fallen into their tentacles and is soon to have his blood sipped, with 'a sustained and cheerful hooting'? Wells has, it's true, tried to cover himself a little over this by explaining earlier, 'Their peculiar hooting . . . was, I believe, in no sense a signal, but merely the expiration of air preparatory to the suctional operation.' But, despite the handling-with-rubber-gloves decorum of 'the suctional operation', it's still difficult to account for 'cheerful'. What has happened is that, as usual, excitement at the thought of men being preyed upon has sent Wells's imagination off into a world of lurid flesh-creepiness. The Martians have caught their gastronome exuberance from him—though, considering the quality of the sustenance they had packed for the journey, it would hardly be fair to blame them if their arrival on earth had awakened some flickerings of enthusiasm:

Their undeniable preference for men as their source of nourishment is partly explained by the nature of the remains of the victims they had brought with them as provisions from Mars. These creatures, to judge from the shrivelled remains that have fallen into human hands, were bipeds, with flimsy siliceous skeletons . . . and feeble musculature.

After a stringy regimen like this, it's no wonder those big vestigial mouths flood with redundant saliva at the sight of the well-fleshed Surrey locals or that a cheerful note intrudes into their pre-prandial hooting.

For Wells, the Martians serve a double purpose: partly, they represent a didactic menace to mankind, and partly they are nightmare creatures to be fitted out with attachments fashioned by his heated imagination. The salivating mouths (a feature shared with Moreau's Beast People) are one aspect of this, but the thing which most grips his interest is their tentacles. In the late story *Star Begotten*, Joseph Davis is presented as naïve in that 'At first he pictured a Martian as something hunched together like an octopus, tentacular, saturated with evil poisons, oozing un-pleasant juices, a gigantic leathery bladder of hate.' On the contrary, it is suggested, they are highly refined and uncorporeal beings, beaming beneficent influences upon the offspring of mankind. But Wells has only himself to blame for the confusion. It is he who established the image of Martians as extra-terrestrial octopuses. This is certainly how they appear in *The War of the Worlds*. Here, the first thing to emerge from the Martian cylinder is 'something resembling a little grey snake', and it is soon joined by similar extremities: 'A lank tentacular appendage gripped the edge of the cylinder, another swayed in the air.' When the Martians come out into the light, they glisten 'like wet leather', and round their mouths are 'sixteen slender, almost whip-like tentacles'—so that the locals soon have them classified: '"Octopuses," said he, "that's what I calls 'em."' Martian technology, too, carries constant reminders of their physical peculiarities. When building their heat-ray machine, they employ 'a leash of thin black whips, like the arms of an octopus'; and they transport themselves around England in an apparatus that has 'articulate ropes of steel dangling from it' like 'long flexible glittering tentacles'. These 'steely tentacles' are used for scooping up human food supplies. The narrator, hiding in a pantry, both sees the mechanical 'reaching and clutching tentacles' at close quarters, and watches the Martians at their own snaky man-handlings. In fact, he is grazed by one of their real tentacles himself—'It was like a black worm swaying its blind head to and fro.' Escaping this, he later encounters another survivor, who is soon expressing strong disgust at the Martians' appendages—'Ugh! Fancy those brown creepers!'

Reconditioned octopuses are, in fact, one of Wells's main stand-bys as a source of *frisson* in his work, especially the earlier books. In one of the articles collected in *Certain Personal Matters*, he remarks that a larger kind of octopus 'coming into a region of frequent wrecks might so easily acquire a preferential taste for human nutriment' and 'in the course of a few score years it might begin to stroll up the beaches and batten on excursionists'. In his story 'The Sea Raiders', written about the same time, this is exactly what they do, except that the casual 'stroll' has been replaced by something more purposeful. A 'peculiar species *Haplotheutis ferox*'—identified on the evidence of 'a half-digested tentacle' and 'a decaying body pecked by birds and nibbled by fish'—is discovered near Land's End by a Mr Jennings (the name, incidentally, of the student who bought Wells the square meal at South Kensington). Then a holidaymaker at Sidmouth, Mr Fison, stumbles with horror on the sight of a human corpse being dined off by 'new and ghastly-looking creatures, in shape somewhat resembling an octopus, and with huge and very long and flexible tentacles, coiled copiously on the ground'; their skin, like that of the later Martians, resembles 'shiny leather'. Spotting him, they make for him at high speed, their tentacles 'pouring over the rocky ridge on which he had just been standing!' Mr Fison gets away; then foolishly returns, with reinforcements, in a boat to track the monsters down. Soon, this little expeditionary force is fighting to survive. After a warning glimpse of 'copious olive-green ribbons' under the water, tentacles rise darkly to the surface; 'tapering, serpentine ropes' wrap round the oars; and 'creeping up the side of the boat with a looping motion came the suckers again'. One man, his arm shrouded with 'a complicated tangle of brown ropes', is pulled overboard and eaten, as is a 'boatload of excursionists' come to offer help. Slaked by their catch, the shoal move on; and, apart from an artist who later disappears with a shriek under the water at Newlyn, there are no further casualties. The story ends by saying 'it is to be hoped' that this is the last that will be heard of 'these terrible creatures'.

The inconclusiveness, with its lingering menace—could they return and, if so, could they be fended off?—is deliberate. And, of course, in modified forms these malign cephalopods do return in Wells's fiction. The Martians in *The War of the Worlds* are one example of this, but there are others. In a story called 'The Crystal Egg', a man claims to be able to view life on the Red Planet by peering into a crystal at a special angle. The glimpses provided by this peep-show are generously equipped with the usual dangling excrescences: the Martians are 'fitted with two bunches of prehensile organs, like long tentacles'; although they also have wings and 'are a bit like bats or cherubs', they 'alight upon their tentacles' and, when not flitting through the Martian atmosphere, are to be seen 'hopping briskly upon their hand-like tangle of tentacles'. One of them catches something in its tentacles as well—one of the 'clumsy bipeds, dimly suggestive of apes' that also inhabit the planet. The picture fades before the sequel can be observed, but not before it has put disquieting thoughts into the minds of the 'bipeds dimly suggestive of apes' who are reading the story.

Martians are not the only kind of extra-terrestrial fauna to have tentacles in Wells's fiction. Some of the Selenites in *The First Men in the Moon* are similarly kitted out: they have 'tentacle hands'. And the most unpleasant specimen of moonlife to encounter is apparently 'the Rapha, an inextricable mass of clutching tentacles that one hacks to pieces only to multiply'. When Cavor is on his tour of inspection of the inwards of the Moon, he notes among the fishermen's catch 'a many-tentaculate, evil-eyed black thing, ferociously active', and it haunts his feverish dreams.

A dream of the Time Traveller's shows similar fears, and with justification. Waking from a nightmare where 'sea-anemones were feeling over my face with their soft palps', he brushes off a marauding Morlock. And in this story there are other instances of Wells's fondness for depicting humans recoiling from predatory extremities. Even the mild Eloi are introduced as briefly creepy— as they wonderingly finger the Traveller, he feels 'soft little tentacles upon my back and shoulders'. The light cast by the subsequent narrative soon causes these wormy miniatures to shrink back to childish digits. But, later, more substantially threatening feelers poke into the story. As the Morlocks close in on the Traveller, 'lank fingers came feeling over my face' (not unlike the 'lank tentacular' appendages in *The War of the Worlds*: another shared attribute is that the Morlocks, like the Martians, are 'chinless'). And when he moves forward in time, he is subjected to more pre-digestive touching:

> I felt a tickling on my cheek as though a fly had lighted there. I tried to brush it away with my hand, but in a moment it returned, and almost immediately came another by my ear. I struck at this, and caught something threadlike. It was drawn swiftly out of my hand. With a frightful qualm, I turned, and saw that I had grasped the antenna of another monster crab that stood just behind me. Its evil eyes were wriggling on their stalks, its mouth was all alive with appetite, and its vast ungainly claws, smeared with an algal slime, were descending upon me.

The Traveller jumps away through time again—almost to the end of the world. There, 'more than thirty million years hence', in the earth's cold, final twilight, he sees, hopping fitfully about on a sand-bank, 'a round thing, the size of a football perhaps, or, it may be, bigger, and tentacles trailed down from it'. There is no other evidence of animal life. Only these favourite organs are allowed to hang on till the end.

Certainly, they always keep their grip on Wells's imagination, and not just when attached to octopuses or extra-terrestrials. In *The Camford Visitation*, for instance, there is an unpleasant literary critic given to gesticulating 'with long tentacular hands that looked bleached'; in *Babes in the Darkling Wood*, one of the drawbacks to Gemini's lodgings is that 'a man with beak and eyes like a cuttlefish . . . scrutinises you as you come in and picks his teeth with one of his tentacles'; and in 'The Flowering of the Strange Orchid' a homicidal bloom attacks its owner with 'exultant tentacles' (a collector ironically called Batten has previously fallen prey to these). Metaphorical octopuses also get into Wells's prose. Attending *Tristan and Isolde* with predatory Mr Ramage, Ann Veronica becomes aware that he is 'stretching hungry invisible tentacles about her'. Surrounded by encumbering futilities in *Brynhild*, Mrs Palace has to fight against 'the relentless tentacles of nothingness', that 'most terrible of monsters'. Mr Blettsworthy has a hallucination about struggling with a 'giant octopus . . . which was slowly and steadily spreading its tentacles over the vessel', and wakes to find himself attacking a piece of rope. *In the*

Days of the Comet shows a girl who has become part octopus: eager to catch a lover, Nettie moves with 'undulations', trailing a green scarf 'like some shy independent tentacle'. *Crux Ansata*, Wells's diatribe against 'the strangling octopus of Catholic Christianity', converts that body into something fearsome from his science fiction. 'Everywhere the Church extends its tentacles', he says: just as, over thirty years earlier, in *The Future in America*, he had drawn attention to 'the Standard Oil group, the "octopus" which spreads its ramifying tentacles through the whole system of American business'. Likewise, the Tono-Bungay enterprise, as it expanded, 'got a tentacle round the neck of a specialised manufacturer or so', and a business tycoon in *The Brothers* has 'financial tentacles'.

Oddly, though, in view of their general role as bearers of leechy menace, tentacles appear beneficent when linked to Wells's two greatest enthusiasms—biology and education. In *Ann Veronica*, there is a tribute to that 'extraordinarily *digestive* science', biology, with its 'tentacular generalisations'. And Sanderson, the headmaster of Oundle, whose innovations Wells applauded in both fiction and non-fiction, is approvingly credited in *The Story of a Great Schoolmaster* with 'a mind like an octopus, it seemed always to have a tentacle free to reach out beyond what was already held'. Often so threatening in Wells's work, tentacles become an asset when they are employed in obtaining food for thought. And always they are fascinating objects for him, being lively reminders of the need to reach out for nourishment and the corresponding need to avoid being reached out for.

Teeth are another feature of the animal world that fascinate Wells: partly because he can insert them into menacing little tableaux—like that in *The Research Magnificent* where Benham encounters a tiger displaying 'its fangs and a pendant of viscous saliva'—and partly because they have travelled so far in evolutionary terms. These fitments of the jaw began as something very different, we are told in an early essay on 'Zoological Retrogression': 'We find what are certainly modified placoid fish scales, pressed into the work of skull-covering, while others retain their typical enamel caps as teeth.' *The Science of Life*, startlingly fusing the homely and the barely imaginable, repeats this idea: 'When Everyman chews his breakfast bacon he does it with teeth which are lineally descended from the shagreen of a cartilaginous fish in the Silurian waters.' And in 'The Scepticism of the

Instrument' Wells recounts that, as a science student, he 'had worked out the development of those extraordinarily unsatisfactory and untrustworthy instruments, man's teeth, from the skin scutes of the shark to their present function as a basis for gold stoppings'. The transience of teeth also provides the basis for an odd bit of speculation in *Crux Ansata*, where it is suggested that 'the key to a real and authoritative old age for . . . divines of the Dark Ages was probably the inherited soundness of their teeth. Those whose teeth decayed ceased to speak with dignity and authority.' This sad situation, some believe, will be remedied in the next world. Spectral dentures, Sir Eliphaz Burrows declares in *The Undying Fire*, have been bestowed upon his sister-in-law in the afterlife: her 'teeth have all been replaced—a beautiful set. Used now only for articulate speech', of course, because in the beyond 'The dietary is . . . practically non-existent'. Meanwhile, it is pointed out in *The Anatomy of Frustration*, man 'lives far longer than his teeth and combative energy', and this the narrator of *Apropos of Dolores* sees as unnatural: 'We mammals seem to have been evolved for the wear and tear of breeding, the cares of parentage, and then physical exhaustion and death. Our teeth are timed for that.' Teeth are relics of our origins, signs of our kinship with the animal world. *In the Days of the Comet* tells us that 'the Upper Nile savages struck out their canine teeth because these made them like the beasts'. For the same reason, Wells continuously plugs teeth into his narratives. Even today, we 'still have . . . ape's teeth in our jaws', *The Soul of a Bishop* remarks warningly, and *A Short History of the World* insists that 'tooth and claw come early into our earthly history'. They come into quite a lot of Wells's fiction, too—especially *The Island of Doctor Moreau*, which is full of dental horror. On the rescue ship, Prendick is 'shocked . . . profoundly' when a 'huge half-open mouth' flashes upon his notice, showing 'as big white teeth as I had ever seen in a human mouth'. On the island, he is uneasily aware of the proximity of 'scissor-edge incisors and sabre-like canines', and has queasy moments when trying to talk the Beast People into acquiescence and 'one by one the listeners began to yawn (showing the oddest teeth in the light of the sinking fire)'. As he prepares to leave the island, three of these creatures are slinking towards a ghastly heap of human remnants, and, as Prendick catches 'the gleam of their teeth' (the last detail he notes), a 'frantic horror' sends him paddling away in his boat.

Teeth are also generously scattered through Wells's mordant parable *Mr Blettsworthy on Rampole Island.* The cannibal kingdom has, as part of its decor, 'a strange freak of nature, a jutting mass of rock in the shape of a woman with staring eyes and an open mouth . . . and the threat of the mouth had been enhanced by white and red paint, suggesting teeth and oozing blood'. The ceremonial staff Blettsworthy is awarded there is 'decorated with mother-of-pearl and the teeth of sharks'. Sharks' teeth also decorate a more formidable piece of woodwork, the two-hundredweight club used to administer 'the Reproof' to deviant citizens. And they provide articles of feminine adornment, young girls wearing nose-plugs made from them. Human teeth are pointedly in evidence as well, Blettsworthy recalling how blood-thirsty Ardam 'sucked his teeth noisily in anticipation of his meal'. All of this is appropriate since the book's fundamental tenet is that creatures live by preying upon each other. Man, Wells says in *What Are We To Do With Our Lives?*, is 'the creature of a struggle for sustenance'. *Mr Blettsworthy on Rampole Island* sardonically fleshes out this claim into a savage fable packed with literal and metaphorical cannibalism.

Arnold Blettsworthy derives, as he recognises, from a family who 'stand for the gentler civilisation, the civilisation of infinite tact'. Brought up in a world of social and religious complacency, he is given the shock treatment these things so often provoke in Wells. Betrayed by the girl he is in love with (her surname is Slaughter) and his closest friend, he learns 'something of the meanness of trusted fellow-creatures, and something also of the vile cellars in my own foundations'. In an attempt to regain his faith in life and his zest for it, he undertakes a sea voyage. But, increasingly, the world strikes him as unreal, and he is unfortunate in falling foul of the ship's captain (a man as intransigently hostile as the captain who marooned Prendick). As might be expected in Wells, Blettsworthy makes his big mistake at meal-time. Snubbed and made to feel a milksop because he doesn't participate in the meaty bawdry being bandied around by the ship's crew, he tries to hold his own by reciting a few limericks at the captain's table, only to incur an even more crushing response: 'If you can't keep a clean mouth at table . . . Blettsworthy, you'll have to take your meals in your cabin.' Goaded by this, he rashly delivers a parodic retaliation. The captain, he says made noises with his soup at dinner and suddenly it occurred to me to make similar noises with my soup. Everyone else looked startled and the captain regarded me over his soup spoon with a malignant interest that manifestly brightly revived.

I made a prolonged, tumultuous finale to my soup. Then very calmly I put down my spoon and waited patiently and with an expression of quiet interest for the captain to finish his. He did so in a subdued manner and he was very red in the face.

Not long after this event, Blettsworthy finds that he is in the soup as a result of it. When the ship begins to sink, he is locked in a pantry and abandoned on board by the embittered slurper, who chants triumphantly as he himself escapes, 'Eat your Soup! *Eat ya soup!*'

Much later, they will meet again by accident in a Pimlico restaurant, but, before this happens, Blettsworthy has his Rampole Island experience. Descending into hallucination, he has a conversation with a shark, a 'snapping bag of guts', who invites him to dinner down his 'one-way throat' and is put out when Blettsworthy counters with gibes about liking shark steak, 'For it irritated this eater even to think of being eaten.' Then, 'chewing slowly and steadily with their heavy jaws', a band of natives come aboard, and Blettsworthy, taken to their island, discovers that cannibalism is the basic fact of existence there: these are people 'living on each other persistently and ruthlessly'. Soon he is also dining off 'the delicate pork-like meat' that is the staple diet. The island does have its decorums and its euphemisms: 'no allusion was ever permitted to the fact that the only possible big meat on the island, big meat as distinguished from fish, rats, mice and the like, was human flesh. . . . human flesh was never known as human flesh, it was spoken of as the Gift of the Friend'. The process by which this benison is obtained is likewise wreathed in verbal veiling—clubbing to death is 'the Reproof'; the resultant corpse is not eaten but 'reconciled'. But, despite these few instances of mealy-mouthedness, Rampole Island stands as a stark image of the ugly natural facts that lie beneath civilisation. Blettsworthy has already encountered various disturbing urgencies—the furtive grappling of Olive Slaughter and Lyulph Graves; his own excited response to this; the killing of a cabin boy; the captain's surreptitious trove of pornography.

On the island, life's conditions openly emerge as bestially predatory. Since the main food supply arrives via the Reproof and this can only be administered if someone is socially unorthodox, the entire community is hungrily alert to breaches of propriety. Members of the tribe live their life 'from the cradle to the cooking pot' in a state of avid eagerness to prey upon each other. And the flora of the island is equally predatory:

> There was an abundant plant like the English sun-dew but very much larger and more active in its gripping movements. It made great carpets on the damper places and I never once ventured to walk across the prehensile leaves it spread so hungrily. Its sticky, hand-like leaves captured not only flies as the English sun-dew does, but lizards, efts and small birds. Their little shrivelled skins and bones lay everywhere on the morass.

The 'hairy sundew' itself (the adjective making it sound more animal than vegetable) crops up earlier in Wells—in his novel *The Wonderful Visit*, which contains a moor where this 'eater of careless insects, spreads its red-stained hungry hands to the God who gives his creatures—one to feed another'. There is a further, slightly different instance of predatory landscape in *The Undying Fire*, when Job Huss takes a walk to distract his mind from the calamities which have been raining down upon him. His stroll is, however, just about as soothing as that which Prendick went on in his attempt to regain peace of mind by getting away from the noise of Moreau's vivisections. In fact, the first thing he comes across is similar, a rabbit the back of whose head has been bitten open. Looking for 'something more agreeable', he then spots 'a row of little brown objects in a hawthorn bush' and, going closer, finds they are 'some half-dozen victims of a butcher bird— beetles, fledglings, and a mouse or so—spiked on the thorns'. Turning away from this grisly pantry, his gaze is further revolted by the sight of a 'villainous-looking cat' with a 'very mangled' bird in its mouth. Later, Huss thinks of this as 'that day when the world of nature showed its teeth to me'. This, of course, is what is happening to Mr Blettsworthy on Rampole Island. What he witnesses is, he comes to realise, 'a mild caricature of the harsh veracities of existence', a phantasmagoric scenario pulling into view the brutal realities which lie at the heart of what he calls 'all the serenities and amplitudes of the liberal civilisation out of which I had fallen'. Not that this civilisation seems all that serene or ample once he is restored to it. With the outbreak of the First World War, he feels that 'Rampole Island had indeed now spread out and swallowed all the world'. The metaphor used here is appropriate, and it is one that returns with even greater force at the end of the book. Appalled by the Sacco and Vanzetti affair, Blettsworthy begins to fall back into garish dreaming:

> And in my fantasy it was like this, that when these two were at last executed we all killed them, all of us, they were torn to little fragments, handed out, and their flesh was eaten by everyone who acquiesced in their fate. 'Eat,' said a voice, 'since you could not save them!' Such is the cruel over-emphasis of these visions; they magnify verities into monstrosities.

The verity magnified into monstrosity in this novel is, as so often in Wells, the fact that life consists of battening, that in order for one organism to survive another must be sacrificed. And he likes to emphasise that the exploited organism could well be a human being. The cannibalism and carnivorous preying in his books are designed to frighten man into a full awareness of his biological condition. The flesh is made to creep by reminders that it is flesh and, as such, edible, valuable to others in the struggle for survival. But there is a lighter side to the picture as well.

Wells does not only suggest that his characters are edible by surrounding them with salivating mouths, bloodstained teeth, and grasping tentacles: he is also very fond of giving them food names. It would, in fact, be possible to draw up quite a respectable menu from amongst Wells's characters, starting with Amontillado (a Cardinal in *Meanwhile*) and working through to Wensleydale (who appears in *The Sea Lady*). Items would include Plaice, Bream, Winkles, Rabbits; 'Sossidge', 'Sardine' and 'Cabbage' (Aunt Susan's nicknames for her husband in *Tono-Bungay*); Lettice ('More Salad than ever in that green dress', her stepfather remarks in *Apropos of Dolores*); Butter, some Beans; Satsuma, Pomegranate, Bramble, and Cranberry (the last two of these, lords). A smooth villain from *The Wheels of Chance* called Bechamel would supply the sauce, and there is a 'Jampot' in the same novel. Though there is no bread, there are quite a lot of crumbs—Mrs Crumb in *The Holy Terror*, the Countess of Crum in

The Autocracy of Mr Parham, and a whole family of them in *Christina Alberta's Father*—a novel particularly rich in leavings: it also contains a Lambone, a Major Bone, and a Captain Bone (no relation). There are generic names as well—like Grubb—or nicknames—such as 'Wittles and Drink' or 'Suet-and-Bones'. And, even when not actually labelled with food names, Wells's characters like to compare themselves to eatables. 'I . . . get hot, juicy, red—like a grilled chop', explains a cyclist in *The Wheels of Chance*; 'I am a water melon', Mrs Rylands announces in *Meanwhile*; and Aunt Susan in *Tono-Bungay* compares herself to a 'ham'. Sometimes, too, they behave like food. Versatile Mrs Rylands not only resembles a melon but 'Abruptly . . . went like sour milk in thundery weather'; it is remarked in *Marriage* that 'if you slashed Blenkins across, he would probably cut like a cheese'; and *You Can't Be Too Careful* contains a man who 'went on getting older and bitterer like stewed tea'.

Imagery that makes humanity seem palatable is a constant favourite with Wells. In 'A Misunderstood Artist', an aesthetic cook scornfully dismisses a *Punch*-reading philistine as 'Mere dripping'; and in *Select Conversations with an Uncle*, brides under their festive gauze are described as being 'like confectionery'. In addition to the grilled chop, *The Wheels of Chance* mentions girls with 'complexions like cold veal', and its hero has a head 'singularly like an albino coconut'. When a mermaid appears in *The Sea Lady*, our minds are rapidly directed towards the fishmonger's by the news that her tail is 'like a mackerel's'. Mr Snape in *The Dream* has 'small chubby features like a cluster of *champignons*'; and Wells's autobiography bestows similar suggestions of facial edibility on his old teacher, Morley—he has 'a strawberry nose'. *Boon* points out 'egg-faced ladies' in Japanese prints, and Rusper in *Mr Polly* not only has a head like an egg but is frequently told to go and 'Boil it'. Remington in *The New Machiavelli* is like a chestnut; the shrunken old ladies in *Tono-Bungay* seem 'dried-up kernels in the great shell of Bladesover House'; Blettsworthy tries to stomach the captain by thinking of him as a 'human fruit' with a 'rough rind'; Americans are 'stale as old cabbage leaves' in *The Holy Terror*; while, in *The Autocracy of Mr Parham*, the Master of Saint Simon's shrivels to an 'old bit of pemmican'.

People in social situations are particularly prone to presentation as consumer-items. In *Marriage*, a 'salad of writers' is at

hand; *The Passionate Friends* offers a 'salad of family visitors';
Alfred Bunter in *Brynhild* is 'the last social mouthful'; and Mr
Britling ruefully remarks of Lady Homartyn's gatherings, 'not
that I'm an important item at these week-end social feasts—but
she likes to see me on the table—to be nibbled at if anyone wants
to do so—like the olives and the salted almonds'. Rather similarly, George Ponderevo, assembling the ingredients of his
fiction, speaks of 'a hotch-potch of anecdotes and experiences
with my uncle swimming in the middle as the largest lump of
victual'. And a tendency to see the literary as provender spreads
spectacularly through *Brynhild*, where a publisher, claiming that
his lists are 'balanced like a menu', excitedly proclaims,

> 'Here they are! Everything in season. Early peas and hothouse
> grapes. . . . This new fellow, Alfred Bunter—I've got him. . . .
> "Raw expressiveness" is on the blurb. He's my ham.'
> 'Your *what?*' said Mr Palace [author of *Sago Lane*].
> 'My ham—Westphalia ham. Raw—you know.'

Indignantly, Palace reflects that 'Mr Murray never talked about
his "list" to Lord Byron as though that nobleman was hors-
d'oeuvres or entrée, nor Mr Chapman to Dickens in the role of
boiled mutton with trimmings. . . . But, oh! what was the good of
talking about things like that to this—this *grocer?*' The publisher's
approach finds an ally, though, when a literary publicist joins the
narrative, talking of Conrad as 'Pink caviare. Special taste, I
mean. Such richness.'

An odd sidelight on this quirk of Wells's is the apparently
unconscious willingness to cater to his fantasies shown by writers
who associated with him. While none of them gives any sign of
openly recognising the way gastronomic imagery and incident
pervade his work, they often, when writing to him about his
books, turn to the larder as a congenial source of offerings.
Bennett, for instance, writes in 1901, 'What I hunger for is the
successor to *L. and Mr L.* I will make a meal off that, I promise
you.' Gissing in 1898 sends off the enthusiastic bulletin, 'Delighted with *The War of the Worlds*. Devoured it at a sitting'—
something which must have particularly pleased Wells in view of
his frequent anxiety about Gissing's dietary. An article published
in 1904 finds him shaking his head over the fact that his friend's
'meals were of bread and dripping, stewed tea, cheese at times,

soup bought desiccated in penny packets, and suchlike victual'. And, after Gissing began to live with Gabrielle Fleury, Wells's apprehension deepened. France, he had observed in *What Is Coming?* is 'habitually parsimonious'; and Mlle Fleury's mother, who was responsible for the cooking, seemed even more parsimonious than most of her Gallic fellows—so much so, in fact, as to be starving Gissing to death. When, on holiday from France, he visited the Wellses, they were so appalled at his meagre appearance that—according to Morley Roberts's *The Private Life of Henry Maitland*—Mrs Wells 'fed him for all she was worth' and they persuaded him to try an 'over-feeding cure' at a Suffolk sanatorium. Returned to France and Gallic thrift, however, Gissing steadily declined, and even a dramatic last-minute intervention, when Wells gained entry to the death-chamber and plied the invalid with banned sustenance, failed to save him. 'According to Gabrielle, Wells took advantage of the night of the twenty-sixth, when he was alone with the sick man, to feed him beef-tea, wine, coffee, and milk in quantity, in order to build up his strength', Gissing's biographer, Jacob Korg, recounts. Gabrielle's version of the doctor's response to all this was that Wells's actions had killed Gissing.

Another writer who becomes culinary when describing Wells's books is Rebecca West. Some of them, she claimed in her review of *Marriage*, are garnished with a sex-obsession that lies 'clotted' on them 'like cold white sauce'; and a later piece, characterising *Mr Polly* as a 'little pot of sweet jelly', expresses her regret that there are passages of Wells's writing where 'his prose suddenly loses its firmness and begins to shake like blanc-mange'. It is Henry James, however, who offers most verbal delectation in his responses to the books. Punctiliously sending off letters of gratitude for presentation copies, and ecstatic accounts of his reactions to the works, he relies almost uncannily on the sort of imagery Wells must most have welcomed. He is reading *The First Men in the Moon* 'à petites doses as one sips (I suppose) old Tokay'. Wells's short stories 'were each to me as a substantial coloured sweet or bonbon . . . which I just allowed to *melt* lollipop-wise, upon my imaginative tongue'. Sampling *In the Days of the Comet*, he goes on 'tasting and tasting, and it is as if, while this lasts, I had my mouth very full'. *Ann Veronica* he absorbs in 'deep, rich draughts'. After reading *The New Machiavelli*, he is praising Wells's 'capacity for chewing up the thickness of the world in such enormous mouthfuls, while you fairly slobber, so to speak, with the multitudinous taste'. Tribute to 'the great stewpot' of Wells's imagination is extravagantly proffered in his response to *Marriage* (perhaps because—as became evident a couple of years later— James didn't like the book very much):

> I live with you and in you and (almost cannibal-like) *on* you, on you H.G.W. . . . I simply decline—that's the way the thing works—to pass you again through my cerebral oven for critical consumption: I consume you crude and whole and to the last morsel, cannibalistically, quite, as I say, licking the platter clean of the last possibility of a savour and remaining thus yours abjectly Henry James.

Even as late as 1913, despite a warning from Wells that it is 'mixed pickles and I know it', James is reporting of *The Passionate Friends* that he has taken in 'the so full-bodied thing in deep and prolonged gustatory draughts.' Communiqués about his real, as well as imaginary, eating also go off to Wells. He lets him know how he is getting on with his 'Fletcherizing' regimen, a process (peculiarly appropriate to James, perhaps) which involved the prolonged chewing of a morsel of food before allowing it to be digested, and which eventually reduced him to a state of malnutrition: 'my dietary is the *easiest* mere tissue of feeble negatives. I eat but little here below, but I eat that little long—and it's a little of the absolutely obvious.' In view of all this amiable sharing of interests, it seems a bit ungenerous of Wells to have dismissed James's mind, in his autobiography, as 'edentate as a pseudopodium'—toothless as a blob of protoplasm.

As we have seen, though, it is not only literature but also the characters in it that Wells likes to think of as eatable. This is often brought out in scenes of aggression. When a bomb explodes near Reedly in *The Holy Terror*, for example, 'glass cut through his face like a knife thrown at a meringue'. Bedford and Cavor, battling against the Selenites in *The First Men in the Moon*, find they are really engaged in a struggle against crunchy edibles. Punching one of the moon-creatures, Bedford discovers that 'He smashed like—like some softish sort of sweet with liquid in it!', and, when another Selenite is struck, 'he crushed and crumpled—his head smashed like an egg'. There is a moment somewhat akin to this in *The Time Machine* when the Traveller, hitting out at the

Morlocks, says he 'could feel the succulent giving of flesh and bone under my blows'. 'Succulent' is a word more likely to be used by a Morlock to describe flesh, one would feel. It occurs again, though, rather startlingly, in *Mr Britling Sees It Through*. Writing from his military training-camp, Hugh describes his response to bayonet-drill—'bounding forward I imagine fat men, succulent men ahead'—and he includes a drawing of the enemy 'skewered like cat's meat' to drive his point home. The predatory nature of warfare brings cannibalism to Wells's mind. Mussolini, for example, is 'that cannibal' in *Meanwhile*; and in Peter's delirium in *Joan and Peter* the Kaiser crawls up to him over a heap of corpses and begins 'gnawing at his shoulder almost absent-mindedly'. On a lower level, there is an example of comparatively reined-in militancy from a tramp in *Bealby*. Irritated by a 'dough-faced fool' he has encountered, he explains, 'I'd enjoy biting *'im*. I'd spit it out, but I'd bite it right enough.'

One of the things Wells high-mindedly takes issue with about Christianity is that its central ceremony involves the supposed partaking of the saviour's flesh and blood—'God-eating', as he has it in his autobiography. The hallowed images of host and chalice are impatiently swept aside by his determination to let the reader know what's behind it all. Even during his brief period of religious fervour, proclaimed in *God the Invisible King*, he is announcing his disgust at 'obscene rites of circumcision and symbolical cannibalism'. *The Soul of a Bishop*, published the same year, continues the indictment as the Bishop of Princhester expresses his horror at the way Jesus has been 'turned from a plain teacher into a horrible blood bath and a mock cannibal meal'. Surveying ecumenical attempts to survive the rising flood of secularism, Wells grimly observes in *Crux Ansata*, 'Roman Catholicism preserves a strong tradition of cannibalism, and I can give a good guess who will live longest on this conjoint raft.' In *Meanwhile*, Mrs Rylands rejects the comforts of religion with the words 'I don't want to eat God.' Those who do are shown to be a grisly bunch—like the lugubrious vampires, eager for 'imaginary draughts of blood', in *Tono-Bungay*, who assemble once a week in a brick chapel to intone,

There is a Fountain filled with Blood
Drawn from Emmanuel's Veins

after which, they split up for 'obstetric whisperings' and talk that is 'medical in substance'.

A jagged literalism is, in fact, one of Wells's main implements for puncturing religious orotundity. He stumbled upon it quite early in life, horrifying his pious mother, when he was a child, by livening up his recital of the catechism in this way. When questioned as to the ingredients of the sacred feast, he explains, 'it occurred to me it would introduce an amusing element of realism into the solemnity of the recital if I answered "Bread and Butter" and chuckled helpfully'. The response was gratifyingly aghast, and this became the weapon he regularly reached for ever after. A reworking of it is offered in *The Dream*, where a child adjusts the Lord's Prayer to request his 'daily bread and butter'. Taking the Sacrament, Wells finds it reminds him of 'a crumb of trifle'. And attention is drawn to Kipps's aunt making him repeat what she calls the 'Colic for the Day', every Sunday. The spiritual is repeatedly brought down to earth by being farcically encumbered with the corporeal. In *The Dream*, for instance, there is speculation as to exactly what will happen on the day of resurrection. What will those who have been cremated or eaten by sharks do by way of covering, wonders the narrator's father; will they be given substitute bodies—'them as 'ave been eat by lions. Many of the best Christian martyrs in their time was eat by lions. . . . They'd *certainly* be given bodies.' Likewise, in *The Soul of a Bishop*, it is wondered, 'Did the birds eat the fruit in Paradise?' Whether they did or not, some of it turns up in Wells's fiction: looking like 'a kind of phosphorescent yellow tomato', a piece of Forbidden Fruit features as a social embarrassment in his story, 'The Apple'. Catering problems on Noah's Ark are made comically specific in *All Aboard for Ararat*: items from the log include such bulletins as 'Fish And Sea-Gulls Become The Main Articles of Diet. The Elephants Are Put on Half-Rations.' A similar deflating factuality comes into play when Wells is giving miracles a glance, those concerning foodstuffs, needless to say, being the ones that take his fancy most. The changing of water to wine at the wedding-feast comes in handy for enlivening a speech to the London University Labour Party, with Wells cheerily remarking of a dinner-party in Prohibition New York that 'There were quantities of what was called lemonade—lemonade which, to my inexperienced palate, seemed to have undergone the Miracle of Cana.' In *The Happy Turning*, Christ is brought back to explain the Feeding of the Five Thousand: apparently, the multitudes brought 'furtive lunch packets', expecting to be hungry and thirsty—'and when they found there was food to burn, they were ashamed of themselves and pretended not to have brought anything. So that again was put down to my miraculous gifts.' Given Wells's penchant for referring to food and his desire to debunk religion, it could, of course, only be a matter of time before the line, 'Man cannot live by bread alone', made its appearance in his fiction. It does so, most appropriately, in *The Wife of Sir Isaac Harman*, a book about a man who runs a chain of bakeries.

In addition to using Sir Isaac for dealing another sidelong blow at the feeding of the multitude—his wife thinks of him as 'engaged in a kind of daily repetition, but upon modern scientific lines, of the miracle of the loaves and fishes'—the work retails other bad food-jokes. Talking of Sir Isaac, Lady Beach-Mandarin declares, 'I can't *imagine* how a man who deals in bread and confectionery can manage to go about so completely half-baked'; and the music-hall note is kept up by the introduction into the novel of a baker with thirteen children—'a fair baker's dozen', it is nudgingly explained, in case anyone's attention has been drowsing. There is obviously a strong urge in Wells to offer feeble witticisms about food. 'What did Shakespeare live on?' it is asked in *Certain Personal Matters*: 'Bacon' is the schoolboyish reply. In *The New Machiavelli*, a licensing bill is punningly rejected as 'beer-baiting'. Mr Pope in *Marriage* proffers a bit of limp jocosity about 'the man who took the salad . . . with his hand, and when his host asked why he did that, replied: "Oh, I thought it was spinach!"' Stella in *Babes in the Darkling Wood* contributes another dismal gastronomic *mot*: 'I don't think very much of cold mutton and trifle, by way of a fatted calf.' But the most excruciating food-humorist in Wells's fiction is a man encountered in *Joan and Peter* jovially quipping,

Where does the road go to, my boy? . . . Why? it goes to Maidenhead and Cookham. Cookham! Have you heard the story? This is the way the man told the waiter to take the underdone potatoes. Because it's the way to Cookham. See? Good, eh? But not so good as telling him to take peas that way. Through Windsor, you know. Because it's the way to Turnham Green. Ha, ha!

Besides garnishing stale waggishness of this kind, food can be of service in Wells's novels as a weapon. Cutlery, he had realised early on, could be put to this use: on one occasion, he recalls in his autobiography, he threw a fork across the dinner-table at his brother 'and I can still remember very vividly the missile sticking in his forehead'. The memory glints briefly again in some of his books. 'I once threw a fork at my elder brother and it stuck in his forehead, doing no serious damage', Sir Richmond recalls in *The Secret Places of the Heart*; Rud in *The Holy Terror* throws a dinner-knife across the table at his brother 'and nicked a bit off the top of his ear'; and Bealby attacks a fellow-servant with a toasting-fork—'He got a prong into Thomas's chin at the first prod.' The really memorable skirmishes, though, are ones undertaken not with implements but with edibles. Things start off fairly mildly in *The Wonderful Visit* where an angel is threatened with a pan of boiling cabbage water and pelted with beech-nuts, take on a bit more vigour when Mr Lewisham begins throwing buns, and reach a resounding climax in *Mr Polly* when marauding Uncle Jim attacks the Potwell Inn. Though Mr Polly himself falls back on culinary hardware for the battle—he is 'armed with a frying pan'—the decisive damage to Jim (who later fights back gamely with a dead eel) is done by two campers who 'smacked his face with steak and punched him with a bursting parcel of lump sugar, they held him though he bit them'. Injury is inflicted in a similar way in some of the later books. 'I was hit by a potato', a man complains after an affray in *The Holy Terror*; and there is a snappy collision of Wells's habit of turning people into food and his tendency to link food with aggression in *The Autocracy of Mr Parham* when frisky Miss Pomander Poole smacks 'a large ham-faced Jew on the cheek with a pâté de foie gras sandwich'. Nor, of course, is it only in fiction that belligerence makes use of edibles. *The Undying Fire* reminds us that Tasmanian aborigines were 'killed by poisoned meat left in their paths' (and a memory of that extermination was one of the starting-points for *The War of the Worlds*).

There are a few noteworthy variants on the use of food as weaponry in Wells. Theodore in *The Bulpington of Blup* is literally made to eat his words: insulting letters he has written are shredded and 'rubbed into his mouth and face' until he had 'a mouthful of paper'. With more subtlety, an uncle of Mr Lewisham's expresses disagreement by means of gustatory mimicry. Believing socialists to be mercenary agitators who trick the naïve into handing over money which is then spent on high-living, he counters his nephew's earnestly radical arguments 'with the word "Champagne" uttered in an irritating voice, followed by a luscious pantomime of drinking'. In *You Can't Be Too Careful*, the pretensions of Evangeline Birkenhead are felled by a menu. Priding herself on her knowledge of French—'It's such a *brilliant* language. There isn't a word in it that hasn't a *double entente*'—and hoping for a 'teeny, weeny, little *ventre à terre* in Paris', she finds a rival is circulating a parody of her Gallophile *élan*. It is headed 'Menu Malaprop' and includes such items as '*Potage Torture*', '*Maquereau*', and '*Agneau au sale bougre*'.

Food and aggression weirdly cohabit in Wells's mind, sometimes spawning bizarre images. In *The War in the Air*, for instance, as he watches airships scuffle, Bert Smallways 'was grotesquely reminded of fish in a fishpond struggling for crumbs'. The raw natural impulses behind the glittering fracas are allowed to surface in a vividly typical image. Then Wells's excitement at the thought of food pushes him, as so often, to an almost surreal extreme, and, a page or so later, the battle has become a matter of 'puddings trying to assassinate each other'. A struggle for power becomes a struggle for food, and then a struggle between foods. The idea of the eatable proves, as usual, so engrossing that it draws Wells right away from his real concerns. There is another instance of this in *Mr Britling Sees It Through*, when he speaks of his hero's list of investments:

> It was, so to speak, his economic viscera. It sustained him, and kept him going and comfortable. When all was well he did not feel its existence; he had merely a pleasant sense of general well-being. When here and there a security got a little disarranged he felt a vague discomfort. Now he became aware of grave disorders. It was as if he discovered he had been accidentally eating toadstools, and didn't quite know whether they weren't a highly poisonous sort. But an analogy may be carried too far. . . .

From the point of view of the novel, it already has been. Mr Britling's investments—apart from causing this brief rumble of disquiet—play no real part in the book, indeed are barely mentioned again, and the toadstool comparison threatens to tip the matter into total nonsense. All that emerges clearly is that Wells has been glad to find an excuse for elaborating on digestion.

It is striking to what lengths of ingenuity his imagination will go in its desire to convert things into the edible. Furnishings, for instance, can metamorphose in this way. An early essay in *Certain Personal Matters* observes that mahogany has 'a singularly close resemblance to raw liver'; and its 'hepatite tint' so takes Wells's fancy that he later works it into a little poem, 'Ballade of the Bedroom Suite':

> Red as red wine is your rosewood's glow . . .
> Rich your mahogany's hepatite shine.

Over a quarter of a century after this, the image is still being used as Mr Preemby in *Christina Alberta's Father* thinks of 'lumpish sideboards of shiny, liver-coloured wood'. Lady Harman likewise finds interior decor taking on disturbingly fleshy overtones. She shrinks disgustedly from the bedroom provided by her tasteless husband since it is decorated in a hideous pink colour 'between rather underdone mutton and salmon'. Parload of *In the Days of the Comet* fares slightly better in that his apartment has floors 'covered with scratched enamel of chocolate hue'. Quite a few other things in Wells have chocolate poured over them. In *Certain Personal Matters*, he recalls a statue, covered with a coat of paint by its owner, that 'gave one the impression of the Venus of Milo in chocolate pyjamas' (another instance of clothing as sauce occurs in *Men Like Gods* when Lady Stella appears in a 'custard-coloured' robe). The plate glass front to the shop in Raggett Street where Tono-Bungay is manufactured is 'coloured chocolate', and the woodwork inside is also 'painted the universal chocolate'. The characteristic stone of New York, Wells notes too in *The Future in America*, is 'the colour of desiccated chocolate'.

Places, in Wells, are particularly liable to fall prey to culinary colonising. Wimblehurst in *Tono-Bungay* is 'Cold Mutton Fat'. London seems to Amanda in *The Research Magnificent* 'like some enormous juicy fruit waiting for her pretty white teeth'—though in *Meanwhile* it is 'like Bovril . . . so much of the world's life is still concentrated here'. Countries also become eatable—Poland is a 'sucked orange' in *A Year of Prophesying*; and so do continents— in *The War that Will End War*, Wells admits to 'a certain sense of presumptuous absurdity as I sit here before the map of Europe like a carver before a duck and take off a slice here and decide on a cut there', while, in his autiobiography, he evokes the eager anticipation with which he and Jane approached their first trip abroad through images of gastronomic relish: 'we were not going to just nibble at the continent. We were going straight through, at one bite, to Rome.' The entire earth, in fact, can be seen as edible: in *The First Men in the Moon* Cavor explains that his invention, Cavorite, could have 'whipped the air off the world as one peels a banana'; and in *A Short History of the World* respective sizes are established by images of the moon as 'a small pea' and the earth as 'slightly compressed, orange fashion'. Given all this, it is no wonder that when Oswald sees his ward reading travel-books in *Joan and Peter* he is 'reminded of some hungry and impatient guest in a restaurant reading over an over-crowded and perplexing menu', or that Mr Blettsworthy, planning his itinerary, finds 'it gave him a fine sense of mastery to take the whole world and peruse it like a bill of fare'.

There is a scene in *Mr Polly* where Wells expatiates on his hero's literary tastes. He is a great admirer, it appears, of Stevenson's *Island Nights' Entertainments* and 'it never palled upon him that in the dusky stabbing of the "Island of Voices" something poured over the stabber's hands "like warm tea" . . . the joy of the vivid phrase that turns the statement of the horridest fact to beauty!' 'Beauty' would not, perhaps, be most people's reaction to this blend of beverage and gore (which is, incidentally, to be found in 'The Beach at Falesá', not 'The Isle of Voices'— and at a higher temperature: the phrase is 'hot as tea'). But it is entirely typical of Wells that he should respond in this way. The texture, look and taste of food and drink are carefully recorded in his books: caviare in *Tono-Bungay* is 'like salt frog spawn'; champagne in *Joan and Peter*, 'like weak vinegar mixed with a packet of pins'. In *Christina Alberta's Father*, Mr Preemby's metaphorical imagination works upon his pasta disconcertingly: though told he shouldn't cut up macaroni because this 'devitalizes it', he still insists on doing so—' "Otherwise," he said in a confidential aside . . . "I can't help thinking it's earthworms." ' Food, in Wells, can find its way into the most bizarre analogies. A picture of dawn in *The Dream* is a 'Bit too like a slice of ham . . . thin pink streaks'; studying dead languages, always a pet aversion of Wells's becomes in *Joan and Peter* a sort of necrophiliac gastronomy—'like trying to graft mummy steak on living flesh . . .

like boiling fossils for soup'; chest diseases, according to Wells's autobiography, 'clear the mind like strong tea'; Queen Victoria, likened to a cottage loaf in *Mr Blettsworthy on Rampole Island*, spreads railways over the world 'as one spreads bread with butter' in *Joan and Peter*; and, with memorable absurdity, mountaineers in 'Little Mother up the Mörderberg' are said to be 'as solemn over their climbing as a cat frying eggs'.

One of the things Wells's mind most enthusiastically couples with eating is sex. Asked if he likes a certain girl, Mr Parham reflects, 'Like her! He could have eaten her.' This is a response shared by many of Wells's characters and by Wells himself. The basic idea is set out in *The Research Magnificent*, where it is explained that being in love is 'like being hungry. Only very fine hungry. Exquisite hungry.' True to this, amorous predators prowl through quite a number of the books. In *The Research Magnificent*, Benham ('a man who needed *bite* in his life') enters into a relationship with a big cat and becomes one himself. Journeying down the Illyrian coast on honeymoon, he and his wife, Amanda, enliven their relationship with erotically carnivorous rompings:

> She put her face closer and whispered. 'Cheetah! big beast of my heart. Do you hear your mate asking for something?' . . .
>   Suddenly with a nimble hand she had unbuttoned and rolled up the sleeve of her blouse. She stuck her pretty blue-veined arm before his eyes. 'Look here, sir, it was you wasn't it? It was your powerful jaw inflicted this bite upon the arm of a defenceless young leopardess. . . .'

'Defenceless' seems an odd word to use of a leopardess: but they settle happily into their roles as 'the Leopard and the Cheetah'; exchange remarks like 'Cheetah! How can you leave your spotless leopard?' or 'You're a greedier thing than I am, you Black Leopard you'; and, when they are apart, 'the correspondence of these two larger carnivores' is largely about the 'Cub' they have produced. They are actually apart quite often, something Wells is fairly eager to emphasise. For, though 'It is as natural to want a mate as to want bread', it is not so natural, he feels, to be penned in permanently with that mate. 'We should meet upon our ways as the great carnivores do', Benham declares. And Wells is particularly anxious to establish the normality of a life of sporadic, prowling encounter in that the relationship of Benham and Amanda owes much to his own affair with Rebecca West, which began a year or so earlier. In that relationship, as emerges from their letters, Wells was 'Jaguar' and Rebecca West 'Panther'. Big-cat imagery similar to that in *The Research Magnificent* litters their letters: they are 'carnivores'; their love-nest is a 'lair'; they go out to 'catch food' and meet 'at the trodden place in the jungle'. The stimulatingly feral note is qualified by a certain furry cosiness—'I do most tremendous love you Panther.' And Rebecca is warned that she must not show her teeth too often. After they have had a child (named Anthony Panther), it is her business to 'Lie and purr with it' while Jaguar pursues his career elsewhere. When she shows signs of sulking over this, she is sharply reminded that 'The Panther and the Jaguar are beasts of two different species and the Jaguar's natural habitat is up cheerful trees.'

Carnivore fetishism is unleashed again in *The Holy Terror*, only there it is snarlingly debunked, as Lord Bohun, a 'great carnivore', muses about going to the South Seas with his mistress so that they can 'love like tigers':

Could there be anything better in the whole of being than having one's grip on a weakly, resisting, overpowered, living creature, and doing one's will, exhausting the grossest fantasy upon that panting life? All the noble carnivores exist for that, and are they not the lords of creation?

He found himself wide awake in a sadistic reverie. . . . 'Ruthlessness,' he muttered. 'Strange lusts. . . . Quivering flesh. . . . The Tiger is an aristocrat.'

The atmosphere, when carnivores get into Wells's fiction, is not generally so rank, though. Rachel in *The Bulpington of Blup*, who 'thought aloud about the affections of the larger carnivores' and felinely pouts 'I'll *bite* you', introduces cuddlier considerations: 'If I were Circe, dearest, I think I should change you into a nice round-headed golden-brown jaguar with dark spots.' And science, in *You Can't Be Too Careful*, is approvingly patted on the head as a 'young tiger . . . biting mouthfuls out of the Creator!'

That meat-cravings and masculinity are closely associated in Wells's mind emerges clearly in *Men Like Gods*, where we hear that 'the larger carnivora, combed and cleaned, reduced to a milk dietary, emasculated in spirit and altogether be-catted, were pets and ornaments in Utopia'. Male sexual advances are sometimes envisaged as carnivorous leapings. When Isaac Harman closes in on the woman who is to be his wife, 'instantly, amazingly, with the famished swiftness of a springing panther, he caught her body into his arms': similarly, Brynhild Palace is 'seized upon hungrily' by Alfred Bunter. Hunger is frequently used by Wells to signify sexual appetite. *In the Days of the Comet* shows a man involved with two women. His feelings for the first he describes as 'that hunger' and 'the hunger of my heart', while the second 'held me with hungry arms . . . kissed me with a hungry intensity of passion'. William Clissold speaks of 'the hunger for a dear companion'. There are 'love-letters of a devouring sort' in *The War in the Air*. George in *Tono-Bungay* gets into 'a state of exasperated hunger for Beatrice'. And *Crux Ansata* declares that 'The appeal of sex is as natural to a young male as eating.' In Wells the two impulses can be virtually indistinguishable. *Marriage* gives a marked example of this. Taken off to Labrador—'a land in which nearly half the inhabitants die of starvation'—so that she and her husband can sort out their relationship, Marjorie, her 'brain cleared by underfeeding', sees how things should be. 'Dear, if I could make you, you should eat me', she cries to her husband, and he reassures her, 'We'd love each other minced.' Even when his lovers aren't slipping into gamy costumes, sex seems often linked in Wells's imagination with predatory means of attaining nourishment.

But his most pervasive attention, of course, is paid to real eating—'Stuffing into ourselves thin slices of what were queer little hot and eager beasts', as it is described in *The Passionate Friends*. Life, this action shows us unambiguously, is inevitably a matter of battening, of converting things which are not the self into the self. And this process of conversion—digestion—holds a strong fascination for Wells. There is a scene in *Kipps* where the hero surveys an anatomy book:

> Turning over the pages of the *Physiology* again, he came upon a striking plate, in which a youth of agreeable profile displayed his interior in an unstinted manner to the startled eye. It was a new view of humanity altogether for Kipps, and it arrested his mind. 'Chubes,' he whispered. 'Chubes.'

This may be a new view of humanity for Kipps but it is a very standard one for Wells. When Gemini Twain in *Babes in the Darkling Wood* writes to his girlfriend, 'your tummy (your dear little tummy) peristalts', he is only, in a tenderer form, purveying information that Wells's books are constantly passing on. Reminders of digestion are encountered everywhere. The most baroque case of this is the Invisible Man, who has to cope with the problem of having a see-through stomach. Until he has digested food, absorbed it into his own being, it remains embarrassingly visible, and, as people are likely to be disconcerted by the sight of an ambulant mix of chyle and enzymes, he has to hide until the absorption is complete. He is an extreme instance, but sufferers from more mundane digestive disorders abound in Wells. *The Science of Life* informs us that 'There is indeed no way of eating the correct kind of protein except cannibalism, and even then there exists no way of getting it direct to the blood without unmaking it and making it again.' Wells devotes a great deal of space to charting the effects and irritations that arise from malfunctionings of this process.

In an early essay, 'The Literary Regimen', he claims that 'It is imperative if you wish to write with any power and freshness at all, that you should utterly ruin your digestion. . . . the thing must be done, even if you have to live on German sausage, onions, and cheese to do it. So long as you turn all your dietary to flesh and blood you will get no literature out of it.' This essay is a ponderously jocose piece. It goes on to elaborate a laboured conceit about different types of diet giving rise to different types of literature—quantities of new currant-buns for luridly pessimistic narratives; strong cold tea and hard biscuits for detective stories; and so on. But, in point of fact, much of Wells's fiction does stem from indigestion—experienced not immediately prior to his taking up his pen, but during his formative years (many of his narratives feature mothers who can't cook and dyspeptic young men; and in *Mankind in the Making* Wells emphasises that poor nutrition in early childhood may create 'a derangement of the digestion, a liability to stomachic and other troubles, that may last throughout life'). *The Dream*, which contrasts the shiny ideals of Utopia with the be-grimed realities of the nineteenth century, stresses that one of the drawbacks of the old world was poor dietary and the ills attendant on this. Recurrently, Wells shows this to be the case. *This Misery of Boots*, cataloguing the pinching discomforts of the poor, includes amongst them 'getting pain and miserable states of mind . . . from the indigestion of unsuitable food eaten at unsuitable times'. Karenin in *The World Set Free* remarks on the bad old days when 'They ate a queer mixture of foods, either too much or too little, and at odd hours.' *An Englishman Looks at the World* contains the alarming statement: 'Few people of three score and ten but have spent in the aggregate the best part of a year in a state of indigestion, stupid, angry or painful indigestion.' And *The Sleeper Awakes* has one of its nineteenth-century characters announcing, 'We have to eat, and then come the dull digestive complacencies—or irritations'— though here, things seem just as bad in the future: waking from his 203-year sleep, Graham discovers a world in which workers at the 'Antibilious Pill Department' sometimes 'turn out a myriad myriad pills a day'. Quite a few minor characters in Wells suffer from indigestion: the two old ladies at Bladesover in *Tono-Bungay*, who 'were left . . . in a state of physical and emotional indigestion after their social efforts'; or the window-dresser in *Kipps* who 'nagged persistently, by reason of a chronic indigestion' (Kipps's uncle, also, sends off bulletins such as 'My heartburn still very bad'); or 'a cadaverous man at Roots', the Upholsterers, who suffered from gastric trouble, in *The Bulpington of Blup*; or old Tom Smallways in *The War in the Air*, whose digestion goes awry after his teeth have fallen out; or Mrs Greedle in *Babes in the Darkling Wood*, whose stomach upsets are cured by charcoal biscuits. Schools harbour a fair number of victims, too. It is only after he has moved to Cavendish Academy that Kipps discovers what Colic for the Day really means, starting to experience 'horrible headaches and queer unprecedented internal feelings, resulting from Mrs Woodrow's motherly rather than intelligent cookery'. The teaching at Morley's school, Wells tells us in his autobiography, could be impaired when the master was digesting or failing to digest his midday meal; and at one of the schools in *Joan and Peter* there are two teachers 'who both suffered from indigestion' and would therefore 'quarrel bitterly with boys they disliked and inflict punishments'.

Indigestion is responsible for a lot of bad temper in Wells's characters. Some of Lady Charlotte's choleric outbursts in *Joan and Peter* are put down to the fact that 'A very little stout served to derange her naturally delicate internal chemistry' and 'There is wrath in stout'. Wartime austerity darkens the mood of Oswald in the same novel, forcing him to give up steaks and chops and gloomily subsist on 'the bulky insipidity of a diet that was, for a time, almost entirely vegetarian'. Mr Seddon in *The New Machiavelli* is a turbulent casualty of 'the moods that arose from nervous dyspepsia', while Mr Pope in *Marriage* suffers 'from indigestion and extreme irritability'. The sour secretions of the aptly named Mr Peeve in *Men Like Gods* seep their bile into his writings. And in *Christina Alberta's Father* the temperature rises further as we hear of 'the diuretic, dyspeptic, infuriating and wildly aphrodisiac effects of Burmah Curry upon Major Bone'. Communism, it is suggested in *The Brothers*, is a windy side-effect of dyspepsia, consisting of 'Dogmas made by exasperated refugees with chronic indigestion'; while Calvinism, it seems from *The Shape of Things to Come*, owes its origin to malfunction of the liver, since it started in Geneva and 'Everyone who comes to Geneva gets liver.' Dictatorship is also shown as having a gastric origin: the most fearsomely splenetic of Wells's dyspeptics is the Holy Terror, Rud Whitlow, who is a 'bilious little boy', suffers throughout childhood from 'headaches and bilious fits', and at university is to be distinguished by his 'large, white, bilious face'.

Kidney-derangement occasionally occurs, giving rise, it seems, to a particularly poisonous type of personality (Wells once informed his sons' governess, 'when a man loses his temper for apparently no reason at all, you may be pretty sure that it is his liver, his kidneys, or both, which are at the root of it all'). Lord Barralonga, a loathsome, gnome-like food-profiteer in *Men Like Gods* 'suffers very gravely from a disordered liver and kidneys'; but the most malign instance is Sir Isaac Harman, whose disordered kidneys have depleted him to a state where he 'spends whole days in bed, drinking Contrexéville Water and planning the bankruptcy of decent men'. The Bishop of Princhester in *The Soul of a Bishop* does, it's true, also have a 'slight kidney derangement', but not much is made of this: unlike Wells's other bishops, he is treated sympathetically (because he soon ceases to be a bishop). His digestive disturbances are psychosomatic, the results of 'doubts that are not yet perfectly digested'. Digestion doesn't only affect mood: mood affects digestion—a situation ironically present in *Tono-Bungay*, where, as his quack medicine empire spreads, Uncle Teddy finds that 'with the increasing excitements . . . came dyspepsia'.

Animals can be sufferers from indigestion, too, of course. In his miracle-debunking mode, Wells makes use of this in *All Aboard for Ararat*, where we learn that 'The Whale . . . In a Manifest Indigestion Rejects Jonah Contumeliously And Offensively.' The log of the ark, in which this entry appears, also contained, it may be recalled, bulletins about how the elephants were faring. This is not surprising, since the elephant is a beast whose dietary plight Wells is especially solicitous about. As early as 1895, in a piece called 'The Duration of Life', he is shaking his head over the fact that 'The Elephant must roam over great tracts of country in search of food for his vast framework.' Over thirty years later, in *The Way the World Is Going*, he points out that the creature's situation is even more painful—'Indigestion and malnutrition are as rife in the forest as the slum. Elephant-hunters say they can tell the proximity of a herd by the borborygmic noises the poor beasts emit.' And, ten years on from this, in *Apropos of Dolores*, this mournful note is sounded once again: 'Elephants . . . suffer greatly from wind. They go about the African forests making borborygmic noises. Travellers remark on the overwhelming smell a herd of elephants leaves behind it.'

Despite this continuing interest, flatulent pachyderms are not the chief recipients of Wells's attentiveness to gastric disorder. In *Mr Polly* he builds a whole book around human indigestion. The novel opens with its hero 'sitting on a stile . . . and suffering acutely from indigestion', and we learn 'He suffered from indigestion now nearly every afternoon in his life.' The disorder, it appears, is long-established. As Mr Polly's mother was an inept cook, 'by his fifth birthday the perfect rhythms of his nice new interior were already darkened with perplexity'; and, during his six years at a drapery, he has been steadily 'increasing his indigestion'. But what has most extensively clouded his life with 'the black mood of the replete dyspeptic' is his marriage to Miriam, who 'cooked because food had to be cooked, and with a sound moralist's entire disregard of the quality or the consequences'. The book recounts his escape from this: basically, it is the story of a man leaving a bony woman who is a bad cook for a plump woman who is a good cook, and settling down with his new partner to a life of gastronomic bliss in an inn once called 'Potwell', now rechristened 'Omlets'.

Food and reactions to it take on further connotations in this book. What is wrong with Mr Polly is that he is being denied refreshment and nourishment in more than the purely culinary sense. Once, he had a healthy appetite for life: out on a walking holiday as a young man, his response to inn-meals was zestfully appreciative—'The going in! The sitting down! The falling to!' But, with a dreary marriage and the imprisonment of the little shop, his existence becomes heavy with stodge. Attempts to give it a bit of savour—by ingesting high-flavoured, cheap commodities like 'pickles and vinegar and the crackling on pork' or 'a ruddily decorated tin of a brightly pink fish-like substance known as "Deep Sea Salmon"'—only lead to inner troubles and dark moods. As Wells says, with perhaps a memory of the Invisible Man's plight, 'If Mr Polly . . . had been transparent, or even passably translucent, then perhaps he might have realised, from the Laocoon struggle he would have glimpsed, that indeed he was not so much a human being as a civil war.' Mr Polly's food disagrees with him as much as his life does. His indigestion acts as a kind of barometer registering his morale. When he is able to take a holiday because of his father's legacy, 'His indigestion vanished with air and exercise.' After he has become engaged to Miriam, however, his landlady's Welsh rarebits make him feel suicidal. Throughout the subsequent years of innutritious matrimony, biliousness builds up to crisis-pitch. Then, once he has settled down with the plump woman, life becomes full 'of interest and wholesome food and successful digestion'. Like a gourmand idyll, the novel that opened with the spectacle of a lone and miserable dyspeptic ends with the picture of a plump couple going contentedly in to supper. In fact, they are now a fat couple, Mr Polly having spread comfortably and his partner expanded from 'the plump woman' to 'the fat woman'.

It is quite in keeping with the book's concerns that the partner Mr Polly finds happiness with should not even be given a name but be seen largely in terms of embonpoint. Her obesity is, as she herself realises, emblematic: 'The magistrates wouldn't 'ave kept on the licence to me if I 'adn't been fat', she explains. Her conversation rather unnecessarily draws attention to the same idea: '"I've never held with fasting," said the plump woman.' And she takes her attachment to food so far as to use it to convey her thought-processes: after she has been debating whether or not to offer him a place at the inn, 'the way she brought the cheese showed Mr Polly that the business was settled in her mind'. Miriam's character is similarly set before us by her physique and attitude to food. Her gawky, pallid appearance is like an embodiment of the skimpy, unwholesome fare she provides. When Mr Polly revisits her towards the end of the book, the musty eggs that he is given serve to emphasise that she has nothing fresh to offer. Food is likewise used to bring out the callous, morbidly vampiric responses of the guests at the funeral of Mr Polly's father. 'Bit vulturial', Mr Polly thinks as he watches them tucking in to the cold meat. The fact that the same crew are on hand to celebrate his marriage to Miriam by another bout of public guzzling makes the two occasions ominously similar. Conversation at the wedding-feast keeps striking an appropriate note of avid vulgarity: ' "Sit down, everyone," cried Mr Voules. "Leaning against anything counts as sitting, and makes it easier to shake down the grub!" ' Priorities are bluntly established: ' "wot about drinking the 'ealth of the bride?" "Eat a bit fust," said Uncle Pentstemon, speaking with his mouth full, amidst murmurs of applause.' And the occasion ends with the prophetic observation that marriage is 'nat'ral—like . . . wind on the stummik'. As we have seen, food and culinary implements play their part in the battles waged to keep Uncle Jim, 'the Drorback', from repossessing the Potwell Inn. They do this so effectively that he is driven away, and eventually drowns: when his body later bobs back into the narrative, it is 'All whitey and eat away'.

Food, then, pervades the book, sometimes as quirky, obsessional embellishment, but often as a central idea, since the novel is so much concerned with the need for nourishment and the havoc wrought by inferior substitutes for it. Indigestion is both presented in all its mundane reality and used as a metaphor for other types of heart-burning—just as in *Tono-Bungay*, a novel which appeared a year before *Mr Polly*, patent medicine racketeering is detailed with comic panache and used as a central focus for the book's portrayal and indictment of deliquescent capitalism. Real ills are displayed in *Mr Polly*; spurious remedies in *Tono-Bungay*.

As Wells acknowledges in his autobiography, *Tono-Bungay* owes its basic idea to the month he spent working as a chemist's assistant at Midhurst, where, under the guidance of a Mr Cowap—who, 'like uncle Ponderevo, really did produce a heartening Cough Linctus'—he 'rolled a few score antibilious and rhubarb pills . . . learnt to sell patent medicines'. The book, like Ponderevo's business empire, ramifies vastly away from this, but much of its comic energy derives from Wells's familiarity with the world and jargon of patent medicines. A distaste for what they are doing—'bottling rubbish for the consumption of foolish, credulous, and depressed people'—is certainly felt. From the beginning of the enterprise, George is aware that 'The stuff was . . . a mischievous trash, slightly stimulating, aromatic, and attractive, likely to become a bad habit and train people in the habitual use of stronger tonics and insidiously dangerous to people with defective kidneys.' But the various advertising ploys are presented with hilarious relish. Gleefully, Wells captures the techniques of creating disquiet—'Many people who are MODERATELY well think they are QUITE well'; 'You are Young Yet, but are you Sure Nothing has Aged your Gums?' He zestfully records attempts to market the product as 'natural' ('TONO-BUNGAY. Like Mountain Air in the Veins') or 'scientific' ('Do you know what a Phagocyte is? . . . what Tono-Bungay really is is a sort of Worster [*sic*] Sauce for the Phagocyte. It gives it an appetite. It makes it a perfect wolf for the Influenza Bacillus'). And, just in case the point is still being missed, he includes a ludicrous parody by George's friend, Ewart: 'Why are Birds so Bright? Because they digest their food perfectly! Why do they digest their food so perfectly? Because they have a gizzard! Why hasn't man a gizzard? Because he can buy Ponderevo's Ashpit Triturating, Friable Biscuit—which is Better.' *Tono-Bungay* teems with references to advertising and mention of vaguely medical commodities—'Mother Shipton's Soothing Syrup', 'Cracknell's Ferric Wine', 'Sorber's Food', 'Decorticated Health-Bread'. Such concerns are present, too, in other books by Wells. Over the years, his works spotlight the advertising of such products as Bumper's British Boiled Jam, Wilder's Canned Peaches, Gobble's Sausages, Partington's Pure Packet Teas, Nabob Pickles, Harvester's Black Pepper, Staminal Bread, and The World Famed Easewood Sausage. As a natural sequel, patent medicine ads appear, offering ways of putting right digestive damage. In *Tono-Bungay*, Wells employs, for the most part, a tone of comic outrage. In the other books, his response is more clamorous. *Anticipations*, for instance, looking forward to a better future, assures us that, when it arrives, 'Probably many papers will refuse to print nasty and distressful advertisements about people's insides at all', and the 'flatulent falsehood' of these pieces will be severely penalised. Likewise, once an age of understanding has dawned after the earth's atmosphere has undergone a

tonic change in *In the Days of the Comet*, the narrator looks back
with disgust at the hoardings of yesteryear:

> Most of these referred to comestibles or to remedies to follow
> the comestibles. . . . The greater number, I may remark, of the
> advertisements that were so conspicuous a factor in the life of
> those days, and which rendered our vast tree-pulp newspapers
> possible, referred to foods, drinks, tobacco, and the drugs that
> promised a restoration of the equanimity these other articles
> had destroyed. Wherever one went one was reminded in
> glaring letters that, after all, man was little better than a worm,
> that eyeless, earless thing that burrows and lives uncomplain-
> ingly amidst nutritious dirt, 'an alimentary canal with the
> subservient appendages thereto'.

Wells may not seem too securely placed for criticism of those who
see man in alimentary terms, or, in view of some of his own
activities (such as urging Macmillan to publicise his books by
means of billboard men, or to stick up posters at Portsmouth
station saying 'Kipps Worked Here') very comfortably situated
for the launching of a high-minded attack upon advertising. But
attack it he frequently does. A further horror retailed by *In the
Days of the Comet* is that 'visceral counsels'—pill-advertising and
the like—are to be seen painted on the sides of bathing-machines;
whilst, in the account of the near future given in *The Sleeper
Awakes*, commercial propositions are blazoned across the cliffs
of Dover. Also, the optimism voiced in *Anticipations* is not really
borne out by some of Wells's glimpses into what is to come.
'Purkinje's Digestive Pills' feature ominously in 'A Story of the
Days to Come', and, as we have seen, the Antibilious Pill
Department is churning out its placebos in the world into which
the sleeper awakes (a world made raucous by advertising
dioramas, and containing such nutritional ingenuities as
mechanical wet-nurses mounted on tripods). *The Future in America*
shows Wells pondering on the successes of J. Morgan Richards,
the man who got Carter's Little Liver Pills rolling, and noting the
way his advertising ensured that 'all sorts of proprietary articles
landed well home in their gastric target'. Right at the end of his
fictional career, in *You Can't Be Too Careful*, he depicts a martyr to
such endeavours—Mrs Tewler, who 'died, as a great number of
people died in those days, of a surfeit of patent medicine advertise-

ments'. The world she lives in, Wells explains, has seen 'a steadily expanding business of pills, aperients, tonics, sustaining foods', since

> enterprising business men, realising that a vast majority of their fellow-creatures suffered from internal pains and discomforts due to the consumption of well-advertised but unwholesome foods, to the unhygienic quality of their housing and employment, and to the survival at a low level of existence of multitudes of individuals who would have been far better dead, devoted themselves to their exploitation.

Accordingly, subsisting on a 'medical menu', Mrs Tewler is duped and doped to death: 'She felt under-nourished, and, instead of taking wholesome food, she consumed a cup of feeble tea with a meaty flavour, that the salesmen assured her with vivid illustrations, had the strength of a whole ox in it. . . . She picked herself up with a viciously drugged wine.'

There are other characters in Wells who turn to drugs for one reason or another. Easton's Syrup, a stimulant, is sipped by many. Sir Richmond Hardy, for instance, confesses, 'I've been taking a few little things . . . Easton Syrup for example' (his doctor dismisses this with, 'Strychnine. It carries you for a time and drops you by the way': strychnine was also an ingredient of Tono-Bungay). The Bishop of Princhester's visions are triggered off by a special drug—'It isn't in the Pharmacopoeia'. Prothero finally appears as an opium-fiend, at the mercy of 'the evil thing in his veins'. George in *Tono-Bungay* fears Beatrice may be addicted to chloral. In one of the short stories there is a compound called 'The New Accelerator' that speeds people up; and in another, 'The Purple Pileus', Mr Coombes gets the force to assert himself through nibbling at fungus (rather as Bedford and Cavor are catapulted into exuberance by the bits of moon-plant they eat). Wells becomes suspicious, too, about what is being put into the food people are putting into themselves. *Phoenix*, for instance, sees him brooding on the damage he feels drugs have inflicted during the war: 'I am disposed to think that the deliberate drugging of troops by excitants has played a large part in the present war and that the fantastic cruelties of the Germans are due to a temporary insanity produced in this way'; and he widens his dark speculations to include the British bread supply:

The control of food under the novel totalitarian conditions that have been forced upon all the belligerent peoples has produced hitherto unthought of facilities for administering invigorating vitamins and stimulants to everyone. The 'national wholemeal loaf' provides a means for this even in Great Britain, and until the disorganisation of a positive military defeat arrests it, it is no doubt being done to a much greater extent to the Germans. Everywhere people are being under-nourished, over-strained and drugged.

Fatal doses of one kind or another dispatch a number of Wells's characters. William Clissold's father, and Lady Mary in *The Passionate Friends*, both poison themselves, and Amanda's father in *The Research Magnificent* commits suicide by drinking prussic acid. Rud Whitlow and Dolores are both given poison—one by design; the other, just possibly by accident. Graham in *The Sleeper Awakes* narrowly escapes poisoning.

Before this, though, Graham has had the opportunity of sampling the more innocuous cuisine of the future—'pink fluid with a greenish fluorescence and a meaty taste'—and has been struck by the elegantly labour-saving apparatus accompanying it—'a light table on silent runners carrying several bottles of fluids and glasses, and two plates bearing a clear substance like jelly'. Similar fare—'attractive amber-coloured jelly', 'a dark blue confection that promised well'—is set before Mr Mwres in 'A Story of the Days to Come' (written about the same time as *When the Sleeper Wakes*, the first version of *The Sleeper Awakes*). These bland comestibles, so decorously remote from their animal origins, are contrasted with the barbarism of contemporary provender:

It was a very different meal from a Victorian breakfast. The rude masses of bread needing to be carved and smeared over with animal fat before they could be made palatable, the still recognisable fragments of recently killed animals, hideously charred and hacked, the eggs torn ruthlessly from beneath some protesting hen,—such things as these, though they constituted the ordinary fare of Victorian times, would have awakened only horror and disgust in the refined minds of the people of these latter days. Instead were pastes and cakes of agreeable and variegated design, without any suggestion in colour or form of the unfortunate animals from which their substance and juices were derived.

Victorian foodstuffs are made mortifyingly unpleasant here; and in *The Sleeper Awakes* an instructive contrast is also drawn between nineteenth-century table manners and those of the future:

> He noted a slight significant thing; the table, as far as he could see, was and remained delightfully neat, there was nothing to parallel the confusion, the broadcast crumbs, the splashes of viand and condiment, the overturned drink and displaced ornaments which would have marked the stormy progress of the Victorian meal.

The possibility of an even more serene substitute for this tempestuous state of affairs is floated in 'The Man of the Year Million', where Wells imagines man 'no longer dining, with unwieldy paraphernalia of servants and plates, upon food queerly dyed and distorted, but nourishing himself in elegant simplicity by immersion in a tub of nutritive fluid'. More likely culinary changes are suggested in *Anticipations*, where we hear that the drawbacks of contemporary cooking—'the coaling, the ashes, the horrible moments of heat, the hot black things to handle, the silly vague recipes, the want of neat apparatus'—are to be replaced by 'a neat little range, heated by electricity and provided with thermometers, with absolute controllable temperatures and proper heat screens', so that it 'might easily be made a pleasant amusement for intelligent invalid ladies'.

In the *Days of the Comet* and *The Dream* also express distaste for contemporary cuisine. But, despite this, there are plenty of pleasantly rotund cooks and domestics on hand in Wells, dishing up appetising food. In *The Wealth of Mr Waddy*, the uncompleted manuscript of a novel that turned into *Kipps*, there is 'a Godsend, one Mrs Satsuma' who 'could cook admirably'. *Love and Mr Lewisham* contains a portrait of Wells's landlady from Midhurst, motherly Mrs Munday, who is horrified by hasty and indifferent eating—'It's ruination to a stummik—such ways.' The near future presented in *In the Days of the Comet* includes a glimpse of 'a broad-shouldered, smiling, freckled woman' who runs an inn and says, 'It's a pleasant place here when people are merry; it's only when they're jealous, or mean, or tired, or eat up beyond any stomach's digesting, or when they got the drink in 'em that Satan comes into this garden.' She seems quite a long way from the neat valetudinarians envisaged in *Anticipations*, and clearly belongs to the same benign species as the plump woman of the Potwell Inn. Occasionally, an unpleasant cook or landlady turns up in Wells—there is one in *The Undying Fire* who makes a heated appearance accompanied by 'a smell of burnt potatoes'. But, for the most part, those of his women who earn their living by cooking or serving food are jovial, rotund creatures given to bad syntax and eccentric pronunciation. Thus, Mathilda Good, a landlady in *The Dream*, 'much larger than any lady I had hitherto been accustomed to', explains: 'I got 'elp of a sort that won't slide downstairs on a tea-tray or lick the ground floor's sugar lump by lump, knowing the lumps was counted and never thinking that wetness tells, the slut!' A similarly Gampian note is heard in 'The Truth about Pyecraft', a story about 'The fattest clubman in London . . . a great rolling front of chins and abdomina'. Eager to become thin, this 'Great, uneasy jelly of substance' downs an old Indian recipe for 'Loss of Weight'—only to discover that it takes effect with dramatic literalness and he starts to float like a 'gas-filled bladder', still obese but weightless; in a desperate attempt to get his feet back on the ground (lead underclothes eventually provide the answer), he keeps demanding food until his landlady, 'An obviously worthy woman', worriedly breaks out, ''E keeps on calling for vittles, sir. *'Eavy* vittles 'e wants. I get 'im what I can. Pork 'e's 'ad, sooit puddin', sossiges, noo bread. . . . E's eatin', sir, something *awful*.' In *Babes in the Darkling Wood*, there is a virtuoso character-part performance from a domestic called, aptly enough, Mrs Greedle. She talks in the usual lower-class convention about 'a bit of 'am and a hegg or so and a nunion for taste', and

> felt whatever criticisms might be passed upon her fancy dishes, her soofles, crimes, mooses, kickshaws, glasses, gallant tins, soup-raims, rag-whos?, consommers and debauches—tomato soup the latter is, with a bit of cream on the top—her arlar thises and arlar thats—nevertheless at good old village cooking, at your bubble-and-squeak or your nice onion stew or your hot-pot or what not, she knew her business to a T.

There is a side of Wells that is always eager to escape into a world of unbuttoned Dickensian repletion where plump women with takingly absurd speech-patterns appear to derive their keenest pleasure from feeding others. Here, amidst much petit-bourgeois jocularity, his characters settle down to meals with jovial, appreciative relish.

It is a state he captures with beautiful enthusiasm in *Mr Polly* when the hero is out hiking through the English countryside with his two friends from the draper's:

> The arrival at the inn was a great affair. No one, they were convinced, would take them for drapers, and there might be a pretty serving-girl or a jolly old landlady. . . .
> There would always be weighty inquiries as to what they could have, and it would work out always at cold beef and pickles, or fried ham and eggs and shandygaff, two pints of beer and two bottles of ginger-beer foaming in a huge round-bellied jug.
> The glorious moment of standing lordly in the inn doorway and staring out at the world, the swinging sign, the geese upon the green, the duck-pond, a waiting wagon, the church tower, a sleepy cat, the blue heavens, with the sizzle of the frying audible behind one! The keen smell of the bacon! The trotting of feet bearing the repast; the click and clatter as the table ware is finally arranged! A clean white cloth! 'Ready, Sir!' or 'Ready, Gentlemen!' Better hearing that than 'Forward, Polly! Look sharp!'

The fresh zest of this, the pleasurable move from one comfortably stimulated sense to another—the sight of the countryside, the sound of the cooking, the smell of the food—is attractively recorded: as is the gratification of receiving service and courtesy for once instead of being pushed forward to offer them. Rare or long-deferred opportunities for gastronomic enjoyment are made the most of by Wells's characters. After a legacy rescues him from the drapery fare—'chiefly bread and margarine, infusions of chicory and tea-dust, colonial meat by contract at threepence a pound, potatoes by the sack, and watered beer'—one of Kipps's most relished indulgences is to make

> a very special thing of his breakfast. . . . there would be a cutlet or so or a mutton chop . . . haddock, kipper, whiting, or fish-

balls, eggs, boiled or scrambled, or eggs and bacon, kidney also frequently, and sometimes liver. Amidst a garland of such themes, sausages, black and white puddings, bubble-and-squeak, fried cabbage and scallops, came and went. Always as camp followers came potted meat in all varieties, cold bacon, German sausage, brawn, marmalade, and two sorts of jam; and when he had finished these he would sit among his plates and smoke a cigarette, and look at all these dishes crowded round him with beatific approval.

Responsiveness to food is well-developed in many of Wells's characters, and it is not rare to find them expressing it in rapturous apostrophe. Bedford, on returning home from his moon voyage, starts to think of 'earthly food', and ' "Bacon," I whispered, "eggs. Good toast and good coffee." ' Old Tom Smallways lets his mind drift back to eating in pre-war days, and 'For a time . . . resigned himself to the pleasures of gustatory reminiscence. His lips moved. "Pickled Sammin!" he whispered, "an' vinegar. . . . Dutch cheese. *Beer!*" '; while Mr Polly, approaching the Potwell Inn, is seized with anticipatory ecstasy: ' "Provender," he whispered . . . "Cold sirloin, for choice. And nutbrown brew and wheaten bread." '

All this whispering suggests an almost religious reverence for the commodities being called to mind: and bits of imagery from church do sometimes get into Wells's writings about food. Lady Grieswold, in *Meanwhile*, takes 'some more stuffed aubergine as if that act was in some way sacramental'; Bealby, watching a meal being fried, notes 'the hymning splash and splutter of the happy fat'; Mr Blettsworthy comments enthusiastically of a bowl of soup that 'It chanted with onions'; while Trafford remarks, 'I like the little sausages round the dish of a turkey . . . like cherubs they are, round the feet of a Madonna' (the plump lady's 'jolly chins', in *Mr Polly*, similarly cluster beneath her mouth 'like chubby little cherubim about the feet of an Assumption-ing Madonna').

On other occasions, the low-voiced response has a slightly different suggestiveness. In *Marriage*, whole pages are devoted to the swapping of food anecdotes by Trafford and Marjorie, and after she has been treated to a graphic account of how to handle a corn cob—'you take it up in your hands by both ends . . . and gnaw'—'Her face flushed a little at a guilty thought, her eyes sparkled. She leaned forward and spoke in a confidential undertone. *"I'd like to eat a mutton chop like that,"* said Marjorie.' These intimate confessions have been brought on by their famished sojourn in the wastes of Labrador. Though this experience has been undertaken so the couple may sort out their marital priorities, 'long discussions of eatables—sound, solid eatables' hold a high place on the agenda: ' "Dinners," said Trafford, "should be feasting, not the mere satisfaction of a necessity. There should be—*amplitude*. I remember a recipe for a pie . . . it began with: 'Take a swine and hew it into gobbets.' Gobbets! That's something like a beginning." '

Cold and hunger cause the salivatory fantasising going on here; and Wells is generally fond of denying his characters food for a while so he can register their appetite when they finally get at some. Probably his most gluttonous eaters are the moon-calves watched by the starving Bedford and Cavor. The first of these to be glimpsed has a 'fat-encumbered neck' and a 'slobbering omnivorous mouth'. Soon, it is joined by other 'animated lumps of provender', which 'lay against their food like stupendous slugs, huge, greasy hulls, eating greedily and noisily, with a sort of sobbing avidity'. These 'busy, writhing, chewing mouths' combine with 'the appetising sound of their munching' to torment Bedford and Cavor with a spectacle of 'animal enjoyment that was singularly stimulating to our empty frames'. Delightedly, Wells records the breakdown of the men to a state where they are prepared to eat anything. Bedford—whose 'mouth had become too dry for whispering'—admits, 'My mind ran entirely on edible things.' Tortured beyond endurance by the 'tempting fleshiness' and evidently 'biteable texture' of the moon-plants, he succumbs, starts to chew, is followed by Cavor, and 'For a time we did nothing but eat.' They have just, of course, made a long journey from earth; and travel normally gives Wells's characters an appetite. The Time Traveller is hungry when he arrives in 802,701, and ravenous when he gets back to his own day. Prendick is starving when rescued by Montgomery. Even the Angel who comes down to earth in *The Wonderful Visit* rapidly develops corporeal cravings—'do you know, I have the most curious sensations in my mouth—almost as if—it's so absurd!— as if I wanted to stuff things into it'. It being explained to him that this process is called eating, he quickly goes on, 'please show me how to eat. If you will. I feel a kind of urgency.' Similarly, in *The Autocracy of Mr Parham*, a spirit has scarcely materialised at a seance before it is demanding, 'Meat—sound meat in plenty. At present I'm still depending in part upon that fellow's nasty ectoplasm. I'm half a phantom still.' Ordeal by hunger is undergone by the narrator of *The War of the Worlds*—he admits, rather like Bedford, 'My mind ran on eating'—and by Bert Smallways in *The War in the Air*. And there is an unexpectedly ferocious moment in *Love and Mr Lewisham* when Wells turns briefly aside from his protagonists to show what has happened to some money that they have been swindled out of. Lucas Holderness, having got their guineas, makes a short, unforgettable incursion into the narrative in order to purchase food, and, after buying bread, 'bit a huge piece of the roll directly he was out of the shop, and went on his way gnawing. It was so large a piece that his gnawing mouth was contorted into the ugliest shapes. He swallowed by an effort, stretching his neck each time. His eyes expressed an animal satisfaction.'

Opposed to this craning, needy desperation—which makes Holderness seem like one of the moon-calves—are those moments in Wells when characters express their mood or personality by means of food. We are told of Miss Stanley in *Ann Veronica* that 'It was her distinctive test of an emotional state, its interference with a kindly normal digestion. Any one very badly moved choked down a few mouthfuls; the symptom of supreme distress was not to be able to touch a bit.' Accordingly, Lady Charlotte, in *Joan and Peter*, conveys that she is *in extremis* with the words, 'In the last twenty-four hours . . . I have eaten one egg, Mr Sycamore. . . . And some of that I left' (her nephew Oswald, on the other hand, broods bitterly on the way her unproductive life has been sustained by greedy intake and 'found himself estimating the weight of food and tanks of drink she must have consumed, the carcases of oxen and sheep, the cartloads of potatoes, the pyramids of wine bottles and stout bottles she had emptied'). The comfortless altruism of Altiora Bailey, in *The New Machiavelli*, is shown in the fact that, when she gathers together her 'interesting people in or about the public service', 'she fed them with a shameless austerity that kept the conversation brilliant, on a soup, a plain fish, and mutton or boiled fowl and milk pudding, with nothing to drink but whisky and soda, and hot or cold water, and milk and lemonade'. Sir Isaac Harman's disposition becomes loudly apparent as we witness him 'sitting at the breakfast-table eating toast and marmalade in a greedy, malignant manner', and hear that, by way of greeting his wife, he 'scrunched "morning" up amongst a crowded, fierce mouthful of toast'. Cranky Lady Beach-Mandarin, in the same novel, runs a 'Shakespeare Dinners Society—nothing he didn't mention eaten'. And there are more extreme examples of food-aestheticism—like the artistic cook in 'A Misunderstood Artist' who produces 'Nocturnes in imitation of Mr Whistler, with mushrooms, truffles, grilled meat, pickled walnuts, black pudding, French plums, porter—a dinner in soft velvety black, eaten in a starlight of small scattered candles'; or Aubrey Vair, the poet of 'In the Modern Vein', who praises his wife's chips as having 'exactly the tints of the dead leaves of the hazel'. The irascible domestic tyranny of Mr Pope, like that of Sir Isaac Harman, sometimes takes the form of aggressive mastication: when his wife attempts to refill his coffee-cup, he 'said with his mouth full, and strangely in the manner of a snarling beast: "No' ready yet. Half foo'."' In *The Autocracy of Mr Parham*, General Gerson, who has 'simian fits', shows himself to be even more bestial: 'He liked common and rather dirty food eaten standing, with the fingers instead of forks.'

What ways of eating most usually reveal in Wells's novels, though, is class origin. Many of his characters are seized by trepidation in situations requiring some degree of gastronomic finesse. Hoopdriver, in *The Wheels of Chance*, is 'cowed by a multiplicity of forks' and over-awed by the waiter in a Chichester inn. A young student, in 'The Story of the Late Mr Elvesham', is 'bothered by the stones of the olives' when taken to dinner in an expensive Regent Street restaurant. Blenker, in *The Wife of Sir Isaac Harman*, 'crumbled his bread constantly' and 'dropped his glasses in the soup' while 'the soups and sauces and things bothered his fine blond moustache unusually'. Kipps is continually being brought down by 'complicated obstacles to food': in particular, there is his meal at the Royal Grand Hotel which turns into a crescendo of public embarrassment as he moves from using the wrong cutlery to mangling and scattering a *vol-au-vent* to sending a chunk of his ice *bombe* shooting across the floor. Wiser characters take steps to avoid *faux-pas*—as when, with the upsurge of their fortunes, Aunt Susan and Teddy Ponderevo become 'social learners': 'The two of them learnt the new game rapidly and well; they experimented abroad, they experimented at home. At Chislehurst, with the aid of a new, very costly, but highly instructive cook, they tried over everything they heard of that roused their curiosity and had any reputation for difficulty, from asparagus to plover's eggs.' Thankfulness for having been saved from embarrassment at the dinner table is expressed in several novels. Mr Preemby is pleased 'there was nothing difficult to eat at tea', and Lady Harman—who comes from an impecunious background—is relieved to find herself confronted with 'nothing strange or difficult but caviare'. Any problems she experiences in handling this would certainly engage Wells's sympathies. As he reveals in his autobiography, talking of a dinner-party given to commemorate the demise of Henley's *National Observer*, it was a hurdle he himself had earlier come up against:

> I sat at the tail of the table, rather proud and scared, latest adherent to this gallant band. And because I was there at the end I was first served with a strange black blobby substance altogether unknown to me. I was there to enjoy myself and I helped myself to a generous portion. My next door neighbour —I rather fancy it was Basil Thompson—eyed the black mound upon my plate.
> 'I see you *like* caviar,' he remarked.
> 'Love it,' I said.
> I didn't, but I ate it all. I had my proper pride.

A sense—indeed, a fear—of being watched as they eat afflicts quite a number of Wells's characters. In *The Sleeper Awakes*, we hear that the Victorian lower middle-class was accustomed 'to feed with every precaution of privacy', and that 'its members, when occasion confronted them with a public meal, would usually hide their embarrassment under horseplay or a markedly militant demeanour'. Contributing to these anxieties are the novels' etiquette-vigilantes. In *The Wonderful Visit*, Mrs Hinijer, the vicar's housekeeper, objects to the way the Angel 'eats with his fingers at minced veal'. The narrator of 'In a Literary Household' says his wife Euphemia finds an acquaintance 'unpleasant . . . on account of his manner of holding his teacup'. Lady Burrows in *The Undying Fire* objects to Mr Dad's 'rather emphatic table manners', while Lady Stella in *Men Like Gods* comments critically on the fact that Fr Amerton is 'a little awkward with the forks and spoons'. In *The Secret Places of the Heart*, Sir Richmond Hardy finds it uncomfortable to dine in the presence of his wife, since 'Her refinement threw a tinge of coarseness over his eager consumption of his excellent clear soup.' But the person tormented most by an 'inbred fear of the table' is Kipps. Hungry for lunch, he enters a hotel dining-room but 'at the sight of a number of waiters and tables with remarkable complications of knives and glasses, terror seized him, and he backed out again'. When he does, later, summon up the courage to eat in public, 'He felt that everyone was watching him and making fun of him, and the injustice of this angered him. After all, they had had every advantage he hadn't.'

Lack of advantages—social, physical, and intellectual—and the subsequent stunting of life are often portrayed in Wells's fiction. When, towards the end of *Kipps*, he remarks, 'I see through the darkness the souls of my Kippses as they are, as little pink strips of quivering, living stuff, as things like the bodies of ill-nourished, ailing, ignorant children', he epitomises in a characteristic image one of his dominating ideas: the idea that knowledge is nourishment, that its denial hinders the proper development of human potential. We are, Cavor remarks in an intoxicated moment in *The First Men in the Moon*, 'the creashurs o' what we eat and drink'. We are also the creatures of what we read and hear; and Wells constantly compares mental assimilation to physical. As William Clissold puts it, 'there is what is fed to us—*dietary* shall I call it?—in which I include not only meat and drink and the want of them, but the reception or lack of all we can inhale or inject into our systems, fresh air or unexpected ideas'. *You Can't Be Too Careful* shows Wells finding an ally in this way of thinking—a Mr Jennings White who 'would sweep away the word "education" altogether, as a tainted word, and have us talk of *Eutrophy*, good nourishment of body and mind'; and in *Science and the World-Mind*, published a year later, Wells is still enthusing over his discovery—'I confess I find it a most attractive word.' Food for thought is a metaphor elaborated copiously throughout Wells's writing. We hear that the Selenites store knowledge 'in distended brains much as the honey-ants of Texas store honey in their distended abdomens': and this is very much the way in which Wells sees the relationship between the human brain and knowledge. What he calls, in *The Bulpington of Blup*, 'that hungry young brain-cortex' is often to be seen pursuing knowledge in his books. Many of his characters, like Fanny in *The Dream*, are witnessed 'reading voraciously, greedily'; many like

Remington of *The New Machiavelli*, possess 'a mind of vigorous appetite'; many, like Bolaris in *The Brothers*, can claim to be 'a glutton for books' (especially Rud Whitlow, who, in his school-days, 'bolted the feast of knowledge and threw it up again with ease, completely undigested'; and George Ponderevo who has made excursions into Bladesover library that were 'Oddly rat-like . . . darting into enormous places in pursuit of the abandoned crumbs of thought'). England, Wells tells us in *The Future in America*, is making 'mentally hungry' men by the thousand in her elementary schools; and he is eager to inspect the intellectual fare on offer to them. Mainly it appears to be inferior stuff, as is stressed again and again. 'Much absolute rubbish is fed to this great hunger,' says William Clissold, 'and still more adulterated food. This appetite, which should grow with what it feeds on, is thwarted and perverted.' An example of this is on display in *Marriage* in the disadvantaged shape of Dowd, a technical assistant who had

> read with a sort of fury, feeding his mind on the cheap and adulterated instruction of grant-earning crammers and on stale, meretricious and ill-chosen books; his mental food indeed was the exact parallel of the rough, abundant, cheap and nasty groceries and meat that gave the East-ender his spots and dyspeptic complexion; the cheap text-books were like canned meat and dangerous with intellectual ptomaines, the rascally encyclopaedias like weak and whitened bread, and Dowd's mental complexion, too, was leaden and spotted.

In *Mankind in the Making*, Wells had similarly looked with disgust at a disorganised public-library catalogue, asking, 'What can you expect from such a supply but a pitiful mental hash? What is the most intelligent of mechanics likely to secure for himself from this bran pie?' Tainted mental dietary is frequently the subject of hostile comment in his work. Carstall, in *The Holy Terror*, de-nounces 'hungry sheep' who 'swallow . . . dead old religions no longer fit for human consumption' or 'devour their silly news-papers'; Muriel, in *The Wealth of Mr Waddy*, has a 'romantic turn of mind nourished to excess on an exclusive dietary of novels'; while Belloc, in *Mr Belloc Objects*, is dismissed as besotted by the heady brew of his own fantasising—confounded in argument, 'He takes a fresh sip or so from his all too complaisant imagination' and, fortified by this, is able to ramble on again. Surveying Wellesley College in *The Future in America*—'How far . . . are these girls thinking and feeding mentally for themselves?'—Wells is disquieted to learn that they are being offered such bland intellectual pabulum as a special version of the Italian Renaissance, softened and strained of any impurities: 'a great civilization . . . *canned*, as it were . . . and freed from any deleterious ingredients'. At Cambridge, it emerges from *Babes in the Darkling Wood*, things are even worse: students there are given 'stale and decaying canned food. Is it any wonder that you find the bright youngsters turning from that to eat cheap, fly-blown stuff from the barrow at the corner, which at any rate has hormones?'

To think of literature in terms of food is almost a reflex action for Wells; and, of course, he can indicate precedents for this— George Newnes, for instance, who, as *The Dream* recounts, 'went on to the idea of a weekly periodical full of scraps of interest, cuttings from books and newspapers and the like. A hungry multitude, eager and curious, was ready to feed greedily on such *hors d'oeuvre*. So *Tit-Bits* came into existence.' In Wells, proprietors of magazines and journals tend to talk as though they are running a restaurant. 'They buy our paper to swallow it, and it's got to go down easy', a newspaper-man says in *The Sea Lady*, whilst in *The New Machiavelli* someone objects, 'We can't turn out a great chunk of printed prose like—like wet cold toast and call it a magazine.'

Reading is seen as a kind of mental eating, and other types of intellectual activity can be viewed in the same way. 'I nibble at religion', confesses Lady Mary in *The Passionate Friends;* and Rowland Palace in *Brynhild* has an uneasy moment when he notices his wife storing up his words: 'she was going off with them to gnaw them in quiet. And immediately he knew that they were—innutritious.' Lack of interest, in this same book, takes the form of contemptuously rapid consumption: Brynhild's father says he 'swallowed the Thirty Nine Articles at a gulp and thought no more about them. If he had masticated them they might have got into his system and given him trouble.'

Wells's own writings and beliefs, however, are to be digested and absorbed. *The Common Sense of War and Peace* carries the exhortation, 'Read me . . . assimilate me to yourself (and assimilation may very well mean a digestive change and improvement)', while *'42 to '44* offers a preliminary warning that 'taken altogether this book is "strong meat for babes"'. Deliberately, Wells's books are aimed at improving the condition of what *Mankind in the Making* calls 'the flabby, narrow-chested, under-trained mind'.

The equation of food with ideas of a mind-broadening nature is made most memorably perhaps in *The Food of the Gods* (despite the fact that this title had already been used for a book about cocoa, Wells insisted on appropriating it for his own work). This novel followed *Mankind in the Making*, and fantastically fills out some of its theories. Like *Tono-Bungay*, too, it deals with booster-nourishment, but, in this case, what is offered turns out to be genuine. 'The Food of the Gods . . . Herakleophorbia . . . The nutrition of a possible Hercules' is a compound which vastly increases the size of organisms. It is introduced in a typically Wellsian scene when the narrator attends a magic-lantern show and is detained, out of curiosity, by a strange noise emerging from the gloom. Waiting until the lights go up, he discovers that 'this sound was the sound of the munching of buns and sandwiches and things that the assembled British Associates had come there to eat under cover of the magic-lantern darkness'. Bizarre masticatory detail, here as so often in Wells, pulls a disproportionate amount of attention to itself—though, on this occasion, with a degree of aptness since the talk has been about a new kind of nourishment, 'Boomfood' as it comes to be known. Soon, having leaked into general circulation, this potential-expanding provender is causing havoc. Chickens, fed on it, become so large that they can eat a cat. An emu-sized pullet tries to make off with a child. Giant rats almost succeed in devouring a doctor, and do consume a horse. Enormously distended eels wriggle ashore at Sunbury and kill sheep. Pangbourne sees a battle with gargantuan ants in which 'Three men were bitten and died.' A science-teacher, out collecting specimens, narrowly escapes with his life after being set upon by monster water beetles: 'attached to Mr Carrington's cheek, to his bare arm, and to his thigh, and lashing furiously with their lithe brown muscular bodies, were three of these horrible larvae, their great jaws buried deep in his flesh and sucking for dear life'. With tenacious voracity, even after the bodies have been chopped away, 'the severed heads remained for a space, still fiercely biting home and still sucking, with the blood streaming out of their necks behind'.

It is characteristic of Wells's imagination to dwell fascinatedly upon such details. The ghoulish relish comically attributed to a newspaper-seller in the novel is not, in fact, all that remote from the author's own excited gloating: 'Doctor . . . eaten by rats. 'Orrible affair—'orrible affair—rats—eaten by Stchewpendous rats. Full perticulars.' Grisly bits of mortuary detail about those who have fallen prey to various hypertrophied predators keep being pushed towards us. The 'larger bones of a cat picked very clean and dry' are discovered after the giant chickens have passed that way. And the rearer of the chickens may, it seems, have met a similar fate: after he has disappeared, a glass eye which could be his turns up along with 'something which may or may not have been a human shoulder-blade, and in another part of the ruins a long bone greatly gnawed and equally doubtful'. Wounds, too, are itemised with loving attention, as when a doctor is savaged: 'bitten he was and badly—a long slash like the slash of a tomahawk that had cut two parallel ribbons of flesh from his left shoulder'. The major part of the novel presents Boomfood as something which causes disaster. Its dangerously magnifying effects on the smaller carnivores are enthusiastically recorded, as are the manglings and mayhem that follow. It comes, therefore, as something of a surprise to find, later in the book, that Wells intends the Food to be seen as a boon to mankind. Horror is first modulated to farce with an account of one of the children who have thrived on the Food, young Caddles who 'ate a swede as one devours a radish. He would stand and eat apples from a tree, if no one was about, as normal children eat blackberries from a bush.' Then, there is another abrupt shift to a tone of lofty philosophising, from which we gather that the Food is meant to symbolise all that can increase man's potential, help him to greater things—not something which, by enlarging predators, constitutes a danger to the race. Those who have not consumed it represent small-minded, rancorously-limited responses to life. The book ends on a note of windy, vaguely biblical afflatus: 'Great and little cannot understand one another. But in every child born of man . . . lurks some seed of greatness—waiting for the Food.'

'Our modern community', Wells insists in *World Brain*, 'is mind-starved and mind-hungry. It is justifiably uneasy and suspicious of the quality of what it gets. The hungry sheep look up and are not fed.' In *The Outlook for Homo Sapiens* he writes, 'I will confess I dislike the restriction and distortion of knowledge as I dislike nothing else on earth. In this modern world it is, I hold, second only to murder to starve and cripple the mind of a child.' What he is working for, he explains in *The Conquest of Time*, is 'a world of intelligent Euphoria . . . a world, that is to say, of easily accessible good nourishment for mind and body', a world where 'Normal people free from fear will learn by a natural appetite, and go on learning as naturally as they eat and go on eating.' The most obvious way in which he caters for this appetite is by his 'historical and biological digests', for, as he recalls in *The Outlook for Homo Sapiens*, the vast sales of *The Outline of History* revealed to him 'a world-wide hunger for adequately summarised knowledge on the part of multitudes whom the schools had sent empty away'. It is not only his overtly pedagogic books that are concerned to offer something the mind can get its teeth into, however. Wells is always eager to present and process what he sees as crucial facts in such a way that they are both appetising and easily assimilable. One such fact that his books, fiction and non-fiction, keep feeding into the mind is the paramount importance of mental and physical nourishment. In his autobiography, Wells declares that some of his work is 'as white and pasty in its texture as a starch-fed nun'. When it deals with eating, though, it is anything but blanched and stodgy. Then, what he called, in 'The Scepticism of the Instrument', 'a mind nourished upon anatomical study' combines with the memories, resentments, and urges of a body once enfeebled by malnutrition to infuse his writing with a colourful and often ferocious intensity.

2 The Slave Goddess: Wells and Sex

Sex, *The Secret Places of the Heart* reminds us, can be looked at in two ways—as bringing about *'a renewal of life in the species'* or *'a renewal of energy in the individual'*. It is the second of these aspects that fascinates Wells. His interest in the first is relatively cursory and largely stimulated by individual circumstances. Only two of his books, *Anticipations* and *Mankind in the Making*, could be said to deal at any length with human reproduction. He wrote each of them when his wife was expecting a baby. *Anticipations*, insisting that 'the main mass of the business of human life centres about reproduction' and dismissing a childless life as 'essentially failure and perversion', appeared in 1901: so did Wells's first son. 'Mrs Wells and I have been collaborating (and publication is expected early in July) in the invention of a human being', he explained to Arnold Bennett. *Mankind in the Making*, proclaiming that 'Exceptionally good people owe the world the duty of parentage', coincided with Wells's undertaking of this duty for a second time—with the arrival of his son Frank in 1903.

Both books stress the importance of producing fine progeny, the significantly-named *Mankind in the Making* going into italics to emphasise its belief that *'Any collective human enterprise, institution, movement, party or state, is to be judged as a whole and completely, as it conduces more or less to wholesome and hopeful births.'* When it comes to determining how such births can be ensured, however, certainty departs. *Anticipations* points ominously to what is not wanted: 'the spectacle of a mean-spirited, under-sized, diseased little man . . . married to some underfed, ignorant, ill-shaped, plain and diseased little woman, and guilty of the lives of ten or twelve ugly ailing children'. For such as these, we are given to understand— 'born of unrestrained lusts, and increasing and multiplying through sheer incontinence and stupidity'—the citizens of a more enlightened age, the New Republicans, will have 'little pity and less benevolence'. But what exactly will be done to staunch their 'reproductive excesses' is never stated. Wells just hints darkly at unspecified aversion therapy: 'the multiplication of those who fall behind a certain standard of social efficiency' will be made 'unpleasant and difficult'; they 'can easily be made to dread it'. Posses of eugenic zealots will 'rout out . . . all the places where the base can drift to multiply'; and, as for sub-standard ethnic groups—'those swarms of black, and brown, and dirty-white, and yellow people, who do not come into the new needs of efficiency'—'Well, the world is a world, not a charitable institution, and I take it they will have to go.' In *Mankind in the Making*, there is an attempt to look rather more positively at the fact that the world 'is no more than a great birth-place' into which 'a huge spout, that no man can stop, discharges a baby every eight seconds'. But Wells's survey of eugenic literature yields no very fruitful suggestions as to how the standard of these deliveries can be improved. We are, he has to admit, 'not a bit clear what points to breed for and what points to breed out'. A quality such as beauty, for instance, is hopelessly diverse and nebulous, and, in any case, there is no way of knowing how it can be generated. 'The sentimentalized affinities of young persons in their spring are just as likely to result in the improvement of the race in this respect' as anything the scientists—'groping in a corner where science has not been established'—have come up with. *The Shape of Things to Come* sees this state of affairs extending into the foreseeable future: there, as far ahead as 2060, human eugenics is still problematical.

Not much, it seems, can be done before birth to modify 'that raw material which is perpetually dumped upon our hands'. After birth, Wells demonstrated, there can be distinct indifference towards it. He left home as soon as his first son was born, rambling round southern England for some weeks, much to his wife's dismay. Some of his characters take the urge to play truant from their offspring even further. Trafford and Marjorie, abandoning their brood without a qualm, go off for a long stay in Labrador. Benham in *The Research Magnificent* (a book published not long after Rebecca West had borne Wells a child) thinks of maternity as 'a rare and sacramental function', but leaves his wife to perform it alone. Though she plies him with 'philoprogenitive' literature, he prefers to globe-trot round Asia during her pregnancy, and after reappearing to inspect 'the Cub', soon departs hot-foot for India again.

Mr Britling, it is true, declares, 'you don't really know what love is until you have children. . . . the love of children is an exquisite tenderness: it rends the heart'. But he is exceptional in that the parental impulse, in Wells's books, is usually a female prerogative. 'I cannot recall a single philoprogenitive moment,' Sir Richmond assures his analyst, when discussing sexual fantasies in *The Secret Places of the Heart*: whatever attracted him to his dream women, 'Certainly it wasn't babies.' Many of Wells's other males might agree; and he himself informed Rebecca West, 'I *hate* being encumbered with a little boy and a nurse, and being helpful' (she was later to be struck by the 'very large number' of letters in which he referred to their child, Anthony, 'with indifference and hostility'). His female characters, on the other hand, can be dotingly bedecked with offspring. In *The Sleeper Awakes*, we hear of 'that figure of a grave, patient woman . . . mother and maker of men—to love her was a sort of worship', while Stratton in *The Passionate Friends*, obsessed with another woman, tremulously draws his son's attention to 'that dear spirit of love who broods over you three children, that wise, sure mother who rules your life'. 'Mummy', it is worth noting, was one of Wells's pet names for his wife Jane; and she lived up to her maternal title conscientiously, even to the point of going out to buy baby-clothes when it was revealed that Amber Reeves, the daughter of prominent Fabians, was about to have a child by Wells. In *The Passionate Friends*, Lady Mary points out that 'womankind' is 'specialised for the young, not only naturally and physically as animals are, but mentally and artificially'. And Wells's women can be fairly ruthless in pursuit of their specialism. In *Brynhild*, Mrs Palace opts enthusiastically for maternity—'I'm going to have—*children*'—and finds it 'a very interesting and satisfying role. "The juices" played up loyally.' The juices are, however, rather more loyal than Mrs Palace, the first of whose five children is—although he doesn't know it—not her husband's. Subterfuge and pregnancy also collude in *Christina Alberta's Father*, where Christina Alberta's mother, finding herself pregnant by a man who has left her, quickly seduces feeble Mr Preemby into marrying her by means of a 'passionate pounce' and kissing that is 'quite different . . . from anything he had ever met around Norwich'. Even Wells's most resolutely infertile lady, Dolores, pretends to be having a baby in order to force Wilbeck to marry

her: after which, 'the child began to evaporate. A sort of annun-
ciation in reverse occurred.' In *Love and Mr Lewisham*, Ethel, close
to losing her husband, repairs their marriage with the riveting
announcement of her pregnancy.

Resentment at female fecundity is sometimes expressed in the
novels. Embittered Oswald in *Joan and Peter* puts it particularly
savagely: 'Women were just things of sex, child-bearers, dressed
up to look like human beings. . . . They were the cheap lures of
that reproductive maniac, herself feminine, old Mother Nature.
. . . Sterile themselves, life nested in them'. The same image of
Nature as a monstrous female avid for impregnation is presented
almost twenty years later in *The Anatomy of Frustration*: 'She
clutches us into a crisis, squeezes out of us what she is after and
throws us aside.' And, though visions of the procreative urge as
a sort of female rapist are unlikely to enter the prim mind of
Martineau in *The Secret Places of the Heart*, even he complains,
'Nature has set about this business in a *cheap* sort of way. . . . she
just humbugs us into what she wants with us.' The indignation
expressed here—at the species taking priority over the individual—
accords oddly with Wells's regular insistence elsewhere that
this ought to be the case; and the attitude to propagation is
markedly at variance with the pious tributes being offered by the
father-to-be at the beginning of the century. In fact, apart from
a special interest in the subject as a result of forthcoming
parenthood, Wells is not at all given to regarding sex as a
procreative matter. It is its effect on him, not the human stock,
that he finds really engrossing.

Wells's writings about sex are very personal and often autobiographical. A sexually communicative—not to say boastful—
urge was always prominent in him. During his brief spell as a
teacher in Wales, he sent off bulletins to friends, keeping them
up to date on the progress of his wooing of the local minister's
daughter, 'a creature with soul'; and carefully included bits of
amatory evidence: 'The letters are getting warmer now as per
enclosed specimens.' Over two decades later, during the fuss over
his affair with Amber Reeves, he is writing in a similarly con-
scious-of-audience way to his friend, Elizabeth Healey, 'Believe
everything scandalous and nothing mean about me and you'll be
fairly right'; while a more man-to-man note is struck in his
correspondence with Arnold Bennett. Here, speaking of what
happened after Amber married someone else, he explains,

by the bye, it may interest you to know that that affair of philoprogenitive passion isn't over. . . . Interesting and remarkable psychological reactions followed. The two principals appeared to have underestimated the web of affections and memories that held them together. The husband, a perfectly admirable man, being married attempted to play a husband's part—(which was asinine of him). Violent emotional storms have ensued and there is a separation and I think it will be necessary out of common fairness to him to give him grounds and have a divorce—and run a country cottage in the sight of all mankind.

A preening sense of being watched—discernible here in such stagey talk as 'principals' and 'in sight of'—frequently emerges in Wells's writings about sex: as does the rather gloating cockiness of another letter to Bennett, written when Wells was still involved with Rebecca West, who often had to pass as his secretary when they travelled together. Chuckling self-indulgently over 'my temporary hymenic indiscretions', it announces, with a rubbing of hands, 'I think I shall get through to Amalfi all right and there a warm-hearted secretary will look after me night and day.'

This sexual swagger shows itself in some of the novels. *Ann Veronica* ('the Young Mistress' Tale' as he called it to Bennett) was notoriously autobiographical, a defiant public flaunting of some aspects of the Amber Reeves affair—even though, Wells assures us in his autobiography, 'It was only a slight reflection of anything that had actually occurred.' *The New Machiavelli* offers another bravado replay of that scandal. And there are many other instances of sexually autobiographical material in the books. Wells's first marriage, to his cousin Isabel, is depicted in Mr Lewisham's relationship with Ethel and George Ponderevo's sexually disappointing union with Marion in *Tono-Bungay*. Catherine Robbins—or Jane, as Wells called her—with whom he eloped a couple of years after marrying Isabel, provided a model for the portrait of passionless Mrs Britling, sharing with her husband a 'marriage in neutral tint'; and there is a sharp cameo of one of Wells's mistresses, the writer Elizabeth von Arnim, in the same book, as Mrs Harrowdean. Also, of course, the three-sided situation in which Wells had found himself—painfully torn between Jane and Isabel (for whom he retained strong feelings for years)—is reflected in many of the novels, and was to reoccur in his life. A man divided between two women appears in over a dozen of the books. And, once married to Jane, Wells soon felt the external pull again. To keep their marriage going, they agreed that he should be allowed *passades*, affairs of physical enjoyment without any dangerous emotional involvement: what William Clissold refers to as 'casual encounters . . . passades . . . brief passions of pursuit and success'. The main risk was that these would become too serious, a problem Wells encountered on a number of occasions and recorded in his novels. After the affair with Amber Reeves had given rise to its frictions and its fictions and lapsed into non-existence (she is distantly glimpsed in *Marriage* as 'a markedly correct and exclusive mother of daughters'), Wells became involved with Rebecca West, and continued to be so for ten years. She appears in various guises in his fiction, dependent on the state of their relationship at the time. The most prolonged account is in *The Research Magnificent*, where she is Amanda, but there is also a portrayal of her as Martin Leeds, the carbuncled artist in *The Secret Places of the Heart*, and Helen, the egocentric actress in *The World of William Clissold*. This last novel contains, too, in the portrait of Clementina, an announcement of the fact that Odette Keun had entered Wells's life. When she left it, nearly ten years later, taking what Wells regarded as his own property in the South of France with her, she was pulled back into his fiction and hilariously savaged in the vituperative pages of *Apropos of Dolores*.

It is not only in the scrapbook sense that Wells's writings about sex are personal. They also constantly pass on his obsessions and idiosyncrasies. The first of these to be developed, as he recalls in his autobiography, was a sexual fixation on Britannia and other emblematic females on display in *Punch*. Speaking of 'the stimulating influence of Britannia, Erin, Columbia and the rest of them upon my awakening susceptibilities', he explains that this was because they were 'bare armed, bare necked, showing beautiful bare bosoms, revealing shining thighs, wearing garments that were a revelation in an age of flounces and crinolines'. 'My first consciousness of women,' he says, 'my first stirrings of desire were roused by these heroic divinities': and in the case of Britannia they were later reciprocated, it seems, to judge from a bizarre letter Wells sent Rebecca West in 1917, announcing

I am a Male
I am a Male
I am a MALE
I have got Great Britain Pregnant.

The 'plaster casts of Greek statuary that adorned the Crystal Palace' also worked their spell—one under which many of Wells's male protagonists fall as they awaken sexually. The 'deep breasted Venuses and Britannias' who took such a hold on his budding susceptibilities do the same to many of his characters. William Clissold confesses, 'My desires were developed in relation to nude pictures and statuary.' Sir Richmond Hardy similarly remembers: 'My first love was Britannia—as depicted by Tenniel in the cartoons of *Punch*. . . . I just clung to her in my imagination and did devoted things for her. Then I recall, a little later, a secret abject adoration for the white goddesses of the Crystal Palace.' Remington in *The New Machiavelli* responds to the lovely casts more potently: 'The plaster Venuses and Apollos that used to adorn the vast aisle and huge grey terraces of the Crystal Palace were the first intimations of the beauty of the body that ever came into my life. As I write of it I feel again the shameful attraction of those gracious forms.' George Ponderevo has had a similar experience in South Kensington—'in the big art museum I came for the first time upon the beauty of nudity'; and his response to Marion is made vivid and fixed by the fact that, one afternoon, returning from 'the gallery of casts from the antique', his mind 'all alive' with a 'newly awakened sense of line', he perceives 'her body drooping forward from the hips just a little—memorably graceful—feminine'. Mr Brumley in *The Wife of Sir Isaac Harman* seems a product of the same conditioning: he not only mentally endows abstractions like Goodness and Justice with 'rich feminine figures', but keeps a life-size model of the Venus de Milo in his bow-window. On a humbler level, Harry Mortimer Smith of *The Dream* falls in love as a boy with 'an undraped plaster nymph' sitting on a spouting dolphin in some public gardens.

Other characters form an ideal from pictorial art, an especial favourite being the Delphic Sibyl from the Sistine Chapel—whose 'mighty loveliness' Wells had 'pondered immensely over' in a book of engravings at Up Park. Stratton in *The Passionate Friends* remembers a photograph of this in his father's study 'that

for a time held my heart'; hanging over Mr Brumley's desk, there
is 'that pretty little slut of a Delphic Sibyl'; Theodore Bulpington,
who has also fallen prey to the alluring fresco, is delighted, on
meeting Margaret, to realise he 'had seen her a thousand times!
She had the same broad brow, the same sweet eyes . . . the Delphic
Sibyl, thirteen years old. With a taste for greengage jam. It was
wonderful, incredible'; and the Sibyl takes flesh again as one of
the Utopian beauties encountered in *Men Like Gods*. Remington
treasures an engraving, too: it is 'a half length of a bare-
shouldered, bare-breasted Oriental with arms akimbo, smirking
faintly', and he says it 'became in a way my mistress'.

Many of the mistresses in Wells's fiction owe their lineaments
to the imprint of such stimulating *objets d'art*. Women in his books
often tend towards the statuesque, while men frequently hanker
after what *The Anatomy of Frustration* calls 'a strong, quietly
animated goddess-slave. Or a strong, quietly animated slave-
goddess.' Sir Richmond, seeking a 'companion goddess',
explains, 'I liked to dream of a blonde goddess in her own
Venusberg one day, and the next I would be off over the
mountains with an armed Brunhild.' This dream of mythological
promiscuity is briefly realised by Mr Palace, lured away from his
wife Brynhild into the arms of Lady Cytherea, who has played
Venus to his Paris in a charade. Theodore Bulpington achieves
a long afternoon in a 'little Venusberg' with Rachel, an 'extremely sympathetic Venus in mufti'. Lady Catherine stands
over Mr Sempack in *Meanwhile* 'like Venus in a semi-translucent
mist'. Alice in *Apropos of Dolores* is 'all the Venuses' to Wilbeck,
and Dolores presents herself to him as an 'emotional Diana'. In
The Sea Lady, there is a battle of the goddesses when Chatteris,
torn between his bluestocking fiancée and a possessive mermaid,
feels he must decide between 'Pallas Athene' and 'Venus
Anadyomene'. In the end, Venus, 'the sea goddess', wins, leading
him off into the deeps. A hall porter who has witnessed this act
of triumph was, we are told, 'difficult to follow in his description
of the Sea Lady. She wore her wrap, it seems, and she was "like
a statue"—whatever he may have meant by that.' The bewilderment is surely disingenuous. This description of the splendid
lady—'One arm was bare . . . and her hair was down, a tossing
mass of gold'—immediately places her in the familiar gallery of
Wells's monumental lovelies. Helen Walshingham, with whom
Kipps becomes nervously involved, represents a more realistic

version of the statue-woman as menace. When Kipps serves her in the draper's, 'She smiled like a satisfied goddess as the incense ascends', but, once he inherits a fortune, 'that period of standing humbly in the shadows before the shrine was over, and the goddess, her veil of mystery flung aside, had come down to him and taken hold of him, a good strong firm hold'. Trepidation takes hold of Kipps, too—and consoling thoughts of homely, unthreatening Ann Pornick. Fleeing Helen after she has turned up at a dinner party, in Olympian deshabillé, displaying her 'dazzling' deltoids and making him feel 'she had become as remote, as foreign, as incredible as a wife and mate' as 'the Cnidian Venus herself', he marries lowly Ann instead, and the author genially pats them on the head: 'in due course these two simple souls married, and Venus Urania, the Goddess of Wedded Love, who is indeed a very great and noble and kindly goddess, bent down and blessed their union.'

Most of Wells's heroes, however, are made of more ambitious stuff. They want the goddess in their arms, not stooping down to smile upon their homely nuptials—though they are not averse to their women seeming to be above them for a while. Temporary elevation of the female, something which makes her ultimate subordination the more gratifying, is a marked feature of Wells's novels. One of his main ways of achieving this is by placing his women on high objects. Walls provide convenient pedestals, besides allowing a quick glimpse of black-stockinged leg, in *Tono-Bungay* and *Mr Polly*. George recalls an incident with Beatrice when he was

on the park side of the stone wall, and the lady of my worship a little inelegantly astride thereon. . . . Just her pose on the wall comes suddenly clear before me, and behind her the light various branches of the shrubbery that my feet might not profane, and far away and high behind her, dim and stately, the cornice of the great façade of Bladesover rose against the dappled sky.

It is from this lofty vantage point that she gets him to declare he is her 'humble, faithful lover', and then kisses him. A variant on this scene occurs the following year in *Mr Polly* when the hero encounters a schoolgirl perched on the wall of her expensive school: 'She certainly looked quite adorable on the wall. She had a fine neck and pointed chin that was particularly admirable from below, and pretty eyes and fine eyebrows are never so pretty as when they look down upon one.' The last phrase here can have two meanings—something earlier taken advantage of at the end of *The Wheels of Chance*. In that novel, Hoopdriver, a draper's assistant, becomes romantically involved with a girl who is 'emphatically "above" him'. For a while, they take on the roles of Knight and Lady: she calls him 'Knight-errant', and looks down approvingly as he chivalrously bends to light the lantern of her bicycle. Eventually, she is whisked back to 'those social altitudes of hers' by an indignant stepmother. Before this, she goes for a farewell walk with Hoopdriver and 'stood on ground a little higher than he, so that he had to look up to her. . . . She seemed to look down at him. Of course, she looked down at him, he thought.' Similarly, in the scenes from *Tono-Bungay* and *Mr Polly*, the elevation is not merely physical. Beatrice's background includes the stately home where George's mother is housekeeper, and Mr Polly is keenly aware that he is of lower social standing than Christabel, the girl who is 'looking queenly down' on him. Unlike Hoopdriver, though, he objects to his lady's desire to keep everything within the realm of chivalric ritual—' "Knight," she cried. . . . "Knight there!" '—and exasperatedly informs her, 'I'm not a knight. Treat me as a human man.' Others are more satisfied with the *châtelaine* response—Stratton in *The Passionate Friends*, for instance, who is graciously rewarded after helping Lady Mary climb into a tree so that 'she was looking down upon me':

> 'Stephen dear,' she said, 'dear, dear Boy; I have never wanted to kiss you so much in all my life. . . .'
> She bent her fresh young face down to mine, her fingers were in my hair.
> 'My Knight,' she whispered close to me. 'My beautiful young Knight.'

Again, there is a difference of social position here—'Matrimonially I was as impossible as one of the stable boys', he realises—and this is a recurrent situation in Wells's earlier novels. Hoopdriver, Kipps, George Ponderevo, Mr Polly, Stratton are all captivated by the haughty fascination of the lady (something Wells himself was not indifferent to: Beatrice Webb commented acidly on his 'dining with duchesses and lunching with countesses', and Amber Reeves complained that, after she had eloped to Le Touquet with him 'He kept hankering to go back whenever he got invitations from Lady Desborough or anyone').

Being looked down upon by a woman regularly gives Wells's males a *frisson*. Graham, in *The Sleeper Awakes*, gets his first tantalising glimpse of high-minded Helen Wotton in this way: 'He looked up and saw passing across a bridge of porcelain and looking down upon him a face that was almost immediately hidden.' A variant on this combination of nobility and architectural aids to elevation occurs in Wells's script for a film that was never made, *The King Who Was a King*. Suddenly found to be the heir to the Claverian throne, Paul Zelinka has to leave his first love, magnanimous Margaret, for a more socially appropriate partner, Princess Helen of Saevia. The film's finale is set on 'a staircase of great architectural beauty'. Helen 'stands on the topmost step . . . looking down very tenderly at Margaret', while Margaret 'looks up at Helen very beautifully'. This tableau is held until 'A view of the whole staircase concludes.'

Lofty locales such as these always attract Wells's lovers. In 'A Dream of Armageddon', a passionate couple spend much of their time pacing emotionally about on a 'high terrace', exchanging remarks like 'Come and see the sunrise upon Monte Solaro.' Miss Grammont in *The Secret Places of the Heart* arouses Sir Richmond's interest by the fact that when he first sees her, at Stonehenge, she is 'standing on one of the great prostrate stones in the centre of the place'. Some time after this, their relationship has prospered to a point where they are ready to declare themselves as lovers; and the understanding between them is expressed—as if in code—by an agreement to climb to higher land: '"I think we go up the hill?" said Sir Richmond. "Yes," she agreed, "up the hill." Followed a silence.' Sexual or matrimonial overtures are frequently associated with heights in Wells's fiction. In *Kipps*, Helen Walshingham engineers a proposal from the hero when they climb to the top of the Keep at Lympne. While Mrs Walshingham remains prudently below, 'high out of the world of every day . . . Kipps and Helen found themselves agreeably alone'. Their talk hovers on the verge of declaration; then, as they prepare to descend the staircase, Kipps proposes and Helen, bending over him from a higher step, laughingly accepts. In *Marriage*, Marjorie is trapped into a similar situation after unattractive Mr Magnet has announced, 'I want you to see the view from the church tower.' To her initial bewilderment, 'as they went through the street, he called her attention again to the church tower in a voice that seemed to her to be inexplicably charged with significance'. Then, as realisation dawns, she 'felt chiefly anxious to get to the top of that predestinate tower and have the whole thing over'. When it comes to the point, however, breathlessness impairs Magnet's performance

> when at last they got to that high serenity, Mr Magnet was far too hot and far too much out of breath to say anything at all for a time except an almost explosive gust or so of approbation of the scenery. 'Shor' breath!' he said, 'win'ey stairs always—that 'fect on me—buful scenery—Suwy—like it always.'

Inability to climb is, in Wells, a sure sign that there is something wrong with someone's sexual drive. Lady Harman, for instance, before her marriage, cherishes an ideal of a man with whom 'she intended to climb mountains. So clearly she could not marry Mr Harman.' Then, disastrously, she backs down from this prospect, marries Mr Harman, a non-climber, and returns predictably frustrated from a honeymoon during which his skill-less attentions have 'obscured a marvellous background of sombre mountain'. Another let-down honeymoon occurs in *Brynhild*, where Mr Palace spoils the invigorating splendour of the Bernese Oberland for his bride since 'nearly all his discourse was deprecatory. For him even the Alps never rose to their highest.' Joseph Davis, in *Star Begotten*, has a particularly demanding wife. Though he takes her to the top of the Matterhorn during their honeymoon, she is not entirely fulfilled and 'at the summit . . . seemed to be pleased but still gravely looking for more'.

That mountains are both aphrodisiac and sexually testing is revealed with special force in *The New Machiavelli*. Hiking through the Alps, on his first trip abroad, Remington realises the experience 'made me feel my body. . . . I saw the sheathed beauty of women's forms all about me.' Goddess-like creatures cast in the usual statuesque mould are dotted around the exhilarating contours of the countryside, and include a girl 'like Ceres' who smiles invitingly at him. When Remington, who has marched past her with his college chum, suddenly breaks out, 'Why don't

I go back and make love to those girls and let the world and you and everything go hang? Deep breasts and rounded limbs—and we poor emasculated devils go tramping by with the blood of youth in us!', his friend responds with prissy irony, 'I'm not quite sure, Remington . . . that picturesque scenery is altogether good for your morals.' Events prove him correct. Immediately after this, Remington encounters a young woman at a hotel who seductively announces, 'My husband doesn't walk. . . . His heart is weak and he cannot manage the hills.' Remington follows her lead: 'I said I loved beautiful scenery and all beautiful things and the pointing note in my voice made her laugh.' Soon, they are climbing into bed so that, at last, he loses his virginity. After the heights of this experience, his marriage to Margaret falls decidedly flat. Ill-advisedly, they opt to spend their honeymoon at sea-level amongst the 'tepid smoothness' of the lagoons of Venice. Here, Remington becomes increasingly restless, eventually informing his wife that he feels an urge to 'climb mountains, take the devil out of myself'. As a substitute, he suggests going on a walk to Chioggia, 'but the long stretch of beach fatigued Margaret's back, and gave her blisters, and we never got beyond Mala-mocco'. Later, she is to disappoint him again by her inability to climb Vesuvius without becoming tired. Isabel, with whom he eventually elopes, has far more idea how to conduct things, tending to rendezvous with Remington at such stimulating sites as the Kew Pagoda or a high cliff-top.

Topography also takes on amorous significance in *The Passionate Friends*. Early in their relationship, Lady Mary tells Stratton, 'if you and I were to be together . . . I should want it to be among beautiful forests and mountains'. After getting on the wrong track by marrying other people, they finally meet by accident in the mountains. Their innocent wanderings here are misinterpreted, and Mary turns to suicide as an escape-route: a decision she obliquely communicates to Stratton by explaining that when they meet again it will be 'In a lonely place . . . among mountains. High and away. . . . Great rocks.' After her departure for this destination, Stratton thinks of her as 'a sunlit lake seen among mountains', an image not dissimilar to that he earlier used to describe their first, intensely platonic, night together: 'We were as solemn as great mountains'.

This metamorphosis of the noble into imposing rock forma-tions is not unusual in Wells. Mr Sempack in *Meanwhile* regularly suggests an analogy of this kind to his acquaintances. Though Lady Catherine objects, 'He isn't *really* a precipice', Mrs Rylands insists, 'he had the quality of rocky scenery that had arisen and tossed its mane and marched. "Tossing its mane" mixed oddly with rocky scenery, but that was how it came to her.' And a letter from her husband, describing Sempack as 'like some Alpine relief map', endorses her view. Looking upon his ex-wife in the same way, Mortimer Smith in *The Dream* knows exactly where to go to be reminded of her: 'There was a little show of landscapes at the Alpine Gallery and several were pictures of Downland scenery and one showed a sunlit hillside under drowsy white clouds. It was almost like seeing Hetty.' Marjorie Trafford—another keen climber: 'It particularly appealed to her that they were to walk among mountains'—does not actually resemble elevated land but has a peak named after her: 'Marjorie Ridge' in Labrador. Ann Veronica, having had a father who stood over her 'like a cliff', intends to go one better when it comes to producing offspring of her own: 'I want children like the mountains.' She and Capes, in fact, are among Wells's most devoted mountaineers. The chapter recounting their elopement, called 'In the Mountains', shows them scaling peaks of ecstasy: 'They found themselves . . . talking love to one another high up on some rocks above a steep bank of snow that overhung a precipice.' And at the end of the novel, over four years into marriage, they are rapturously recalling the heightened experiences of that earlier time: 'But the mountains, dear! We won't forget the mountains, dear, ever.' Similarly, Benham and Amanda's 'Spirited Honeymoon' in *The Research Magnificent* ranges through Switzerland, the Austrian Tyrol, and Northern Italy: 'Amanda had never seen mountains, and longed, she said, to climb.' Later, we are told she 'fell in love with Monte Rosa' and 'wanted to kiss its snowy forehead'. Likewise, Wells's wife Jane, he reveals in *The Book of Catherine Wells*, 'fell in love with the Alps' and developed a 'passion for high places'. Contrary to what this taste would be made to signify in his fiction, though, Jane played an unglamorously temperate role in her husband's life.

But, if mountains are associated with summits of physical experience, it is flying that is used to convey the most soaring passions. Beatrice Normandy in *Tono-Bungay* collapses instinctively before George when he glides above her in his aeroplane as she is out riding:

She had already got her horse in hand when I came up to her. Her woman's body lay along his neck, and she glanced up as I, with wings spread, and every nerve in a state of tension, swept over her.

Then I had landed, and I was going back to where her horse stood still and trembling.

We exchanged no greetings. She slid from her saddle into my arms, and for one instant I held her. 'Those great wings,' she said, and that was all.

Trafford, soon to prevent Marjorie from entering into a tame match with Mr Magnet, crashes his plane down upon the lawn where they are playing croquet. Elizabeth Horthy, 'that last romantic', in *The Shape of Things to Come*, dramatically kills herself, after being thwarted in love, 'by flying her machine to an immense height and throwing herself out. She went up steeply. It was as though she was trying to fly right away from a planet which had done with romance.' Conversely, self-obsessed Dolores has 'an exaggerated idea of the dangers overhead', and Wilbeck finds trips by air a convenient way of escaping her company.

As the spectacle of high-born Beatrice prostrate before George's rising prowess makes quite clear, Wells's women can be pulled from an initially superior position and pushed emphatically below man's level. This, it soon emerges, is where he feels they really belong. Female inferiority of various kinds is both implicit and explicit in his books. The highest compliment he can pay to women, in fact, is to bestow on them an honorary virility. Ann Veronica, skilled in ju-jitsu—'I believe you've crushed a gland or something', an opponent gasps after she has choked off his advances—tells herself, 'I'm not a good specimen of a woman. I've got a streak of the male.' Many of the other women Wells approves of could say the same thing. Beatrice Bumpus, who awakens the hero's calf-love in *The Dream*, had a 'jolly frank and boyish face', while Hetty, whom he marries, is 'slender as a tall boy in her khaki breeches'. In *Meanwhile*, Mrs Rylands' 'ruffled hair made her look like a very jolly but rather fragile boy', even though she is nine months pregnant. Miss Grammont in *The Secret Places of the Heart* causes Sir Richmond to think 'the word "girl" . . . seemed even less appropriate for her than the word "boy". . . . He could talk with her as if he talked with a man like himself.'

Her father, it transpires, having decided, 'I'm going to make a man of you', has devoted his attention 'to a kind of masculinization of his daughter'. Miss Leeds, another claimant on Sir Richmond's affections, not only has the Christian name Martin but 'the face of a sensitive youth rather than the face of a woman', and her hair is 'parted at the side like a man's'. She is a portrait of Rebecca West (praised in *What Is Coming?* for her 'virile common sense', and endowed, as Amanda in *The Research Magnificent*, with 'a boy's complexion'). Lady Mary, another honorary hermaphrodite, describes herself as 'an abnormality—with whiskers of inquiry sprouting from my mind'. Christina Alberta adopts male postures—standing in front of the fire, 'shapely legs wide apart and hands behind her back in an attitude that would have shocked all her feminine ancestors'—and her boyfriend is nervously aware that she seems more masculine than he is: 'She was so direct and free in her thoughts and talk that she made Bobby feel that his own mind wore a bonnet and flounces.' The heroine of *Joan and Peter*, another emancipated girl much admired by the author, 'drives like a man', and announces her intention of learning plumbing, bricklaying, and carpentry, since 'doing running repairs hardens a woman's soul'. In *Marriage*, when Trafford gets himself into difficulties in the wastes of Labrador, Marjorie works 'like two men' to rescue him, muttering to herself, 'Why don't they teach a girl to handle an axe?' Isabel in *The New Machiavelli* is said to write 'in exactly the manner of an able young man' and 'with the stark power of a clear-headed man'. It is evident, too, that the accolade of having performed as well as a member of the opposite sex is one she would be proud to receive: when she and Remington face crisis, she states sturdily, 'You and I, Master, we've got to be men.'

The slavish note also audible here frequently accompanies amorous exchanges in Wells's work. Verbal obeisances to the male come from his heroines with surprising directness. In *The Sleeper Awakes*, Helen Wotton, herself a statuesque paragon of nobility, reverentially gasps out to Graham such apostrophes as 'Father and Master. . . . The world is yours' or 'Oh! Father of the World—Sire! I knew you would say these things.' Blue-blooded Beatrice Normandy gratifyingly informs proletarian George, 'You are my prince, my king.' Essenden in *The Shape of Things to Come* has attracted similar tributes: 'In some of her scrawled notes to him it seems Elizabeth called him "my King".' And the depths of abasement shown by Ann Veronica when they are up in the mountains startle even Capes, who has written 'a vigorous and damaging attack' on the 'case for the primitive matriarchate and the predominant importance of the female throughout the animal kingdom':

> 'I say,' she reflected, 'you *are* rather the master, you know.' . . .
> She slid her cheek down the tweed sleeve of his coat. 'Nice sleeve,' she said, and came to his hand and kissed it.
> 'I say,' he cried, 'Look here! Aren't you going a little too far? This—this is degradation—making a fuss with sleeves.'

An even more masochistic grovelling is exacted from Marjorie after Trafford has got her to agree to go off to Labrador:

> For some reason his tearing her up by the roots in this fashion had fascinated her imagination. She felt a strange new wonder at him that had in it just a pleasant faint flavour of fear. Always before she had felt a curious aversion and contempt for those servile women who are said to seek a master, to want to be mastered, to be eager even for the physical subjugation of brute force. Now she could at least understand, sympathise even with them.

Unfaithful wives, in Wells, display a desire to be knocked around. Wilbeck in *Apropos of Dolores*, learning of his wife's infidelity, 'thought of giving Alice a memorable shaking and spanking and then . . . realized that that was precisely what she wanted'. It becomes apparent to William Clissold, after Clara has confessed to having a lover, 'that she would have liked a little strangling'. Guilty Amanda in *The Research Magnificent* begs for chastisement: ' "Cheetah dear! I would love you to kill me." . . . Her eyes dilated. "Beat me." '

More often, though, it is intellectual domination that Wells's women crave. Throughout the ages, he explains in *The Work, Wealth and Happiness of Mankind*, woman has had to defer to the male, so that 'If it is not in her nature to concede leadership it is woven now almost inextricably into her persona by the power of tradition.' Moreover, 'in none of the open fields, except domestic fiction, can it be claimed that any women have yet displayed qualities and initiatives to put them on a level with the best men'.

As might be expected, therefore, 'Her recent gains in freedom have widened the choice of what she shall adorn or serve, but they have released no new initiatives in human affairs.' In *Marriage*, the distinguished scientist Sir Roderick Dover, 'an altogether satisfactory person' with 'a leonine courage in his mind', puts the case quite bluntly—'Women . . . are inferior—and you can't get away from it'—going on to add, 'We've tried it long enough now, this theory that a woman's a partner and an equal.' Far from being this, they appear to be around the level of high-grade chimpanzees in the eyes of Dr Martineau in *The Secret Places of the Heart*: 'It was a fixed idea of the doctor's that women were quite incapable of producing ideas in the same way that men do, but he believed that with suitable encouragement they could be induced to respond quite generously to such ideas.' Quite a few of Wells's heroines tamely acquiesce in this belief. Joan sees Peter as 'a bigger and cleverer creature than herself; he compelled her respect. He had more strength, more invention, more initiative, and a relatively tremendous power of decision', and 'she did not believe that she herself had any great power of further growth except through him'. Using an image perhaps considered appropriate—'I'm like Susan Wilkes the dressmaker, I can't do anything until I have a pattern'—Brynhild Palace expresses a similar view. There is, she feels, 'an absolute lack of positive initiative in women', an 'ideological barrenness'. This can be fertilised, however, if they are receptive to a male's fruitful ideas: Stella Kentlake, for example, says she has been 'impregnated' by the theories of Gemini Twain. Hoping to become creative, many of Wells's women attach themselves as helpers (and often, it turns out, hinderers) to men with a mission: Isabel and Margaret to Remington; Marjorie to Trafford; Lady Mary to Stratton; Amanda to Benham: Princess Helen to Paul Zelinka. The respective roles are spotlit most glaringly in *The Brothers*, where Catherine tells her lover, Bolaris, a charismatic leader-figure, 'I have played a woman's part in the world, and that is to look on while things are being done. And learn.' Eventually, Bolaris, who has shared her 'profound disbelief in a woman's capacity for intellectual initiative', is killed; and the story ends with the pathetic spectacle of Catherine imploring her lover's corpse, 'Tell me what I am to do.'

Before this, though, she and Bolaris have been able to make an unexpected use of their private relationship in the public struggles raging round them. 'Lampobo', a 'little language' they have concocted for amorous intercourse, comes in handy as a code. Infantile love-talk does not serve this purpose in any other books by Wells, but it pervades them. In *'42 to '44*, he claims that 'The first thing two lovers set about doing is to invent new names for one another and to devise a little language of their own.' He himself was very given to this. In the 'lekkers' he sends his wife Jane (her name itself a fond invention), he continually lapses into baby-talk and nicknames, even writing a poem called 'Chanson' about the habit:

> It *was* called names
> Miss Furry Boots and Nicketty and Bits,
> And P.C.B., and Snitterlings and Snits,
> It *was* called names.

Play-pen lispings are also coyly resorted to in the letters to Rebecca West, his 'faifful panfer' and 'Fing I like talking to'. Partly recording that affair, *The Research Magnificent* picks up the same note—' "How could we ever keep away from each uvver?" she whispered.' Quite a few of Wells's lovers enter into sexual relationships as if they were a nursery. Tenderness is made to sound like something from the kindergarten. Mr Lewisham calls Ethel 'Dillywings' and 'Dear Little Wife Thing', and her name for him is 'Husbinder'. William Clissold's wife archly addresses him as 'Flosopher-lost'. George Ponderevo makes up, with his wife and spaniel, a cosy world of 'Mutney and Miggles and Ming'— though he eventually 'tired of the baby-talk' and abandons it and them. Alice, Wilbeck's first wife in *Apropos of Dolores*, also welcomes baby-talk and nicknames. And that pet-names can imply a jovial stooping towards the childish or the not-quite-human is brought out by his admission that he always found a nickname 'more sincere', when addressing Dolores, than words like 'dearest' or 'darling'.

Despite his ideal of the goddess on the heights, Wells's attitude towards the female in reality can be very down-to-earth. *The Work, Wealth and Happiness of Mankind* declares flatly, 'there is work to be got out of her', adding the proviso, 'She needs, as the automobile people say, "reconditioning" so that she can return to the open road of life afresh.' After any requisite stripping-down and servicing, Wells's women are generally designed for either, or both, of two roles—epitomised in his reference to the 'warm-hearted' secretary who would minister to his needs by night and day. Woman is to provide erotic solace and recreation of a pleasurably childish kind (hence the romper-talk), and she can also be of use as a dedicated dogsbody to a busy man. The first of these views is conveyed with startling frankness in a letter to his wife: 'I want a healthy woman handy to steady my nerves and leave my mind free for real things'; and it breaks out in statements of his need for 'some sort of body slave', or such plaintive cries to Rebecca West as 'I want a breast and a kind boddy'. She also received instructions about her 'duty as a custodian of genius'—'You have got to take care of me and have me fed and have me peaceful and comfortable'—but, to Wells's chagrin, refused to see this as her basic function, and insisted on attaching importance to her own life. As one who had, as he admits in his autobiography, 'neither imagination nor sympathy for the woman's side of life', he found this enraging. And he met it elsewhere, too. It was not only Rebecca West who kept sliding irritatingly away from what he regarded as the approved feminine positions—lisping love-doll and admiring amanuensis. From his first wife onwards—'what she said spoilt the picture I wanted to make of her in my imagination'—women thwarted his designs and refused to be contained within the frame of his fantasies. This is reflected in the books.

Women, in Wells, are tremendous saboteurs. The most deadly instance of this is Doris Thalassia Waters, the somewhat emphatically named mermaid who hunts down Chatteris in *The Sea Lady* (a story intended, Wells said in his autobiography, to show that 'love . . . breaks things up'). Having pursued her quarry from the South Seas, she flips seductively ashore near Folkestone, bewitchingly destroys both Chatteris's political career and his engagement, and then—'Bubblin' over' with laughter, as a witness puts it—leads him off to drown in the sea. Her fingers, as she does this, are clutched in his hair and she has 'her head back, laughing. . . . As much as to say, "Got 'im."' Less dramatically, but repeatedly, other women in Wells's fiction injure men by dragging them out of their element. *Love and Mr Lewisham*, which appeared a couple of years before *The Sea Lady*, is a good example of this. Like many of Wells's protagonists, Lewisham has a 'dream of incessant unswerving work'. He intends to dedicate himself to learning, but female intrusion into his studiously disciplined existence soon puts paid to this—as the picture of his wife driving him to fling Huxley's *Vertebrata* into the fireplace makes evident. In fact, from the earliest moments, when the sight of her blossom-trimmed hat distracts him from his Latin verse translations, attention to Ethel keeps pulling Lewisham's life away from the course that he has charted in his Schema—the map of an 'arranged career', an 'ordered sequence of work and success, distinctions, and yet further distinctions', that is pinned admonishingly on the wall of his study-bedroom. Academically, he goes to pieces; he leaves the 'great building' in South Kensington in failure; and, after a bitter outburst—'In one year . . . all my hopes, all my ambitions have gone'—slumps into a dim domesticity. The book's ending shows him—and perhaps the author—trying to make the best of this. After a period of estrangement, the couple become reconciled, with Ethel expecting a child. But it is hard to view this reunion very opti-mistically. Throughout the novel, Ethel has been associated with dishonesty and subterfuge. When Lewisham first speaks to her, she is cheating by writing a boy's imposition for him, and lying by pretending she doesn't know who Lewisham is. Later, she is discovered rigging the spectral manifestations at a fraudulent seance. And, even after the reconciliation, there is 'one untellable indiscretion' that she holds back from her husband. Besides being duplicitous, Ethel seems shallow when set against Miss Heydinger, the straggle-haired student Lewisham meets at South Kensington. Though encumbered with some blue-stocking absurdities, she increasingly emerges as a fairly admirable figure—emotionally as well as intellectually more interesting than Ethel. When Lewisham is made to break with her, there is, once again, a sense of something valuable being ejected from his life by the person he has married. This image of the wife as philistine and vandal looms large on the novel's final page. The book's closing paragraphs show Lewisham dropping the torn-up pieces of his Schema into a waste-paper basket Ethel has just bought for him.

In *Tono-Bungay*, George is likewise pushed off course by Marion. As with Lewisham, his initial response to the woman he marries is partly based on a misunderstanding. Lewisham is enchanted, on receiving his first letter from Ethel, to find she addresses him as 'Dear': 'it seemed to him the most sweet and wonderful of all modes of address, though as a matter of fact it was because she had forgotten his Christian name and afterwards forgotten the blank she had left for it'. George is tenderly struck by the sight of Marion—reading, he assumes—in one of the bays of the Education Library. Later, he discovers that the appetite she is satisfying is not an intellectual one: 'she never read. She used to come there to eat a bun in quiet.' Like Lewisham, too, confronted by his girl's obvious lack of mental sparkle, he constructs a consoling myth: 'if her ignorance became indisputable, I told myself her simple instincts were worth all the education and intelligence in the world'. What these simple instincts do to his own education and intelligence is, once again, fairly catastrophic: 'My work got more and more spiritless, my behaviour degenerated, my punctuality declined; I was more and more outclassed in the steady grind by my fellow-students.' Things became so very bad, he reveals, that 'Even a girl got above me upon one of the lists.' It is only after shaking Marion off that he is able to rehabilitate himself by immersion in scientific research. William Clissold is another of Wells's dedicated males whose studious intents meet with temporary female sabotage. 'Sex', he ruefully explains, 'caught me unawares one day and wrenched away the mastery of my life from science. I fell into a passion of desire and I married. It was as if the walls of my laboratory collapsed, and my instruments and notebooks were overturned and scattered by a rush and invasion of stormy, commonplace, ill-conceived purposes.' Nor is this invasion merely metaphorical. One of the harassments Clissold has to cope with is his wife's habit of coming to his laboratory to 'help' him and taking offence at his 'frequent disinclination to knock off and make love to her'.

That involvement with a woman could prove fatally incompatible with a dedicated career is something Wells keeps returning to—rather ungratefully in view of the fact that, as he states in his autobiography, 'for thirty years, I had my business looked after for me by an extremely competent wife'. Despite all Jane's secretarial labours—checking manuscripts, redrawing diagrams, sending off his income-tax returns—the spectre of the disruptive lady is not exorcised and continually manifests herself in Wells's writings. She is to be seen, for instance, in 'A Dream of Armageddon', where a man who has abandoned the 'pride and struggle' of political life in order to be with his mistress, speaks of having 'thrown up . . . all I had ever worked for or desired, for her sake'. Ten years later, in *The New Machiavelli*, this situation is worked into a full-length novel, with Remington's career ruined by his elopement with Isabel. *Anticipations* bleakly predicts of the modern woman that

> She will set herself to realize, as far as her husband's means and credit permit, the ideas of a particular section of the wealthy that have captured her. If she is a fool, her ideas of life will presently come into complete conflict with her husband's in a manner that, as the fumes of the love potion leave his brain, may bring the real nature of the case home to him. If he is of that resolute strain to whom the world must finally come, he may rebel and wade through tears and crises to his appointed work again. The cleverer she is, and the finer and more loyal her character up to a certain point, the less likely this is to happen, the more subtle and effective will be her hold upon her husband, and the more probable his perversion from the austere pursuit of some interesting employment, towards the adventures of modern money-getting in pursuit of her ideas of a befitting life.

Marriage dramatises such a struggle: 'the story', Wells explains in his autobiography, 'tells how masculine intellectual interest met feminine spending and what ensued'. As the first rapture fades, Trafford wakes to discover not so much all passion spent as quite a high proportion of his income. Marjorie's extravagance— 'she bought fruit carelessly, they had far too many joints'— forces him to undertake extra work, as a result of which his research (to which she has already petulantly objected) suffers disastrously. His career and their relationship are only saved by the drastic expedient of a year in Labrador. There, as they take stock of their life, he expatiates on his wife's shortcomings— 'you've done nothing but dress since we married'—and she eagerly agrees: 'I've been a fool, selfish, ill-trained and greedy. . . . Yes, I've been the trouble. . . . What are we women—half savages, half pets, unemployed things of greed and desire. . . . We women—we've been looting all the good things in the world, and helping nothing.' A year later, in *The Passionate Friends*, Lady Mary adds her voice to this anti-female diatribe; unless action is taken, she believes,

we women are going to be the Goths and Huns of another
Decline and Fall. We are going to sit in the conspicuous places
of the world and *loot* all your patient accumulations. . . . All your
little triumphs of science and economy, all your little accumulations of wealth that you think will presently make the
struggle for life an old story and the millennium possible—*we
spend.*

High among the items woman is likely to spend man's money on,
A Modern Utopia points out with disgust, are 'costly sexualised
trappings' and 'distinctive barbaric adornments'. Encased in
these, she cunningly sinks to the level of the lower forms of life
and 'achieves by artifice a sexual differentiation profounder than
that of any other vertebrated animal. . . . one must probe among
the domestic secrets of the insects and crustacea to find her living
parallel'. Flaunting her gender with scents and display, she
becomes 'an unwholesome stimulant turning a man from wisdom
to appearance'. Some men in the books react excitedly to such
enticing feminine externals. Brumley in *The Wife of Sir Isaac
Harman* is immediately struck, on meeting that lady, by her
'manifest spending of great lots of money on the richest, finest,
and fluffiest things'; and, as one who 'responded to countless-
guinea furs', he is especially entranced by the high-priced pelts
that she is swathed in. His imagination keeps eagerly attaching
these to Lady Harman afterwards, so that, with her 'black furry
slenderness' and 'shining furry presence', she almost becomes
another of Wells's big-cat women. The author's attitude towards
female extravagance is less enamoured. *The Work, Wealth and
Happiness of Mankind* intimates that women are likely to consume
the three qualities mentioned in its title because 'They are urged
by every magazine and paper they pick up, by the implications
of almost every book, to regard themselves as spenders, as elegant
or beautiful, at the worst, subtle creatures, for the maintenance
of whose elegance, beauty and subtlety an immense mass of
spending is necessary and justified.' This means that, once again,
woman sinks to lower reaches of the evolutionary scale: her
'persona in the middle and upper class still falls in most cases
into the more primitive classes of peasant or predatory'; she is
'still, as a sex, at the . . . barbaric stage'. Martineau in *The Secret
Places of the Heart* (a book concerned with 'love-making considered
as a source or waste of energy', Wells says in his autobiography)

also indicts woman as a squanderer of natural resources: 'She spends excitingly and competitively for her own pride and glory, she drives all the energy of men over the weirs of gain.' Austerity measures towards women are consequently called for: 'We have to educate them far more seriously as sources of energy. . . . we have to suppress them far more rigorously as tempters and dissipators.'

The main thing that has to be suppressed in women, Wells's writings soon make clear, is egotism. Recurrently his narratives highlight what he calls, in *The King Who Was a King*, 'the essential fact that women do see life much more acutely as an affair of personalities than men do'. This, in Wellsian terms, of course, is to be deplored. Theoretically, his approval always goes to an ability to surmount the limitations of the self and serve the species. This is something his women generally fail to do. Instead of offering what Wells regards as their appropriate brand of altruism—that of catering to the needs of a man with mission— they selfishly wreck careers, impede research, and squander man's resources. There are some exceptions, some women who come to learn their proper role—Princess Helen, for instance, in *The King Who Was a King*. She is, Wells explains, intended to represent 'woman the decisive, emerging from the romantic tradition, attempting to make a personal lover of our Hercules and then realizing the greater power and beauty of his larger and ampler purpose, giving herself to that and gaining herself, him and everything in that self-subordination'. She is also, with her 'white robed beauty' and milady posturings, totally un- real—or, as Wells has it, 'simplified beyond any vividness of characterization'. An inspirational dummy out of the same cupboard as Helen Wotton of *The Sleeper Awakes* and Lady Mary of *The Passionate Friends*, she is so very unconvincing as to cast doubts on the author's genuine belief in the likelihood of her existence. What *Anticipations* calls 'a wife of the distracting, perplexing personality kind' gets portrayed far more graphically.

Wives are generally irksome in Wells's books. Sometimes, they are softly potent little parasites (Ethel Lewisham, Marion Ponderevo); sometimes, they are extravagant (Marjorie Traf- ford). They can be disappointingly unpassionate (Margaret Remington, Edith Britling) or disconcertingly unfaithful (Amanda Benham, Clara Clissold). A whole string of gaunt nags stretches from Miriam in *Mr Polly*, who 'ceased to listen to her husband's talk from the day she married him, and ceased to unwrinkle the kink in her brow at his presence', to Job Huss's wife in *The Undying Fire* and Mrs Noah in *All Aboard for Ararat*. Mrs Huss—who represents a modern version of Job's wife— reveals a resounding lack of wifely sympathy by turning on her husband with such comfortless cries as 'To have cancer now! In these lodgings!' Noah's consort, it transpires, is even worse— 'a vain, restless, jealous exhibitionist, a dishonest and consuming woman'. She is of a promiscuous disposition—as the racial variety of her three sons clearly shows—and makes 'an intense fuss about her passionate possibilities. On that side she became disgusting.' She has 'an essentially feminine mind . . . shallow, quick', and egotistically resents her husband's achievements: 'Her attitude to my work was made up of vehement jealousy and a desire to gain credit for it as its virtual inspiration.'

She is, in fact, a fainter, small-scale reprint of Wells's greatest female monster, the central figure of the book which appeared a couple of years earlier, *Apropos of Dolores*. Despite Wells's disingenuous disclaimers—'some silly influence is at work in the firm of Methuen trying to suggest an identification of Dolores with Madame Odette Keun'—an unmistakable portrait of that lady dominates this book. A fervent admirer of Wells's work—she had 'sobbed with ecstasy' on reading *First and Last Things*—she first met him him in 1923 after an ardent and soul-baring correspondence. The encounter was successful: they made love, though they had never seen each other, in a darkened hotel bedroom in Geneva—'I did not know whether he was a giant or a gnome but it did not matter', Odette declared. And soon, they settled down together in the South of France. *The World of William Clissold* and *The Bulpington of Blup*, written during this time of co-existence, are both dedicated to Odette Keun, the first of them describing her as Wells's 'Self-Forgetful Friend And Helper'. This book also carried a Greek epigraph meaning 'everything passes': and the image of Mme Keun as self-forgetful friend and helper gradually met the fate that this predicts. In 1933, after a great deal of acrimony, she parted from Wells but held on to their villa near Grasse (it was called Lou Pidou, a contraction of *Le Petit Dieu*, her name for Wells). The following year, Wells's autobiography was published, and Odette greeted its appearance with three long articles in *Time and Tide*, pelting her ex-lover with such adjectives as 'small, sickly, common, selfish, vain, angry', drawing attention to 'his perpetually vibrating physical and sexual vanity', commenting on the frequent demands for assuagement made by the latter quality, and concluding 'this man is a pathological case'. Four years later, with *Apropos of Dolores*, Wells took his revenge. The book is most emphatically what he denied it to be—'an "attack" on that vociferous lady at Grasse'. Dolores's Levantine background is similar to Odette Keun's: so is her appearance. With the deft rapidity of one exasperatedly familiar with his subject, Wells makes the likeness unmistakable. Revealing features are caught unerringly, as in a caricature—'that slightly haggard look of animation that has always characterized her', 'a dark hank of hair over one resentful eye and her long, lean, silver-bangled arms about her knees'. Much of the book is an autopsy on a dead relationship. Bits of a life together are exhumed and slicingly dissected. Character-traits are grimacingly pincered-out as give-away symptoms of egotism—Dolores's fondness for 'that intolerable French idiom, "Je trouve"', her habit of interspersing her conversational monologues with a few questions 'concluding with "Yes? No?" to give an indication of the number of words permitted in the reply'. A biologist, Foxfield, is brought in, too, to identify the class from which Dolores derives. It is his belief that 'The need for children is less and will diminish, and that makes an increasing proportion of the women in the world superfluous as mothers, home-makers and—in any honourable sense of the word—women'; hence, the world 'is haunted by the superfluous dissatisfied woman. She darkens the sky.' In the shape of Dolores, she darkens Wilbeck's life. His existence is exhaustingly divided between struggling out of her clutching embraces and reeling under her randomly malignant attacks. After an overdose of sedative has sent her to her final rest—Wells outdoes Odette's character-assassination by killing her off in his own writing—Wilbeck is particularly eager that her tombstone should carry the legend 'Pax Dolores', not 'Resurgam'. Like Foxfield, too, he feels Dolores, behind all her surface idiosyncrasies, typifies 'the natural antagonism of a female egotism in conflict with man's increasing disposition to go his own way and think of things outside her personality and range'. She is, he says, 'a human being stripped down to its bare egotism . . . assertion and avidity incarnate . . . the foundation stuff of humanity . . . a common woman in a state of chemical purity'.

One of Dolores's most rabid impulses is jealousy. As her suspicions burgeon—to the point of accusing him of incest with his daughter—Wilbeck starts to think of life as 'a fantastic arena of struggling people with lassoes, hooks, crooks, nets, adhesive ribbons, chains, handcuffs'. This alarming panorama of 'the cravings of possessive love' is true to much that happens in Wells's fiction. Jealousy is the sexual emotion he presents most vividly. In his autobiography, he claims 'it lies at least as close to the springs of human action as sexual desire'; in his books, it appears as a far more widespread force. Desire is not often depicted in Wells's fiction. George Ponderevo lies awake because of Marion, 'writhing, biting my wrists in a fever of longing'; and, after seeing Clara swimming, William Clissold takes frustrated passion a little further: 'in the night I would lie in bed and bite my wrists and arms black and blue with the violence of my desire for that wet body in its closely clinging dress'. But usually we do not see Wells's characters heated by 'the red blaze', as Remington calls it. According to William Clissold, this hot urgency is 'merely the red centre of a far ampler desire—a desire for possession, assurance, and predominance'. And it is possessiveness that Wells focuses on. *First and Last Things* maintains that 'The ordinary civilized woman and the ordinary civilized man are alike obsessed with the idea of meeting and possessing one peculiar intimate person, one special exclusive lover who is their very own', while *The Dream* regretfully notes that, in the bad old pre-Utopian days, 'The pride and self-respect of a man was still bound up with the animal possession of women—the pride and self-respect of most women was by a sort of reflection bound up with the animal possession of a man.' Many of Wells's novels seem written to bear this out. *The Passionate Friends*, for instance, as its title is meant to intimate, concerns itself with whether lovers can retain their independence and be not possessive partners but passionate friends. Lady Mary marries Justin rather than Stratton because she believes, 'I shall be free—free! . . . He isn't so fierce; he isn't so greedy.' As regards Justin, she could hardly be more wrong. His 'ruling passion', it emerges, 'was that infinitely stronger passion than love in our poor human hearts, jealousy.' He displays it, first, by locking her away in a remote Irish castle, and, later, by only allowing her out with a spy called Miss Summersley Satchel. As regards Stratton, though, Lady Mary is correct. He is violently jealous—'I wanted her as barbarians want a hunted enemy, alive or dead. It was a flaming jealousy to have her mine'—and sees evidence of the emotion everywhere. A chapter called 'The Arraignment of Jealousy' widens the survey out from sexual jealousy to include 'the ancient limiting jealousies which law and custom embody' and 'The bloodstained organised jealousies of religious intolerance, the delusions of nationality and cult and race'. But, despite these generalisations, it is sexual jealousy which dominates the book—tormenting Stratton, maddening Justin, paining Stratton's wife, and even ruffling Lady Mary. 'I was violent to my toilet things', she shamefacedly reveals to Stratton, when confessing that jealous tantrums seized her after hearing of his relationship with Rachel.

The ravages of the green-eyed monster are also on view in *The Wife of Sir Isaac Harman*, which appeared the following year. Like Justin, Harman is a wife-imprisoner—Lady Harman is incarcerated in the Surrey countryside. And, like Justin, he employs a female spy to hover round his wife: it is the same spy, in fact—Miss Summersley Satchel—though her last name has now changed unaccountably to Satchell. A 'clutching, hard-breathing little man', Sir Isaac has 'a supremely acquisitive and possessive character'. His notion of an ideal pet is a bull mastiff, and his edition of *The Taming of the Shrew* has underlinings and 'deeply scored' marginalia drawing attention to such sentiments as 'I will be master of what is mine own: / She is my goods, my chattels.' The embodiment of everything that's grasping, he is fitted out with 'compressed lips', 'clenched teeth', and 'white knuckles'. When thwarted, he is to be seen 'squeezing his lips', 'gripping his hands more tightly behind him', and showing 'a face of pinched determination'. Rigid with possessiveness, he comes about as close to *rigor mortis* as is possible while still retaining life; and, after his death—brought on by hardening of the arteries—'His hand was thrust out as though he grasped at some invisible thing.' The object of this *post-mortem* clutch, it soon emerges, is unlucky Lady Harman. The human gin-trap she has married tries to hold her posthumously through provisions in his will.

The Research Magnificent, published the next year and containing a chapter called 'The Assize of Jealousy', keeps up the obsession with the topic. Here, Benham's composure is severely shaken when he finds Amanda's affections have wandered while he has been globe-trotting. Learning what Wells would regard as a fairly basic lesson, he remarks with some surprise, 'I think I have been disposed to underrate the force of sexual jealousy. . . . I thought it was something essentially contemptible, something that one dismissed and put behind oneself in the mere effort to be aristocratic, but I begin to realise that it is not quite so easily settled with.' William Clissold learns this lesson, too. Trying to be liberal, he has 'preached the tolerations of the herd', but 'the exclusive passion of the lair' is in his blood and, under pressure, takes him over. While he has been peering through his microscope at micas and felspars, his wife and a young artist have been pencilling one another in the nude. When Clara confesses that this has led to an affair, Clissold experiences an 'agreeable and exciting impulse' to get his hands around her neck and 'squeeze it, squeeze it' until she is dead. Clara's lover is called Philip Weston; Amanda Benham's lover was called Philip Easton: a similarity which neatly, if unintentionally, underlines Wells's insistence that such situations recur the world over. Certainly, the facts of jealousy, possessiveness, and infidelity pervade his books. Detailed exploration of the personalities caught in these patterns of behaviour interests him less. It is easy to recall that many of his books have at their centre a sexual triangle: the names and characters of those involved are far harder to remember. The personnel remain simplistic but continually the scenario is returned to.

In Wells's fiction, no one is safe from an attack of 'jealousy . . . that inflammation of the mind, that bitterness, that pitiless sore', as *The Passionate Friends* describes it. Lady Mary's rarefied existence fails to shield her from a bad attack. And even being married to a comic character does not guarantee immunity. After a lifetime of respectable monogamy and decently farcical foibles, Teddy Ponderevo suddenly goes off the rails and takes a mistress, souring his formerly cordial relationship with Aunt Susan. The most intense portrayal of sexual jealousy and its hot accompaniments, however, is *In the Days of the Comet*. Like a much earlier narrative by Wells, 'The Cone', this is set in the Potteries and features a character made murderous by jealousy. In 'The Cone', a simmeringly vengeful husband lures his wife's lover into visiting the local blast furnaces. Here, though the air is thick with warning symbolism, the lover is persuaded to climb up above the cone that tops the furnace. Then the inflamed husband pushes him down on to it, so that his blood is 'boiling in his veins'. Despite its lurid imagery and yelled insistence on the punishment fitting the crime—'Fizzle, you hunter of women! You hot-blooded hound! Boil! Boil! Boil!'—the story is disturbingly pungent, largely on account of its searing descriptions of physical agony. Clinging to a massive chain before toppling right down to the cone, the lover 'could smell the singeing of his hands'. Destructive heat is given an acrid actuality that makes it sickeningly memorable as we watch 'a charred, blackened figure, its head streaked with blood, still clutching and fumbling with the chain, and writhing in agony—a cindery animal, an inhuman monst-rous creature that began a sobbing intermittent shriek'. Initially, Wells intended to write a whole novel—of which 'The Cone' is a fiery fragment—set in the Potteries. Nearly ten years later, with *In the Days of the Comet*, he did so. Again, jealousy, hot-blood, lust, heat, and redness coalesce to keep the narrative incandescent. Against a garish background of blast furnaces, Leadford burns with feverish rage at the discovery that the girl he loves is involved with another man: 'The thought of Nettie, my Nettie, and her gentleman lover made ever a vivid inflammatory spot of purpose in my brain.' His jealous hatred mounts to a 'boiling paroxysm of fury', as industrial unrest convulses the Potteries and war erupts in the international sphere. Links between the larger-scale belligerence and Leadford's frenzy are made clear: 'The thing was . . . an enormous irrational obsession; it was, in the microcosm of our nation, curiously parallel to the egotistical wrath and jealousy that swayed my individual microcosm.' Then, a comet trails its gases through the earth's atmosphere, and all is changed. These pacifying vapours quench the nastier passions, leaving only nice ones. Jealousy disappears and monogamy goes with it: Nettie is amiably shared by Leadford and her other lover; Anna, Leadford's wife, joins the calmly unpossessive little commune, too.

Monogamy was notoriously alien to Wells. One of the early jocose pieces in *Certain Personal Matters* remarks waggishly, 'Wife-choosing is an unending business. This sounds immoral.' In his life, partner-choosing was certainly a fairly unending business: one can see why he was amused, as *The Future in America* records, to be confronted by the question, 'Are you a Polygamist?' when applying for permission to enter the States. The unnaturalness of monogamy is a theme to which he frequently warms. Ewart in

Tono-Bungay, bringing together two of Wells's preoccupations, suggests as an ideal a City of Women. Here, each woman will have her own home 'with a little balcony on the outside wall'; leaning down from this, she will smile and talk to the suitors below; and 'she will have a little silken ladder she can let down if she chooses—if she wants to talk closer. . . .' In a very early essay, 'Human Evolution', Wells cautiously advances his belief that 'most men find monogamic life marriage involves an element of sacrifice', and then starts hopefully wondering whether such a sacrifice is strictly necessary nowadays: 'Charity is in the air, and why should not charming people meet one another?' In his later novel, *In the Days of the Comet*, a comet is in the air and charming people do meet one another. From a position of buoyantly placid polygamy, they look back with wondering pity at the clutching frenzies of former times: 'The old-world theory was there was only one love—we who float upon a sea of love find that hard to understand.' In former days, they realise, 'love was a cruel proprietary thing'. Very different is the post-cometary world where Anna composedly allows Leadford his *divertimenti*—'If I could hear notes that were not in her compass, she was glad, because she loved me, that I should listen to other music than hers.' In *A Modern Utopia*, the previous year, Wells had suggested that 'Utopia should not refuse a grouped marriage to three or more freely consenting persons.' *In the Days of the Comet* is obviously designed to illustrate this Utopian ideal; but it is noticeable that it does remain Utopian, only achieved after something out of this world has altered human nature.

Campaigning for polygamy and greater sexual freedom, Wells's fiction is very harsh on promiscuity or lewdness. Sleazy romping comes in for much hostile comment. As a student, staying in dubious lodgings at Westbourne Park, his autobiography reveals, he was inveigled towards this after lunch on Sundays, when

> dalliance became the business of the afternoon. The married couples retired to their apartments; the lodger went off to a lady. I was left to entertain a young woman, who was I think, a sister of my landlady's husband. . . . I sat on a sofa with her and caressed and was caressed by her, attempting small invasions of her costume and suchlike gallantries which she resisted playfully but firmly. Her favourite expressions were

'Ow! *starp* it' and 'Nart that.' I remember I disliked her and her resistances extremely and I cannot remember any definite desire for her. I am quite at a loss to explain why it was I continued to make these advances. I suppose because it was Sunday afternoon, and I was too congested with unusual nourishment to attempt any work.

In addition to these post-prandial frolickings, there was provocative behaviour from his landlady which 'excited me considerably, bothered me with contradictory impulses, disgusted me faintly and interfered rather vexatiously with the proper copying out of my notes of Professor Huxley's lectures'. This woman—no doubt a prototype of the research-disrupting females of the novels— and her scuffling circle represented, Wells felt, 'a sort of humanity, coarser, beastlier and baser than anything I had ever known before': they were 'like simmering hot mud'.

George Ponderevo responds with similar distaste to the leering bumpkins of Wimblehurst, compressing his loathing of their 'sluggish, real lewdness—lewdness is the word' into a cloddish image of the archetypal 'blade' of the district, with 'his slow knowingness, the cunning observation of his deadened eyes, his idea of a "good story", always, always told in undertones, poor dirty worm!' Opposed to this grubbiness is the ideal proposed in *A Modern Utopia*: 'a straight and clean desire for a straight and clean fellow-creature'. This hygienic state of affairs is to be found between Ann Veronica and Capes. She is 'young and clean', he says, 'as clean as fire', possessing a 'nice clean hardness'; if he were 'a clean, free man', he would ask her to be his partner. Then, less than a week after they have spent a day together which had 'all the clean freshness of spring and youth', they decide to elope, since 'It's the only clean way for us'—though they must defer this till the end of the college session so they can 'clean up everything tidy'. Semantic carbolic is also vigorously used in *The Passionate Friends*. Lady Mary's voice has a 'clean strong sharpness' and, with it, she declares herself the enemy of 'timid grubbiness'. Her affair with Stratton is 'clean and scandalous' (unlike the murky behaviour of those who 'sin in the shadows'). When he tactlessly urges her to be his wife and 'make a clean thing of it', she becomes indignant: 'Isn't it a clean thing *now*? . . . Do you mean that you and I aren't clean now?' And he hastily assures her, 'Oh, clean . . . clean as Eve in the garden. But can we keep clean?' They hope she will achieve 'a clean sort of divorce'. But Justin, wrongly described by one of his friends as 'clean as they make them', behaves with dirty vindictiveness, and the lovers are separated. A relative now urges Stratton to 'make a clean job' of his life and marry Rachel, 'that clean girl'. At first, he tries to deflect her affections elsewhere, to a student who is 'such a fresh, clean human being'; then, realising how 'clean and sweet' she is, turns to her himself.

Other novels show the sorry plight of women who have lost their cleanliness. Benham imagines unfaithful Amanda, who 'had spoilt her own fur', lamenting, 'a dirty, lost, and shameful leopard I am now, who was once clean and bright'. Beatrice, in *Tono-Bungay*, refuses to marry George on the grounds that she is 'a woman smirched'; and, though he pleads with her, 'Start clean and new with me', she is adamantly hopeless: 'A woman when she's spoilt is *spoilt*. She's dirty in grain. She's done.' Dr Carstall in *The Holy Terror* would agree with this diagnosis. He gruffly opines that 'most who go loose stay loose. And a loose woman who is getting old is a damn nasty thing.' Even when younger, they seem fairly nasty, if we take as typical Puppy Clarges, the angular vamp of *Meanwhile*. She is 'strident and hard, a conflict of scent and cigarette smoke, with the wit of a music hall and an affectedly flat loud voice . . . . she was occasionally indecent and she professed to be unchaste. . . . The very thought of Puppy and a lover was obscene.' Puppy is romping on the Italian Riviera. *The World of William Clissold* disapprovingly locates similar fauna in the South of France, where

> they will dance like automata to imitation negro music, they will flirt without discrimination, they will set out upon timid, dishonest, nocturnal adventures and arrange their poor little adulteries and fornications . . . and so come at last belatedly to inartistic lasciviousness or speechless grossness and sleep.

A moral climate favourable to the evolution of such patterns of behaviour is seen as the prevailing atmosphere of the 1920s. During this period, Wells feels, an upsurge of cheapening promiscuity was accompanied by an avalanche of dirty books. Not only was England in 1920 'out for everything it could do sexually', *The Shape of Things to Come* remarks, but

Literature, always so responsive to its audience, stood on its head and displayed its private parts. It produced a vast amount of solemn pornography, facetious pornography, sadistic incitement, resexsualised religiosity and verbal gibbering in which the rich effectiveness of obscene words was abundantly exploited.

What was particularly distressing to Wells, as his *Guide to the New World* reveals, was to find Aldous Huxley, 'that strange abnormal grandson of my master and teacher', contributing to this: 'His mind is evidently enormously obsessed by thoughts of sex and bodily vigour, and in his Brave New World he makes sexual and athletic elaboration the chief employment of human leisure. To that he thinks our reason leads us.' Wells's reason leads him away from this prospect. Like Sir Richmond in *The Secret Places of the Heart*, he believes, 'One does not want to live for sex but only through sex. The main thing in my life has always been my work.' *The Shape of Things to Come* briskly states that 'properly interested people are not overwhelmed by sex'. A similar no-nonsense line is taken in *Guide to the New World*: 'healthy, educated children and men and women, with a lively interest in life, do not succumb to these fundamental urgencies. They will be untroubled by either morbid excess or morbid abstinence and jealousies.' As *God the Invisible King* has it, 'The sword must neither be drawn constantly nor always rusting in its sheath.' The sensible nudes found leading model lives of temperance and co-operation in *The Dream* and *Men Like Gods* obviously embody this ideal state. A regulated sex-life, balanced so it does not interfere with their civic functioning, is one of the attributes of the mature Utopians (in earlier life, they are allowed a phase of more hectic sexuality). Of the Samurai, Wells's elite group in *A Modern Utopia*, we are told, with characteristic imagery: 'In this matter, as in all matters of natural desire, they held no appetite must be glutted, no appetite must have artificial whets, and also and equally that no appetite should be starved. A man must come from the table satisfied, but not replete.' This ungorged but comfortable state is one Wells feels he has achieved himself, as he makes clear in *First and Last Things*

Now in this matter of physical appetites, I do not know whether to describe myself as a sensualist or an ascetic. If an ascetic is

one who suppresses to a minimum all deference to these
impulses, then certainly I am not an ascetic; if a sensualist is
one who gives himself to heedless gratification, then certainly
I am not a sensualist. But I find myself balanced in an
intermediate position.

This portrait of himself as a sexual moderate is hard to reconcile
with the widely-attested image of Wells as 'Don Juan among the
intelligentsia', which he mentions in his autobiography. He is
more accurately caught in lines describing William Steele in *The
Anatomy of Frustration*: 'Temperamentally he was extremely
heterosexual; yet intellectually he was disposed to ignore sex.'
There was a great deal of sexual activity in Wells's life: perhaps
because of this there is not much mental lingering over it.

Heated sexual imaginations are doused with ridicule in the
novels. Wilbeck draws disgustedly amused attention to Dolores
spotting syphilis in pimples, pursuing pubescent youths with
emancipated queries, and having her prurience contemptuously
tickled by Foxfield, who invents orgiastic tales of marine life:
'She was much excited by the idea of sea water as something into
which an infinitude of spawn and gonads were perpetually
liberated.' Brynhild Palace is revolted when she meets 'smutty
little girls of thirty or forty' who are rather similar—'always
talking of "taking lovers" and never really getting at them. Some
of their "affairs" sounded like collecting autographs or stealing
spoons for fun.' *The Work, Wealth and Happiness of Mankind* notes
a sad increase of such phenomena: 'The dissipated middle-aged
woman is becoming almost as common as the dissipated middle-
aged man. In the pleasure resorts of Europe and North Africa
one meets now the wealthy, lonely American wife or widow,
looking for the consolation of masculine intimacy and picking up
the "gigolo", the dancing partner, as a protégé, a companion and
often a venal lover.' Hedonist playgrounds of this kind are
converted into euthanasia reserves in some of Wells's prediction
books. *Anticipations* claims that 'Whole regions will be set aside
for the purposes of opulent enjoyment—a thing already happening, indeed, at points along the Riviera to-day.' And in such
locales, Wells remarks with satisfaction, the compulsive pleasure-
seeker will follow 'his primrose path to a congenial, picturesque,
happy and highly desirable extinction'. Opposed to these
moribund playboys are the New Republicans, admirably civic

figures who dispassionately look upon their love-making as 'a concession to the flesh necessary to secure efficiency'. Members of this group, we are told, 'will probably dress with a view to decent convenience . . . they will avoid exciting colour contrasts and bizarre contours': rather like Helen Wotton in *The Sleeper Awakes*. In keeping with her status as 'one of the most serious persons alive', she is clad in 'a silvery grey robe'. Trailing nobly around in it, she provides the moral support necessary to help Graham cope with all the 'luxury, waste and sensuality' of life in the twenty-second century. Though susceptible to female allure—he is beguiled by the red-haired daughter of the Manager of the European Piggeries, and makes the acquaintance of a dancing-girl, whom he 'found . . . an astonishing artist'—Graham retains a strong revulsion from the easy, copious sensuality of this civilisation. And it is made quite clear that he is wise to do so. One innovation he hears about is that of the Pleasure Cities—'strange, voluptuous, and in some way terrible. . . . Strange places reminiscent of the legendary Sybaris, cities of art and beauty, mercenary art and mercenary beauty, sterile wonderful cities of motion and music.' These pleasure-dominated zones, it is later explained to him, 'are the excretory organs of the State, attractive places that year after year draw together all that is weak and vicious, all that is lascivious and lazy . . . to a graceful destruction. They go there, they have their time, they die childless, all the pretty silly lascivious women die childless, and mankind is the better.' The fun-palace is a camouflaged extermination-chamber.

Hedonism, wasting time and energy, is in Wells a feature of civilisations in decline. 'Morals and Civilisation', published in 1897, observes that 'the enfeebled reprobation of sterile and sterilising indulgences, is one of the common features of all civilisations passing from the militant to the static state of civilization'. The erotically romping weaklings of *The Time Machine*, scarcely aware that they are Morlock-fodder, illustrate this point. Graham, looking down on a twenty-second-century dance-hall in *The Sleeper Awakes*, gets a similar view of enervated pleasure-chasers. Lightly clad and appetisingly bedecked, a crowd of effete good-timers sway excitedly together. Many of the women, Graham realises with particular disgust, are mothers who have handed over their children to automated crèches equipped with dandling machines and mechanical wet-nurses (the modelling of whose breasts, no opportunity for voluptuous refinement having been missed, is 'astonishingly realistic').

The ideal, Wells insists, is for a man to ensure, by avoiding both erotic deprivation and excess, that he can get on with his work without undue hindrance from 'the irksome, restricting, obstructive obsession with sex', as he puts it in *The World Set Free*. Realism and a constant urge towards autobiography, however, ensure that many of his male protagonists are endowed with a packed and promiscuous sexual history, which they sometimes rather swaggeringly lament. William Clissold, who has done 'quite a lot of promiscuous love-making', declares himself 'what the eighteenth century called a rake'. Mr Britling, seeing himself as a 'Pilgrim of Love', has, like Clissold, moments of slaked revulsion when he dutifully regrets all the working-hours his excitements have squandered. Remington, another erstwhile philanderer, confesses to Margaret before he marries her, 'there is another side to my life, a dirty side', explaining 'I'm streaked.' Capes in *Ann Veronica* shares this attribute, as his own confession before settling down reveals. Impressing on Ann Veronica that he has 'a streak of ardent animal' in his composition, he owns up to adultery and promiscuity, and tells her, 'I'm smirched. . . . I'm damaged goods.' Sir Richmond in *The Secret Places of the Heart* is another prowler. He has 'been—about women—like a thirsty beast looking for water'. As with Capes—and Wells—he has reacted to marriage as though it were a starting-pistol: 'instead of my marriage satisfying me, it presently released a storm of long controlled desires and imprisoned cravings. . . . I was unfaithful to my wife within four years of my marriage.' Wells himself, after marrying, did not wait so long. Of his relationship with his first wife, he said, 'After six "engagement" years of monogamic sincerity and essential faithfulness, I embarked, as soon as I was married, upon an enterprising promiscuity. The old love wasn't at all dead, but I meant now to get in all the minor and incidental love adventures I could.' He began—'Quite soon' after his marriage—with a Miss Kingsmill who had come to the Wellses' house to retouch negatives. When speaking of his sex drive, Wells's autobiography sometimes makes it sound like a tendency to some recurrent ailment which 'was to hamper and confuse my progress very considerably'. His attitude to his affairs seems to be one of exasperated need, considering them—as Sir Richmond did his— 'at once unsatisfying and vitally necessary'.

Hypocrisy coupled with compulsive womanising—public

advocacy of what he regarded as unhealthy repression and private practising of what he regarded as unhealthy obsession—especially disgusted Wells. He encountered it in Hubert Bland, the father of a young Fabian, Rosamund, with whom he was briefly involved. Behind the façade of a respectable marriage to Edith Nesbit, Bland indulged in a private life of hectic promiscuity. Monocled, emphatically Catholic, soberly encased in impeccable City garb, he was, beneath it all, an *aficionado* of the clandestine. Psychologically unbuttoning to other males in private, he

would give hints of his exceptional prowess. He would boast. He would discuss the social laxities of Woolwich and Black-heath, breaking into anecdotes, 'simply for the purpose of illustration'. Or he would produce a pocket-worn letter and read choice bits of it—'purely because of its psychological interest'. He did his utmost to give this perpetual pursuit of furtive gratification, the dignity of a purpose. He was, he claimed to me at least, not so much Don Juan as Professor Juan. 'I am a student, and experimentalist,' he announced, 'in illicit love.'

When he found that Wells was also exploring this area, along with his daughter, the outraged sexual Tory in him thundered to the fore. Bland was in no sense a campaigner for sexual emancipation, Wells's autobiography stresses; he was a fanatical upholder of the *status quo*, craving for rules so he could enjoy the thrill of trespass: 'I wanted to abolish barriers between the sexes and Bland loved to get under or over or through them. The more barriers the better.'

Ramage, the philandering financier in *Ann Veronica* is an ebulliently hostile picture of this type of personality:

His invalid wife and her money had been only the thin thread that held his life together; beaded on that permanent relation had been an interweaving series of other feminine experiences, disturbing, absorbing, interesting, memorable affairs. Each one had been different from the others, each had had a quality all its own, a distinctive freshness, a distinctive beauty. He could not understand how men could live ignoring this one predominant interest, this wonderful research into personality and the possibilities of pleasing, these complex, fascinating expeditions that began in interest and mounted to the supremest, most passionate intimacy. All the rest of his existence was subordinate to this pursuit; he loved for it, worked for it, kept himself in training for it.

In the novel, he is one of several men trying to trap Ann Veronica. Virtually imprisoned by her repressive father, tired of her sentimentally restrictive suitor Manning (who tries to limit her freedom of movement by putting her on a pedestal), she escapes to London, where she learns the near-impossibility of existing decently as an independent girl. Financial problems are one aspect of this—Ramage lends her money then demands sexual interest in return. And a frequent obstacle is misunderstanding. Freedom is confused with licence. Landladies reject her 'with an air of conscious virtue' or, assuming that she is a prostitute, offer rooms adorned with 'vulgar . . . undesirable' engravings. A particularly troublesome annoyance is being given the eye—no light matter in this novel. Soon after arriving in London, Ann Veronica is accosted by a man with a 'hungry gaze'; and, not long after this, is pestered more persistently by a man 'with bluish eyes that were rather protuberant'. Driven from a tea-room by his ogling, she finds it hard to shake him off; and, even when she has done so, his 'bulging blue eyes' get into her dreams. It is Ramage, though, who represents the greatest menace in the ocular molestation line. When he first enters the narrative, attention is drawn to his 'rather protuberant black eyes'. When he later encounters Ann Veronica alone, they become 'rather too protuberant'. And, when she seeks him out in his City office, they bulge even more alarmingly: he starts 'protruding his eyes' at her, making her feel increasingly uneasy at 'how prominent his eyes were'. But their full tumescent power remains latent until he jumps on her in a *chambre privée*, and 'Her eye met his four inches away, and his was glaring, immense . . . a stupendous monster of an eye.' Though Ann Veronica escapes this would-be penetrating stare, Ramage hangs hopefully around the neighbourhood with 'his eyes distended', and eventually makes another inflamed pass at her: 'His eyes', she notes with interest, 'looked a little bloodshot' but are still hungrily 'projecting'. No wonder Mr Stanley disapprovingly declares of Ramage, 'A man like that taints a girl by looking at her.'

The City gent with the secret life is one type of hypocrite.

Another frequently decried by Wells is the sex-starved don. Oxbridge academics and their repressed lives are often the subject of head-shaking commentary in his writings. We hear in *Joan and Peter* that 'such sins as the dons knew of were rather in the nature of dirty affectations, got out of Petronius and Suetonius and practised with a tremendous sense of devilment behind locked doors'. This grubby state of things has been the case for centuries, *The Anatomy of Frustration* suggests, taking Robert Burton savagely to task because 'His sexual satisfactions, if he had any . . . were a mean business of the backstairs and alleys of that monastic university town', Oxford. *The Research Magnificent* gives us a detailed close-up of a contemporary don, Prothero. He is literally as well as metaphorically dirty: 'I quiver with hot and stirring desires', he confesses. 'And I'm indolent—dirty indolent. . . . there are days when I splash my bath about without getting into it.' Calling at his rooms in Trinity, Benham surprises Prothero poring over 'a large red, incongruous, meretricious looking volume' called *Venus in Gem and Marble*. True to the suspicions voiced in *Joan and Peter*, his door is locked, and he is 'looking a little puffy' when he shamefacedly opens it. Unlike the other instances of erotic attachment to statues and mytho-logical artefacts, Prothero's goings-on are obviously to be deplored. He himself, in fact, immediately denounces 'Inflam-matory classics', disclosing that, instead of working, he has spent the morning with 'that large, vulgar, red book' because 'I want— Venus'; and, lest there should be any misunderstanding, he adds defiantly, 'I don't want her to talk to or anything of that sort.' A shocked Benham fears the root of the trouble may be an enlarged liver, but Prothero hysterically places the blame on his 'horrible vice of continence' and the disturbing nature of the season, 'a peculiarly erotic spring'. This has made him 'hot and red and shiny and shameless'; and it is doing the same to his colleagues. 'The majority of my fellow dons who look at me with secretive faces in hall and court and combination-room are in just the same case as myself. The fever in oneself detects the fever in others.' Donnish erotomania is catered for far more satis-factorily in Russia, he believes: 'Binns tells me that, although there is a profession of celibacy within the walls, the arrange-ments of the town and more particularly of the various hotels are conceived in a spirit of extreme liberality.' Travelling in that country later with Benham, he is able briefly to become the beneficiary of such liberality, but, with the return to Cambridge, 'The little man merged again into his rare company of discreet Benedicts and restrained celibates.' Finally, going completely off the rails as a result of his abnormal life, he expires in a *fracas* in an opium den.

'Celibacy, that great denial of life', as *Mankind in the Making* has it, is repeatedly denounced by Wells. Sometimes, real-life practitioners of it are shudderingly alluded to, as when *New Worlds for Old* points to the 'hot dark reservoir of evil thoughts that years of chastity and discipline seem to have left intact in Fr Phelan's soul'. Sometimes, fictional creations show its horrors. Fayle, the dismissively named religious fanatic in *The Brothers*, is a product of celibacy; so is Fr Amerton in *Men Like Gods*, whose writhingly excited denunciations of Utopian nudity cause the Utopians to feel, 'This man with the white linen fetter round his neck is disgustingly excited by the common human body.' Unused sexual energy can spill over into religion. 'What is your theologian's ecstasy', Dr Moreau demands, 'but Mahomet's houri in the dark?' It can also be displaced into politics, as Rud Whitlow in *The Holy Terror* repulsively shows. His autocratic impulses come from his 'autosexual' personality. Keeping himself very much to himself erotically—'he did not like to give himself away to a fellow creature even amorously'—Rud becomes increasingly withdrawn from reality. Attempts to interest him in women flop absurdly: even an alluring masseuse, Miss Chubby Fielder, rubs him up the wrong way. Rud's trouble is diagnosed by Chiffan: 'When a man is happy with his woman and a woman is happy with her man and they are happy with their friends, neither of them *aches*—as he does—to possess the world.' Rud wants to possess the world because he can't possess a woman. Chiffan is quite different. One of Wells's reformed rakes—his wife, to whom he is devoted, is 'the twenty-ninth "real mistress" of his philandering career'—he now lives a life of healthy balance. Awareness of this increasingly disturbs Rud until, after a diatribe of frustrated resentment, he has the man killed.

Another example of sexual disturbance getting unhealthily into politics is what Wells calls in *The Wife of Sir Isaac Harman* 'The Great Insane Movement': the suffragette campaign. This was something about which he felt particularly bitter since, as he records in his autobiography, the ladies involved in it had constituted something of a severe personal disappointment. When the movement began, Wells assumed its members would be statuesque free spirits cast on the model of his early ideal females, and 'prepared to welcome these goddesses'. Alas, 'As the hosts of liberation came nearer and could be inspected more accurately', he 'found reason to qualify these bright expectations': far from comprising a 'great-hearted free companionship of noble women', the suffragettes turned out to be a screeching rabble— typified by the hooligan harpies who fall on a politician in Court dress, in *The Wife of Sir Isaac Harman*, with the shriek, 'Tear off his epaulettes!' Though much concerned with the injustices of the married state and the need for Lady Harman to obtain a decent independence, this book emphasises that the way for her to go is not shoulder-to-shoulder with the suffragettes. In fact, in the form of the derisively named Agatha Alimony, they let Lady Harman down when she seeks sanctuary with them after leaving her husband: 'We mustn't mix up Women's Freedom with Matrimonial Causes. Impossible! We *dare* not!' Agatha Alimony had been given room to discredit herself and the campaign for the vote in Wells's fiction before. She turns up in *Marriage*, at a suffragist gathering in Trafford's house, 'wearing an enormous hat with three nodding ostrich feathers, a purple bow, a gold buckle and numerous minor ornaments of various origin and substance'. From under this heap of millinery—designed to suggest she has more on her head than in it—she emits 'deep trumpet calls', with the intention, Wells exasperatedly believes, of rallying her followers behind the banner of irrationality. Agatha wants, she declares vehemently, 'to annoy scientific men'. Certainly, she annoys Wells and his physicist in the novel, Trafford, who warns Majorie that exposure to such feminist hot-air will make her mind 'liquefy . . . and slop about'. Wet ideas and slushy utterances typify the suffragists. Aiding Agatha's advocacy of the woman's cause on this occasion is a soulful male called Godley Buzard. His theme—it resembles 'a solo on the piccolo'—is the Matriarchate: 'Every One of the Great Primitive Inventions was made by a Woman . . . to Women they owed Fire and the early Epics and Sagas.' This yearning motif was earlier introduced into Wells's fiction by Miss Miniver in *Ann Veronica*:

'The primitive government was the Matriarchate. The Matriarchate! The Lords of Creation just ran about and did what they were told.'

'But is that really so?' said Ann Veronica.

'It has been proved,' said Miss Miniver, and added, 'by American professors.'

'But how did they prove it?'

'By science,' said Miss Miniver, and hurried on.

This wobbly fantasia is obviously built up on a morass of wishful thinking. And Miss Miniver's biology is just as shaky as her anthropology:

> Originally in the first animals there were no males, none at all. It has been proved. Then they appear among the lower things ... among crustaceans and things, just as little creatures, ever so inferior to the females. Mere hangers-on. Things you would laugh at.

This eldritch crescendo is somewhat unnecessarily accompanied by a commentary alerting us to the deficiencies of Miss Miniver's techniques of persuasion: 'arguments indicated rather than stated ... served in a sauce of strange enthusiasm, thin yet intense', etc. A more common way of emphasising the suffragettes' wanton disregard of logic is to allude sarcastically to their substitution of damage for debate. Also gracing the Trafford *soirée*, for instance, is a small lady in glasses who speaks stirringly of women's efforts to bring home to Asquith 'the eminent reasonableness of their sex by breaking his windows, interrupting his meetings, booing at him in the streets and threatening his life'. This heavy irony is a weapon Wells keeps swinging at the suffragettes. Lady Harman and Mr Brumley, at Kew, are guided past ' the old pavilion, the one that Miss Alimony's suffragettes were afterwards to burn down in order to demonstrate the relentless logic of women'. *Marriage* reminds us of the way 'the occasional smashing of a Downing Street window or an assault upon a minister kept the question of women's distinctive intelligence and character persistently before the public'. And in *The Bulpington of Blup* we hear of 'The militant section of the movement which set fire to the contents of pillar-boxes and smashed plate-glass windows as evidence of women's peculiar capacity for government'.

Another thing which fatally detracts from the conviction of the women's cause, Wells suggests, is the thinness of their vocal chords. Considering the notoriously squeaky timbre of his own voice—'thin high-pitched', noted his sons' governess; 'curious, atonic, thin . . . physiologically inexplicable', felt Julian Huxley; 'high, huskily hooting', observed Dorothy Richardson—this is something it might have been thought more prudent for him to keep quiet about. But, in fact, he is persistent in voicing his belief that excited women don't strike the right note. His auto-biography complains about the 'squawking' at suffragette gatherings; and so do some of his characters. After listening to a feminist tirade, Mr Brumley feels 'it was such a poor speech—squeaky'. Ann Veronica shrinks embarrassedly from the way her sisters 'pipe out a demand for votes'. And Lady Mary loftily de-clares of the same phenomenon, 'the effect is more like agitated geese upon a common than anything human has a right to be'.

Wells's dislike of the suffragettes is so intense that he will even briefly side with a character like Isaac Harman in order to mock them. He, we are told, 'had supposed suffragettes were ladies of all too certain an age, with red noses and spectacles and a masculine style of costume, who wished to be hugged by policemen'. Perhaps he had been reading *Ann Veronica*, where a suffragette more or less answering to this description is on display. Miss Miniver's nose, if not red, is 'pink' and 'pinched'; her 'emotional' eyes are 'further magnified by the glasses she wore'; and we are left in no doubt about the fact that she is embracing a cause because men won't embrace her. Like Wells's other suffragettes, she has give-away vocal chords: asked if she doesn't want to be loved by a man, she cries *'No!'* in a voice reminiscent 'of a sprung tennis racket'. Wells keeps harping on the way frustration has seeped into her reasoning, making it soggily bitter:

> 'Of course,' said Miss Miniver . . . 'we *do* please men. We have that gift. We can see round them and behind them and through them, and most of us use that knowledge, in the silent way we have, for our great ends. I wonder what men would say if we threw the mask aside—if we really told them what *We* thought of them, really showed them what *We* were.' A flush of excite-ment crept into her cheeks.
>
> 'Maternity,' she said, 'has been our undoing.'

A chauvinist guffaw at the thought that it's unlikely to be hers concludes the response to this passage, which also aims to raise a laugh at Miss Miniver's attempt to smuggle herself into the line-up of man-pleasing beauties, and her garrulous insistence on women's silent way. This portrait of the suffragette as addle-brained and limply-vindictive frump is surrounded in the book by other acidly-etched vignettes of feminist absurdity. There is a whole chapter recording Ann Veronica's encounter with the movement. Once again, female inability to argue is stressed. When Ann Veronica meets Kitty Brett (a hostile sketch of Christabel Pankhurst), she finds her 'about as capable of intelligent argument as a runaway steam roller'. Other suffragettes prove equally out of control—' "It's like Troy!" said a voice of rapture. "It's exactly like Troy!" ' And there is, for Ann Veronica, a particularly distasteful outburst of hysteria when she is in prison and one of her fellow-suffragettes takes to

> howling before the midday meal. This was an imitation of the noises made by the carnivora at the Zoological Gardens at feeding time; the idea was taken up by prisoner after prisoner until the whole place was alive with barkings, yappings, roarings, pelican chatterings, and feline yowlings, interspersed with shrieks of hysterical laughter.

This frivolous attitude towards food and carnivores disgusts Ann Veronica—who will later spend a decisive afternoon at the Zoo, inspecting a toucan's bill with Capes, and marvelling at 'his practical omniscience' as he explains that animals prefer sugar to buns. Proper reverence for biology and a biologist ultimately saves her. It is in the nature of things, she comes to feel, that, though a woman would not wish to be 'subject to the wrong man', she would fervently aspire to be 'slave to the right one'. Although Capes tells her, 'I have known you for the goddess', the position she adopts is more like that of acolyte. When they first meet, she is his student; after they elope, he is surprised at 'her capacity for blind obedience' to 'his command'; and the essence of their marriage is epitomised in the novel's final moments when she 'flung herself kneeling into her husband's arms'. When working on *Ann Veronica*, Wells wrote to Frederick Macmillan that it was 'the best love story I have ever done'. It is certainly one of the most typical—a distinctly artificial-looking icon of the slave-goddess surrounded by a weird pile of the paraphernalia, from mountains to suffragettes, that his imagination likes to strew around the concept.

3 The Redeveloped Basement: Wells and Habitat

Wells learned from biology that habitat is life's great shaper. Evolution showed him how environment moulded species by its gradual pressures. Fossils stamped upon his mind the fact that failure to fit in must bring annihilation—'The long roll of palaeontology', his essay 'On Extinction' says, 'is half filled with the records of extermination.' Anatomy supplied living proof of the power of environment—*A Short History of the World* points out that man's body still pays homage to its watery origins: 'his lung surfaces', for instance, 'must be moist in order that air may pass through them into his blood'. In *Guide to the New World*, Wells stresses that 'down the whole corridor of recorded history, man has been *made*'. What has made him is his habitat: and this concept is significant to Wells not only as regards the past but also the future. Looking ahead to this in book after book, he urges that man, previously shaped by environment, must now start to shape environment to his own advantage. The necessity for this was not only impressed on him by a training in biology. It was first brought home by the surroundings of his formative years.

A large proportion of Wells's early life was spent below the ground. Until he was thirteen, he recalls in his autobiography, the family mainly lived 'in a completely subterranean kitchen, lit by a window which derived its light from a grating on the street level'. What eventually pulled them out of this 'dismal insanitary hole' was Mrs Wells's return as housekeeper to Up Park (a name that, with its suggestions of height and space, must have sounded especially alluring to the cramped basement-dwellers of Bromley). Even here, however, life turned out to be largely subterranean. Mrs Wells's rooms were two semi-basements with grilled windows. And, in any case, Wells was now being sent out to live and work in various draperies. Amongst the numerous things he disliked about the first of these was the fact that, as he recounts in a letter home, he had to eat in 'a sort of vault underground'. Years later, when he finally escaped from the lowering confines of the retail trade to student life in London, he still failed to stay permanently above ground. Much of the time, he lodged with aunts who occupied a basement, so he had to work 'by the gas light in the underground front room'. And though impressed, like George in *Tono-Bungay*, by his college's 'hugely handsome buildings' in Exhibition Road, he had to descend, in order to participate in its debating society, to an underground lecture theatre. After all this subterranean existence, it's no wonder he was appalled, on joining the ranks of the Fabian Society, to find them meeting, with 'an air of arrested growth', in underground apartments in Clement's Inn. To see supposed social reformers huddled in the kind of setting that had framed his years of want exasperated Wells. Objecting to their premises as much as their procedures, he insisted in his pamphlet *Faults of the Fabian*, 'Our rooms ought to suggest a new and more pleasant way of living, they ought to be light and beautiful and hopeful, instead of being a dismal basement lit through a grating.'

The way of living lit through the grating in Bromley had been both restricted and ramshackle. Poverty meant it was difficult to escape from the shop—the only openings Mrs Wells found for her sons led to dead-end jobs in draperies—and inside the home everything was grimy, ill-matched, misplaced, second-hand, 'frayed, discoloured and patched'. It was an environment, Wells later claimed, that had deformed him physically: he blamed his lack of stature, for instance, not only on meagre meals but also on having been kept too long in a small bed. Certainly, it helped to shape his theories and imagination. What his social improvement schemes show most clearly is an attempt to get as far away as possible from the living conditions of Bromley. His ideal environment is the basement remodelled, with each feature strikingly replaced by its opposite: the dark, underground room is hauled up high into the light; huge windows are fitted; the walls are pushed back or broken down so there is ample space; and instead of muddle there is order everywhere.

The basement formed a matrix for Wells's imagination: and some of the features it forced upon his notice were much reinforced by what he later found elsewhere. Mess, for instance, did not only disfigure the family interior; it characterised the whole of Bromley. Under the guise of Bromstead, this appears near the beginning of *The New Machiavelli* as a semi-rural village—'a little mellow sample unit of a social order that had a kind of completeness'—which is then pulverised and filthied as 'the limitless grimy chaos' of London pours over it. This is what Wells felt had happened to Bromley during his childhood: a tidy community with time-rounded contours was engulfed and splintered into jerry-built fragments by the tidal-wave impact of a massive city bursting outwards. *The War in the Air* displays another instance of the squashed and broken village: Bun Hill, a once 'idyllic' place, now 'flooded by new and urban things'. And, if Bromley seemed merely a spilling further of the dingy disarray of Atlas House, the draperies Wells was sent to duplicated the shop's jail-like aspect— as his reaction on moving into an establishment at Southsea for 'two years of incarceration' makes clear:

> At that moment I could not discover in my mind or in the world, as represented by the narrow side street into which I was looking, . . . the blind alley below me or the strip of sky overhead, the faintest intimation of any further escape.
>
> I turned round from this restricted outer world to survey my dormitory in much the same mood as a condemned prisoner surveying the fittings of the cell he is to occupy for his allotted term.

The drapery as dungeon reappears in a number of Wells's books. *The Wheels of Chance* opens with Hoopdriver's 'chains' falling from him as he leaves the drapery for his annual holiday, euphoric but for 'The shadow of going back, of being put in the cage again'. It ends as he returns to his place of work and 'The gate closes upon him with a slam.' *Kipps* takes the idea of haberdashery as confinement even further: 'we're in a blessed drain-pipe,' a trapped apprentice growls, 'and we've got to crawl along it till we die'. *Mr Polly* sends its hero on a tour of places of imprisonment that Wells had known. He is first immured in a series of draperies, including one with 'an underground dining room'; and then fastened into an outfitter's shop for fifteen years. Though this differs from the Wellses' establishment in that it is not a china dealer's (there is one, next door), it is obviously—with its 'ill-built, cramped rooms' and 'an underground kitchen that must necessarily be the living-room in winter'—a reconstruction of the shop in Atlas House.

Delving into his memories, Wells's fiction frequently unearths dismal abodes like those that walled in his early life. Murky caves of genteel poverty honeycomb his work. 'You were troglodytes!' gasps one of his Utopians in *The Dream*, on hearing of life in the Old World. Confirming this, there are 'troglodytic servants' in *Tono-Bungay* and numerous Wellsian characters who go underground in an effort to survive. Landladies eking out a pinched existence by squeezing into the basement of a house that they let are glimpsed in *The Dream*, *The Wife of Sir Isaac Harman*, and *In the Days of the Comet*. Down on their luck in London, Teddy Ponderevo and Aunt Susan are forced into the regulation basement kitchen. The Chafferys in *Love and Mr Lewisham* occupy one too: and, when he visits them there, we learn 'That descent had a distinctly depressing effect upon Lewisham'—as well it might, considering that the author's memory is here gloomily retracing its steps back to Atlas House. In *Kipps*, a descent to a basement is the turning point of the story. Having climbed a tower to propose to high-class Helen, Kipps backs down from the relationship by turning to Ann, who insists he must abandon his pretensions to loftiness if he wants her: 'that's my door, down there. Basement.'

Humbly, he goes down to it and proposes to her in the underground kitchen. Once they are married, though, and planning to build a house, Ann is emphatic that 'It mustn't be a 'ouse with a basement . . . a downstairs where there's not 'arf enough light and everything got to be carried.' Other escaped basement-dwellers show even more determination to leave it all behind. Uncle Teddy in *Tono-Bungay* is a case in point. Once his fortunes start to rise, he follows an architectural policy of 'Onward and Up', as Aunt Susan puts it. George charts the 'ascendant movement' of this until, as 'invaders of the upper levels of the social system', the Ponderevos take over Lady Grove, a fine old house with 'a very high terrace', looking out 'across the blue distances of the Weald'. Even this is not the summit of Uncle Teddy's ambitions, however. He decides to build a huger house on a higher spot—the resoundingly-named Crest Hill, 'A mammoth house . . . to suit these hills'. Watching the progress of this towering dream-home, George says it 'burgeoned and bulged and evermore grew. I know not what delirium of pinnacles and terraces and arcades and corridors glittered at last upon the uplands of his mind.' Obviously a spectacular compensation for lowly beginnings, this dramatic edifice is matched by one in *The Holy Terror* (a novel in which quite a few characters take to homes in the hills). Rud Whitlow's house here is 'built into a cliff', and it is, Wells revealingly explains, 'Rud's own fancy that he should sleep in a bed upon a dais in a great arched loggia . . . from which he could descend to the open-air life of his grand balcony. His early upbringing in stuffy little rooms had given him a sort of architectural claustrophobia.'

Large windows—over which Wells often enthuses—similarly cast light on his own early claustrophobia. Sempack, the admired sage of *Meanwhile*, has had a house built for him near the summit of a hill: like the anti-basement it is, it spreads itself to the light, so that, working before 'a big plate-glass window', he has 'a view that goes away into distance beyond distance for miles and miles'. Another ideal home is put up for inspection in *Christina Alberta's Father*. This sits 'comfortably on the hill-side', has a gazebo and 'a number of excellent points of view' from which to gaze out at vistas of Sussex, sunsets, and the sea.

The possibility of taking a broad view of things always espe-cially appeals to Wells, but details of interior decor can be the subject of rhapsodic attention too. It is a testimony to the heroine's admirable nature, in *Joan and Peter*, that she plans to build 'Cottages with sensible insides, real insides'; and in both *The New Machiavelli* and *Marriage* a long, appreciative section is devoted to the decorating of fine rooms with splendid furniture and fabrics. Also, Wells's peerings into the future, though often blithely unfocused, can light excitedly on instances of Design Centre ingenuity. *A Modern Utopia*, popping into a hotel in the ideal state, notes approvingly that 'The room has no corners to gather dirt, wall meets floor with a gentle curve, and the apart-ment could be swept out effectually by a few strokes of a mechanical sweeper.' Another bright idea is that 'You are politely requested to turn a handle at the foot of your bed before leaving the room, and forthwith the frame turns up into a vertical position, and the bed-clothes hang airing.' Similar Utopian ingenuities are on display in *Men Like Gods*—such as a bath which was 'difficult to misuse. If you splashed too much a thoughtful outer rim tidied things up for you.'

Wells's interest in domestic architecture did not stay at the level of theory. A restless mover in and out of various homes, he played a part in designing some of them himself. At Sandgate, for instance, he commissioned a house to be built on a hill with a good view, watched fascinatedly and sometimes disapprovingly as it was built, and had tussles with Voysey, the architect, over such matters as the placing of door-handles. Another cause of controversy was Voysey's habit of ornamenting houses he had built with the emblem of the heart. Wells insisted this be turned upside down, and called his home Spade House. He seems to have been wise in choosing the symbol of industry rather than affection to characterise his home. Years later, he consecrated a house built in Provence for himself and Odette Keun to their mutual passion by having a plaque announcing 'Two Lovers Built This House' cemented over the fireplace. The subsequent ups and downs of their affair apparently necessitated much bringing-in of the local builder to remove or replace the proclamation. Arnold Bennett, who visited this house, notes in his Journal that Wells had planned it himself; and comments, 'windows too large'. That there should be abundant light and views was a prime requirement of Wells when setting up home. After he and Jane moved into a Georgian rectory at Little Easton, he had windows added in order to open up the house's prospects. And the Paris flat he occupied with Odette Keun seems to have satisfied both his fondness for views and his enthusiasm for heights by allowing him to look out across the Seine at the Eiffel Tower. The last house Wells moved into, 13 Hanover Terrace, catered to another trait, his dislike of superstition. Despite its unlucky number—his indifference to which he liked to emphasise— he remained there throughout the Blitz, going out, when a bomb fell on the house opposite, to put up a large number 13 beside his unharmed front door. It was in this house that he died on 13 August 1946.

Wells's expansionist impulses are not, of course, confined to house-design. City planning also attracts his eager interest. New York, in particular, is a continuing subject of admiring comment on account of its 'tall vigour', as *A Year of Prophesying* puts it. The keynote is struck in *The Future in America* when Wells excitedly points out that the Cunarder on which he had sailed, and which dwarfed the Liverpool skyline, is now itself dwarfed by massive New York. For pages after this, he is gasping rapturously at the hugeness of it all—'the fierce commercial altitudes', the 'Cyclo-

pean stone arches' of Brooklyn Suspension Bridge. And as he
wanders round 'this New York that has so obsessed me with its
bigness', he receives 'a vision . . . of everything wider, taller,
cleaner, better'. At the book's conclusion, as he sails away, there
is a splendidly evocative image, with the skyscrapers reminding
him 'quite irresistibly of piled-up packing cases outside a ware-
house': what could come out of them is a better future. In fact, he
came to feel, a way of life to match the audacious upward thrust of
the New York buildings never emerged. But Wells's admiration
for the monumental masonry always remains. *The War in the Air*,
dismissing London, Paris, and Berlin as 'shapeless, low agglo-
merations', rhapsodises over New York's 'exquisite ascendant
lines', its 'cliffs of high building' and 'steep canyon of Broadway'.
The tendency emerging here—to see New York as a man-made
mountain—soon becomes standard in Wells's response to the
city. *The Passionate Friends* describes it as a 'cliff of man's making'.
The Dream marvels at its 'cliffs and crags of windows towering
up to the sky'. *World Brain* watches admiringly as its 'great grey
and brown and amber masses, cliffs and pinnacles' soften in the
twilight. And in *Mr Blettsworthy on Rampole Island* the metamorphosis goes a stage further: the 'tall, grey cliffs' that have
loomed over the hero in his long delirium turn out to be the New
York skyscrapers distorted by his fantasy.

New York, with its soaring sky-line, has the height that Wells
requires of an ideal habitat, but it is not wide enough for him.
The community man should be trying to establish, he believes,
must be much more extensive—what *First and Last Things* calls
'the World City of Mankind'. Plato's *Republic*, Wells declares in
The Outline of History, introduced 'a new thing in the development
of mankind . . . the idea of wilfully and completely recasting
human conditions'. Wells himself took to this concept of re-
moulding man's environment with great enthusiasm. Increasingly, his writing is propaganda for what he refers to, also in *The
Outline of History*, as 'The idea of the world state, the universal
kingdom of righteousness of which every living soul shall be a
citizen'. 'Hitherto', he explains in that book, 'man has been living
in a slum. . . . He has scarcely tasted sweet air yet and the great
freedoms of the world that science has enlarged for him.' If the
species is to survive, he argues, it must escape from what *Brynhild*
calls the '*The Cramped Village*', a mean and confined way of life,
into an environment affording ample opportunity for physical

and mental expansion. *The Passionate Friends* speaks of the need to take possession of 'that wide estate of life that spreads about us all'; and if the phrasing makes the world community sound rather like a global Up Park, this is appropriate since, as Wells explains in his autobiography, he considered country-house existence 'the experimental cellule of the coming Modern State'. What his Utopias bear most relationship towards, though, is his own early living conditions—which they emphatically invert. Revealingly, the structure of four of his Utopian books is one of contrast. *A Modern Utopia* projects us to an ideal world 'Out beyond Sirius, far in the deeps of space'. Physically, it is the same as the earth— a planet like our planet, the same continents, the same islands, the same oceans and seas'—but in quality it is completely different. Reprovingly, the book sets what its model citizens have done with their environment against the mess man has made of the same. London, for instance, is transformed into an award-winning assemblage of Wells's favourite architectural features— 'great arches and domes of glass above the wider spaces', 'cliffs of crowded hotels' and so on—unlike the hideous panorama of deformity and low-grade workmanship into which the narrator is plunged on his return—'I am standing beside an iron seat of poor design in that grey and gawky waste of asphalte—Trafalgar Square'. The book has the before and after pattern of a crude advertisement (though it is difficult to locate the exact commodity that has brought about the change)—something even more apparent in *In the Days of the Comet*, which very didactically juxtaposes its pre- and post-cometary worlds. *Men Like Gods* achieves the same effect by a kind of interdimensional catapulting: unregenerate earthlings are accidentally propelled from their fouled environs into a paradisal state which exists parallel to their planet. *The Dream* reverses this process: infected by a cut acquired from some old world rubble, a Utopian is mentally transported back to the squalid past, and his lurid communiqués on what he witnesses appal his listeners.

Glittering seductively on the horizon, promising relief, it seems, from the dusty deprivations of the present, Wells's Utopias are like mirages—shimmering allure with no real substance. The Prologue to *In the Days of the Comet*, taking us into a high tower that affords a view of the new world, virtually admits this: 'one perceived only distances, a remote horizon of sea, a headland . . . vague haze and glitter'. Nothing that follows adds any convincing solidity to this *ignis fatuus* vision of Utopia (which, with the double cloudiness of 'vague haze', could hardly be more nebulous). This is true of Wells's other ideal states. And not only is it hard to envisage them with any precision: it is also impossible to see what exactly has brought them about. *Men Like Gods* does give a 'History of Utopia', a section supposedly explaining how the model world has been achieved; but it would be difficult to imagine anything much less specific:

A fortunate conspiracy of accidents rather than any set design had opened for them some centuries of opportunity and expansion. Climactic phases and political chances had smiled upon the race. . . . Many thousands of people were lifted out of the normal squalor of human life to positions in which they could, if they chose, think and act with unprecedented freedom. A few, a sufficient few, did. A vigorous development of scientific inquiry began, and, trailing after it a multitude of ingenious inventions, produced a great enlargement of practical human power. . . . extraordinary possibilities of control over his own body and over his social life dawned upon the Utopian.

Oddly, too—despite Wells's usual calls for decisive action to bring about Utopia—the passage seems designed to foster fatalism, so great is its stress on the fortuitous and passive: 'fortunate conspiracy of accidents . . . political chances . . . were lifted out of . . . dawned upon'. Strangely, in a writer so concerned with the importance of evolution, the process of change which has crucially reshaped the world and the human species does not get portrayed. Apart from a vague, repetitive insistence on the wonderful results to be gained from being scientific and co-operative, *The Dream* and *Men Like Gods* provide no guidelines on how to progress from the low-level living of the present to the salubrious heights of the future. *In the Days of the Comet*, looking at the removal process a little more closely, offers nothing more substantial than a misty transformation scene.

In fact, this is a work whose contrast-structure throws into particularly sharp relief the vacuity of Wells's ideal state. Surveying the old-world habitat, the early section of the book is crammed to bursting-point with detail. The first chapter opens in 'a little ill-lit room', the contents of which are enumerated with obsessive thoroughness. The plaster on the ceiling is 'cracked and bulging', 'discoloured by . . . yellow and olive-green stains'. The wallpaper is 'faded' and disfigured by 'several big plaster-rimmed wounds' caused by attempts to get nails into the wall. There are hanging bookshelves 'sustained a little insecurely by frayed and knotted blind-cord'. The tablecloth is splashed with ink. The fender is a 'misfit'. In the grate is a 'broken corn-cob pipe'. The coal-box has a 'damaged hinge'. The sash-window is 'rickety'; the door, 'loose-fitting'. And taking the honours in this inventory of dilapidation is a wash-handstand which has been 'chipped, kicked, splintered, punched, stained, scorched, hammered, desiccated, damped, and defiled'. He is itemising 'all this grimy unpleasantness' with 'such particularity', the narrator explains, because 'I see these details of environment as being remarkable, as significant, as indeed obviously the outward visible manifestations of the old world disorder in our hearts.' There is, in this book, a constant parallel between character and habitat. The ramshackle rubbish which the author heaps around the old-world homes is not only matched by the muddled mis-conceptions which clutter many minds, but also, in the public sphere, by the 'promiscuous . . . higgledy-piggledy . . . vast irregular agglomeration of ugly smoking accidents' which makes up the industrial environment around them. Inflammation is another common factor. Hot, exacerbated characters are sil-houetted against a panorama of 'flaring industrialism'. Flecks of red are scattered everywhere to show the feverish heat of the old world. Wearing 'a discoloured red tie', Leadford prowls smoulderingly around, with jealousy making 'a vivid inflam-matory spot' in his brain—especially when he sees his rival in the darkness and the man's cigar 'glowed like a blood-red star'. Meanwhile, in the streets, hot-headed workers menacingly mass together 'as corpuscles gather and catch in the blood-vessels in the opening stages of inflammation'; an irascible industrialist called Lord Redcar has his motor set on fire; and, out at sea, a naval battle starts, with 'intensely red' sparks pouring from an ironclad and 'red flashes' of gunfire spurting in return. Then what is aptly called 'green moonshine' envelopes the earth, and Utopia arrives. Because of the change of atmosphere, people now meet 'naturally and inevitably upon the broad daylight platform of obvious and reasonable agreement'; there is 'a sense of enlarge-ment'; 'lives that were caught, crippled, starved, and maimed' blossom into fulfilment.

Noticeably, though, the author's imagination is most attracted towards the acts of destruction necessary in the new age. Wells's Utopias are generally preluded by mayhem. *The War in the Air*, *The World Set Free*, *The Shape of Things to Come*, and *The Holy Terror* all show mankind pitched into global carnage before the World State emerges. *In the Days of the Comet* resounds, in its latter stages, with the noise of demolition. Man's environment is so thoroughly smashed and purged before reconstruction that the citizens of the new world have to live for some time in what seems a giant building-site: we hear of 'the Year of Tents, the Year of Scaffolding'. Some pre-cometary edifices do survive. Leadford's mother is transferred from 'that dismal underground kitchen' to 'the upper room of Lowchester House': rather as though Mrs Wells (who died while Wells was drafting this book) had been rehoused in the upstairs quarters of Up Park. But, for the most part, the new world arrives with a flurry of destructiveness. One feature of the rise in mankind's living standards is the revival of Beltane festivals, which become great ceremonial incinerations of old-world furnishings and *bric-à-brac*. 'The actual houses, of course, we could not drag to our fires', Leadford remarks with regret (a situation perhaps partly rectified in *Mr Polly*, where the hero's feats of accidental arson are cheered on with the cry that it would also be a good idea to 'burn most of London and Chicago'). But everything remotely portable gets lugged to the incinerator:

> we brought all their ill-fitting deal doors, their servant-tormenting staircases, their dank, dark cupboards, the verminous papers from their scaly walls, their dust and dirt-sodden carpets, their ill-designed and yet pretentious tables and chairs, sideboards and chests of drawers, the old dirt-saturated books, their ornaments—their dirty, decayed, and, altogether painful ornaments—amidst which I remember there were sometimes even *stuffed dead birds*!

Clothing goes up in smoke as well—apart from a few disinfected samples kept in museums for the appalled edification of future generations—as Wells, flushed with pyrotechnic relish, puts a torch to the grimy impedimenta of his early life. But, when the bonfire has died down, all that is left is misty emptiness. The absorbingly trash-crammed interiors, full of quirky bits and pieces, are replaced by hazy vistas of cliché and abstract noun:

'galleries and open spaces . . . trees of golden fruit and crystal waters . . . music and rejoicing, love and beauty without cease'.

The negative usually comes out better than the positive in Wells. Impatience prefers demolition to construction. As he remarks, in a revealing passage in *What Are We To Do With Our Lives?*,

> To make is a long and wearisome business, with many arrests and disappointments, but to break gives an instant thrill. We all know something of the delight of the *bang*. It is well for the Open Conspirator to ask himself at times how far he is in love with the dream of a world in order, and how far he is driven by hatred of institutions that bore or humiliate him. He may be no more than a revengeful incendiary in the mask of a constructive worker.

There are times when the last sentence is virtually a self-description.

A letter Wells wrote to his wife, complaining about some alterations to their house at Little Easton, also tells us much about him: 'My irritability at home is due to the unsettled feeling due to rebuilding. I do not think you understand what a *torment* it is to an impatient man to feel the phantom future home failing to realize itself. I *hate* things unfinished and out of place. I want things *settled*.' This irritable revulsion from disorder is typical of Wells. 'I dismiss the idea that life is chaotic', he says in *First and Last Things*, 'because it leaves my life ineffectual'; 'I like my world as coherent and consistent as possible', he explains in *World Brain*; and when he met Stalin he declared, 'first, I am for order'. This commitment shows itself in many of the novels. *The New Machiavelli*, for instance, contrasts 'a great ideal of order and economy . . . called variously Science and Civilization' with the damage caused

> All along o' dirtiness, all along o' mess,
> All along o' doin' things rather-more-or-less.

And these lines of Kipling, quoted with approval not only here but also in *Mr Britling Sees It Through*, have a very wide range of application in the novel—from chaotic town-development to muddled thinking to the accidental death of the hero's father when he breaks his neck after toppling from a makeshift ladder. But it is in *Tono-Bungay* that the theme of disorder and its damages is most elaborately developed. The book probes what *Anticipations* called 'the great swollen, shapeless, hypertrophied social mass of to-day', and finds symptoms of degeneration everywhere. Decay and disease—especially cancer, which proliferates by decomposing healthy structures—riddle the book. Following the fortunes of a quack medicine enterprise, Wells keeps referring to real ills. There are constant reminders that Tono-Bungay is thriving because conditions are right for it. It is like a fungus sprouting, quite appropriately, in 'this rotten old warren of England'. In the novel, a disordered and corrupt environment is seen disrupting and infecting lives, behaviour, personalities. The book's welter of rottenness and breakdown is designed to illustrate what was claimed in *A Modern Utopia*: 'everywhere societies deliquesce, everywhere men are afloat amidst the wreckage of their flooded conventions'. Mess is *Tono-Bungay*'s structural principle: the book is given shape by a recurrent motif of irregularity.

Lack of order is emphasised from the very beginning. George explains that he is both a 'lax, undisciplined story-teller' who will 'sprawl and flounder' and a socially displaced person, 'jerked out of his stratum'. Life has tossed him from an ordered but dying world to a living but chaotic one. Bladesover, where his mother was housekeeper, constituted 'a complete, authentic microcosm' of rigidly structured, eighteenth-century society. Looking back, George sees it as a world of 'stations' and 'degrees'. Its inhabitants venerate these: Lady Drew is an expert on genealogies, George's mother is strong on precedence. The system of 'vertical predominance' still obtains: the servants downstairs hear the gentry—'living, like God, somewhere through the ceiling'— moving around above them. But Bladesover is ossified, possessing shape but no vitality—rather like the old church at Eastry, another 'example of the eighteenth-century system', which is 'like some empty skull from which the life has fled'. Its main inhabitants are moribund grotesques arthritically manoeuvring through stiff routines of conversation and behaviour. By the time George has grown up, they are all gone and Bladesover has fallen prey to the incongruous social mobilities of the modern world. It is taken over by 'strange tenants', the Lichtensteins. Similarly, Hawksnest, another great house, is occupied by a hustling newspaper proprietor, while 'Redgrave was in the hands of brewers.' (An even more vulgar fate befalls Shonts in *Bealby*: it goes to 'the Peptonized Milk and Baby Soother people'.)

Typically, George is expelled from Bladesover for refusing to conform to the *status quo*. He fights with one of his betters (and breaks the rules of gentlemanly boxing during this rebellious bout). From the country estate, with its 'airy spaciousness' and 'wide dignity', he is sent to the 'squalid compression' of Chatham. Here, everything is repulsively skewed away from order. The sailors are 'gross and slovenly'; the ships, 'clumsy, ugly, old, and dirty'. The Frapps, with whom he stays, live a life of squalor, religious fanaticism, and incompetence in a little baker's shop. The smallest details of their lives are messily revolting, George remarks: Mr Frapp, for instance, has badly-cut hair, 'disagreeable' fingernails, and flour in his hair, eyelashes, facial creases, and coat-seams. When not muddling around amidst the 'litter' of his sordid premises, he frequents a chapel with a 'spavined' harmonium, where a malformed line-up of fellow-spirits congregates: 'a fat woman with asthma, an old Welsh milk-seller with a tumour on his bald head . . . a white-faced, extraordinarily pregnant woman . . . a spectacled rate-collector with a bent back'.

Religious disbelief makes George a misfit in this community just as social unorthodoxy got him expelled from Bladesover, and he is sent to live with Uncle Teddy and Aunt Susan. Here, the domestic habitat is harmonious, but the wider environment is wrong. Wimblehurst is stultifying to Uncle Teddy—'not his *miloo*', Aunt Susan explains. As so often in Wells, too, the strains of small shop-keeping are felt. Uncle Frapp was 'floundering' in debt. Uncle Teddy goes bankrupt. And, soon after this, removed to London, he and Aunt Susan are inhabiting the familiar Wellsian dungeon, a 'makeshift' flat with the usual 'little inconvenient kitchen in the basement'. The environment around them is equally unalluring—a 'witless old giant of a town, too slack and stupid to keep herself clean'. When George too arrives in this 'chaos of streets and people and buildings and reasonless going to and fro', he tries to exorcise his sense of 'purposelessness' by dedicating himself to science. But, as he becomes involved with Marion, his 'behaviour degenerated', his 'punctuality declined', and he has a 'breakdown' of industry. It is in this demoralised state that he picks his way through 'large quantities of cabbage stumps and leaves' to his uncle's quarters in Raggett Street and joins forces with him in selling 'slightly injurious rubbish' to the 'jaded', 'overworked', and 'overstrained'.

With exuberant inventiveness, Wells then retails the fraudulent ploys used to promote Tono-Bungay, but he never lets us forget that, in essence, this absurd product is 'mischievous trash'. And ultimately the idea of deadly rottenness is starkly set before us—when George journeys to Mordet Island to steal quap, heaps of quaggy mineral filth which, put to commercial use, could just save his uncle's failing fortunes. Characteristically, nothing goes according to plan. Gordon-Nasmyth, who was to guide the expedition, is unable to do so, because—as he explains in a telegram that scrambles his name—he has fractured his leg in a motor smash. Chance and mess having sabotaged the original scheme, George takes over, but is 'sick all through the journey out'. The ship, which is 'rotten and obsolescent', is vermin-infested, and some of the crew are virtually deranged. Mordet Island, when finally reached, proves a hideously extreme example of the processes with which the novel deals. Under air fetid with 'a constant warm smell of decay', there is 'a desolation of mud and bleached refuse and dead trees'. Dotted across this are 'dismantled sheds' and 'worm-rotten and oblique piles and planks', remnants of a station which has been abandoned, as anyone who stayed in it was 'eaten up mysteriously like a leper'. There are also 'two little heaps of buff-hued rubbish . . . quap!' And, looking at this 'rotting sand' with its 'little molecular centres of disintegration', George recognises that 'It is in matter exactly what the decay of our old culture is in society, a loss of traditions and distinctions and assured reactions.' The malign decay which permeates the book is here seen at its most elemental. Horribly contagious, its corrupting and disintegrating powers wreak havoc on the journey home: the contaminated crew develop blisters, inflammation, fever; the ship falls soggily apart.

The situation to which George returns is also one of disintegration. The Tono-Bungay enterprise topples into bankruptcy, with the result that Uncle Teddy's energies leave nothing behind except a monumentally unfinished house on a 'despoiled hillside': much of this, too, has been 'so dishonestly built that it collapsed'—like his financial enterprise. Uncle Teddy himself displays a triple breakdown. He has crumbled morally and committed forgery; he is physically ill—as his quack-medicine

empire prospered, he has moved through flabbiness and dyspepsia to more serious disorders; finally his mind becomes deranged,
and he dies in 'the laxity of delirium and dementia', 'repeating
long, inaccurate lists of figures'.

Society and business-life both seem grotesquely out of control.
Sexually, things are chaotic, too. George is attracted to Marion
partly by a mistake; they 'blunder up to sex' and are 'married
with all the customary incongruities'—more, in fact, since the
officiating clergyman has a cold 'and turned all his n's to d's'.
The wedding procession, amidst the 'irrelevant clatter and
tumult' of London, is 'like a lost china image in the coal-chute of
an ironclad'. And the culmination of it all is a fiasco: George holds
'far short of happiness, Marion weeping and reluctant in my
arms'. Increasingly repelled by her unresponsiveness and their
'ungainly' home life, he is unfaithful; and, 'like children who had
hurt each other horribly in sheer stupidity', they become
divorced.

His later affair with Beatrice shows him finding a more com-
patible partner, but, despite this, the key-note is lack of harmony—
as is conveyed by Beatrice trying to pick out a piece of *Tristan
and Isolde* on the piano, after she has refused to marry him, and
missing a note, failing again, and 'making a feeble jar'. It is not
even clear why she rejects George. Her letter is 'enigmatical'; she
insists cryptically that she is 'spoilt and ruined'. George has a
sense of 'hopeless cross purposes'. And, even before we have read
of their twelve-day affair—in a chapter called 'Love among the
Wreckage'—he assures us that it was all quite futile, of a piece
with the other instances of mess the book conveys: 'Love, like
everything else in this immense process of social disintegration in
which we live, is a thing adrift, a fruitless thing broken away from
its connections. I tell of this love affair here because of its
irrelevance, because it is so remarkable that it should mean
nothing.' The ambiguity which has shrouded their relationship
thickens even further as it finishes; George thinks Beatrice may
have said she was addicted to chloral, but 'Perhaps I am the
victim of some perverse imaginative freak of memory.' Nothing is
definite, and nothing has a dignified shape. Two days after their
harrowing parting, George accidentally meets Beatrice with
another man; and even his pain at 'this chance sight' cannot be
expressed straightforwardly: as he starts to weep, a man who
has been trimming a hedge suddenly bobs into view, so—'Abruptly,

ridiculously'—he has to hide his real feelings. Farcical dissonance hallmarks the book. George and Beatrice's love-affair sputters to a stop in a few jerky and jarring happenings. Similarly, Uncle Teddy's death-bed scene is untidily bathetic: when all are poised to watch him pass on, 'my uncle spoiled the climax, and did not die'; later, he slides away unregarded—'I do not know when he died,' George says.

After this death, George wanders round in a literal fog, feeling life is just a 'phantasmagoria'. Like the quap episode, this is an extreme instance of a factor always present in the book. Other kinds of blurring are encountered everywhere, and nowhere more so than in people's speech. In the novel's deranged environment, the lines of communication are down. Language is as malformed as most of those who use it. Verbal garbling abounds: Mrs Mackridge haughtily braying 'Indade!'; Frapp mouthing 'Wuss . . . Blarsphemy'; the cold-clogged clergyman reducing the wedding-formula to gibberish; the disturbed Rumanian captain who 'would still at times pronounce the e's at the end of "there" and "here"'; Uncle Teddy, as one of the 'Poovenoos', going disastrously astray with French when he tries to become 'Oh Fay' and avoid 'Goochery' in the belief that 'Le Steel Say Lum'. Speech gets badly fractured: the talk of Marion's friend, Smithie, is 'broken by little screams'; Uncle Teddy, speaking in public, emits sentences that 'unwound jerkily like a clockwork snake' and he dies muttering 'half-audible fragments of sentences'. Lines can be crazily wrenched out of context, dislocating their sense—as in Lady Osprey's intended put-down to George when he says he is interested in flying: 'I was lying on the turf, and this perhaps caused a slight confusion about the primordial curse in Lady Osprey's mind. "Upon his belly shall he go," she said with quiet distinctiveness, "all the days of his life."' And there is another comic interlude when weird, disconnected bits of talk are picked up by George's attention as he wanders around a tea party:

'So she bit his leg as hard as ever she could and he let go.' . . .
　'Had four of his ribs amputated.' . . .
　'Had to have a large piece of silver tube let into his throat, and if he wants to talk he puts his finger on it. It makes him so interesting, I think. You feel he's sincere, somehow.' . . .
　'Preserved them both in spirits very luckily, and there they

are in his study, though of course he doesn't show them to
everybody.'

These pieces of verbal detritus mainly relate to abnormality. And
this is typical. In *Tono-Bungay*, Wells loses no opportunity of
making reference to disrupted order. Details of mess and degeneration are strewn lavishly throughout the book. The newspapers
at Chatham are 'smudgy' and filled with 'vilely-drawn pictures' of
'squalid crimes'; Mrs Mackridge has hair painted on her bald
brow; Marion's complexion is 'bad' and she 'could slash her
beautiful lines to rags with hat-brims and trimmings'; Effie, the
girl George has an affair with, ends up married to 'a wretched
poet' who has 'limp' legs and is 'given to drugs'; when the
Ramboats try to run a farm, they get 'very muddy', kill a cow 'by
improper feeding', and are in financial difficulties within a year;
at the Vicarage near Lady Grove, 'a confusing family', including
daughters with 'pinched faces', are 'dispersed among a lot of
disintegrating basket chairs' and there is talk of Annie Glass-
bound, who is 'Not quite right'; and there are numerous other
instances of slovenly and unhealthy muddle.

Apart from Aunt Susan, who is hobbled by her loyalty to Uncle
Teddy, George—devoted to science with 'her order . . . her steely
certainties'—is the only character who displays competence and
a concern for precision. Quite early in the book, he devises a way
of crating the bottles of Tono-Bungay which prevents 'many
breakages and much waste and confusion'. But, though there is
efficiency in this, it is directed to a shoddy end, the defter
packaging of rubbish. The Mordet Island fiasco shows his expertise even more hopelessly snarled up with chaos and corruption.
He shoots a native 'neatly' in the back—but this means the man
is 'frightfully smashed out in front'; and, after this 'most
unmeaning and purposeless murder imaginable', George finds it
impossible to keep the body buried. An animal pulls it from the
mud into which he has pushed it: so, once more, his concern for
order gets involved with a messy end—'Methodically I buried his
swollen and mangled carcass again.' After which, the body gets
exhumed by natives. Finally, all George's disciplined scientific
work—which has seemed such a contrast to the sprawling
quackery of Tono-Bungay—is put to injurious use: he builds
destroyers. *'Waste'*, he says at the conclusion of his book, might
have been the best title for it. It offers a panorama of the

squandered. Its main female characters are sterile—'childless Marion . . . my childless aunt . . . Beatrice wasted and wasteful and futile'—and this fruitlessness seems symptomatic of a society burned out by 'a wasting aimless fever of trade and money making and pleasure-seeking'. The capacity to reproduce is hampered, just as the willingness to produce is thwarted—as is demonstrated by a procession of the workless trailing through November fog behind 'wet, dirty banners': 'A shambling, shameful stream . . . oozing along the street, the gutter waste of competitive civilisation'. George himself, committed to vigorous and testing intellectual effort, finally turns out to be the greatest case of waste. A corrupt environment channels even his inventiveness and industry to destructive ends. The main lesson he learns from his experiences is the overwhelming influence of habitat: 'I thought I was destined to do something definite to a world that had a definite purpose. I did not understand then, as I do now, that life was to consist largely in the world's doing things to me.'

As George's fortunes show, it is not only an unpropitious physical environment that can warp and deplete lives. Unhealthy concepts, cumbersome and foolish institutions, a directionless or perverse society can do the same. This is something Wells sometimes depicts symbolically. On Rampole Island, for instance, Mr Blettsworthy is surprised to find 'It was a part of the strangeness of these people that in a land where sunshine was pleasing and grateful they were content to live in a gorge through which the wind blew rarely and in which odours brooded long.' The islanders cower in their natural basement, it transpires, because 'The uplands were supposed to be wastes of incalculable danger.' And there is substance to their fears. Before they can move to the higher ground, they need to clear it of its present occupants, Megatheria or Giant Sloths. Assembled—as if by some didactic Dr Moreau—out of various symbolic bits and pieces, these antediluvian creatures unforgettably embody malign torpor and reactionary staleness. They are encrusted with signs of neglect, 'a slimy growth of greenish algae and lichens', and there are weeds growing from their filthy coats. They give off a heavy odour of decay, 'like rotting seaweed mixed with night-soil'. When they move, they seem 'to cringe along . . . in almost the attitude of an Oriental on a praying carpet' and propel themselves 'in rheumatic jerks, usually with a grunt of self-preoccupation'. They conceive 'only when startled out of their ordinary habits of life and seriously frightened'. Despite their clumsy appearance, these ungainly assemblages of crawling abjection have a fearsome ability to crush and ravage. Blettsworthy is struck by 'how fast a megatherium in a mood of destructiveness could get over the ground', when challenged by the appearance of something new; and he notes, too, that since they 'live entirely upon fresh shoots and budding vegetation', they have reduced the potentially fertile uplands to a barren waste. Maintaining their dominance by creating an environment in which nothing fresh can thrive, the Megatheria obviously represent the hidebound—a point made explicit when Blettsworthy has a dream in which 'Institutions had become entirely confused with Megatheria and Megatheria with Institutions, and I was organising a great hunt to clean the whole world of the lumpish legacies of the past.' Only when they have been cleared away can people climb out of their 'sunless holes' into 'that civilisation . . . those Great Spaces . . . Under the sun'.

The Rampole Islanders are not the only characters in Wells to be found confining themselves to an inferior environment. 'The Country of the Blind' shows this as well. Here, the inhabitants of a 'now isolated and forgotten valley' have become, over a number of inbred generations, totally blind. Tumbling accidentally into their world, a mountaineer called Nunez assumes that, since he can see, he will dominate and lead them. Instead, the independent views he holds because of his vision provoke more and more hostility. The valley-people resent his unorthodox perceptions and propose to rid him of them by putting out the 'greatly distended' eyes they think have made him mad. With fabular starkness, Wells depicts how a man who sees the reality of his surroundings can arouse defensive coercion in those who have settled for blind acceptance of myth. And typically, he presents the most insidious pressure towards obscurantism as coming from a woman. Nunez's fiancée delicately urges him to face the surgeon's knife and be gouged into conformity—until, in panic, he abandons the dark valley and scrambles up onto the sunlit heights.

Blettsworthy and Nunez escape from allegorical examples of restrictive environment. Theodore Bulpington deliberately retreats into an unhealthy mental state. A portrait of Madox Ford—and, Wells said in his autobiography, 'a very direct caricature study of the irresponsible disconnected aesthetic mentality'—he is shown as only in his element when in a fantasy world. The title of the book in which he figures proclaims his ideal. 'The Bulpington' is his imaginary, larger-than-life concept of himself; 'Blup', a distorted version of 'Blayport', the town where he passed his childhood, is the imaginary, romantic realm in which he feels most at home:

> There was something unstable and elusive about Blup. It was never quite Blayport; it was much rockier; and soon it got detached and began wandering about the country. Its scenery acquired a touch of the Highlands even while it was still a haunt of sea-going men; it made itself a tortuous rocky harbour like a Norwegian fiord. . . . there were always very still and watchful sentinels upon its ramparts. And at the sunset gun the great embroidered banner of The Bulpington fell down fold upon fold, fold upon fold, gold thread and shining silk, and gave place to the little storm flag that fluttered through the night.

Theodore's 'reverie took to itself scenery', Wells says. It heaps up the picturesque to shut out reality. Ensconced in sterile glamour, he determinedly narrows his horizons: so his life is played out against a background of distorted 'mental hinterland'.

This last phrase—coined by Remington in *The New Machiavelli*—has a clear relation to Wells's own purposes. Knowledge, he argues, is a crucial part of man's habitat. False ideas can distort as surely as physical constrictions: 'In China', *All Aboard for Ararat* declares, '. . . they used to make dwarfs and human grotesques by putting little children to grow up in jars and cases of porcelain. Dogmatic religious teaching is the mental parallel.' And there is a variant on this—pointing out that social systems can also stunt—in *The First Men in the Moon* when Cavor comes upon 'a number of young Selenites confined in jars from which only the fore limbs protruded, who were being compressed to become machine-minders of a special sort' and compares this with 'our earthly method of leaving children to grow into human beings, and then making machines of them'. Space to develop physically, socially, and intellectually is one of the things Wells keeps campaigning for. Wider vistas are not only prime requirements of his dwellings: they are also considered essential for healthy mental life. It is crucial for the species, Wells increasingly emphasises, that man has a clear picture of his origins and history, and thinks hard about his future. During his own lifetime there had been an almost dizzying enlargement of perspective. Before the end of the eighteenth century, he says in *The Outline of History*, the 'enormous prospect of the past which fills a modern mind with humility and illimitable hope, was hidden from the general consciousness of our race. It was veiled by the curtain of a Sumerian legend.' This has now been rung up. Scientists have pushed the human *mise en scène* further and further back. And the vast panorama brought in view is one that Wells never tires of contemplating. He is as fond of running his mind's eye down man-less corridors of past as he is of sending it probing into the future.

The Time Machine is a work in which he does both. At its conclusion, the narrator is colourfully speculating whether the Traveller has fallen 'into the abysses of the Cretaceous Sea; or among the grotesque Saurians, the huge reptilian brutes of the Jurassic times', whether he 'be wandering on some plesiosaurus-haunted Oolitic coral reef, or beside the lonely saline lakes of the Triassic Age'. Future terrestrial environments, however, are set out in the main body of the book. Like most of Wells's writings about habitat, it shows a blend of the biologist and the basement dweller. This latter element is strongly in evidence in the sections dealing with the Eloi and the Morlocks, where the above and below ground polarity is paramount. As the Traveller explains, the relative situations of these two groups represent the dramatic culmination of a tendency already obvious in his own day for the poor and working to be pushed beneath the ground, and the rich and leisured to spread out across it. *In the Days of the Comet* has a disgruntled proletarian crying to an aristocrat, 'You'll ask us to get off the face of the earth next.' George, in *Tono-Bungay*, glancing out of his window at the unemployed, feels 'It was like looking down a well into some momentarily revealed nether world.' And in some of Wells's future states these hints have been acted on. The regimented proletariat in *The Sleeper Awakes* toil like a slave-army far beneath the city 'in the under-ways'. Further on in time, the Morlocks have been pushed down well-like openings into a nether world, while the Eloi inhabit the tamed earth. Then, what *The Science of Life* calls 'the extraordinary plasticity of each of the main types of life's construction under the influence of different habitats' takes gradual effect. Ease and security relax the Eloi into a degenerate prettiness; darkness and hardship change the Morlocks into something like 'whitened Lemurs'.

The Time Machine partly shows Wells inventively redeveloping environments he has known—the underground room at Bromley, the servant-tunnels at Up Park, and the estate's exclusive parkland. The book dramatises the dangers of oppressive territorial demarcation, and lets subterranean rancour surface in the form of Morlocks. But it does not only look at habitat in order to make social comment. The story is also designed to illustrate how environmental change must ultimately wipe out life on earth. The Traveller stops at three points in the future: what they represent are final stages on the way to terrestrial extinction. The first is bathed in sunset imagery; twilight covers the next; the last is blotted out by a total eclipse. The first episode emphasises the decline of man. The race has split disastrously apart into two degenerate and sub-human species, and neglect is hopelessly eroding the surviving evidence of its former glory. Maimed and decrepit monuments loom everywhere. The first object the Traveller sees is a sphinx-like figure which is 'thick with verdigris' and 'greatly weather-worn' (something which imparts 'an unpleasant suggestion of disease', so that the nearby reference to the 'sightless eyes' of the statue—which later becomes 'leprous'— awakes thoughts of morbid complications rather than the simple insentience of stone). Matching this invalid decor, the Eloi are 'indescribably frail' and look 'consumptive'. The land is like a 'long-neglected garden', and the decorations on the buildings are 'very badly broken and weather-worn'. The dining-hall is 'dilapidated'; its marble table, 'fractured'. The windows are 'broken'; the curtains, 'thick with dust'. Everything is in 'a condition of ruinous splendour'. Everywhere, the Traveller finds crumbling accomplishment. And there is one instance of regression that is weirdly autobiographical: as if reversing his own climb to success, Wells sends the Traveller into 'the ruins of some latter-day South Kensington'; then leads him, via galleries displaying science's achievements, back to the Bromley basement—'As you went down the length', it is explained, 'the ground came up against the windows, until at last there was a pit like the "area" of a London house before each, and only a narrow line of daylight at the top'. At other moments, he is set before gorgeous vistas of degeneration: as when, one 'golden evening', he rests on a 'corroded' seat 'half smothered in soft moss' and surveys 'the broad view of our old world under the sunset of that long day'. Gilded by waning light, this panorama of post-meridian decline opens his eyes to what is happening to his species: 'The ruddy sunset', he says, 'set me thinking of the sunset of mankind.'

Leaving the world's late-afternoon, he then advances to a point where 'steady twilight brooded over the earth'. Under a sky which is 'inky black' and 'deep Indian red', life has shrivelled back to rudimentary forms. The surviving vegetation, it is pointed out, is 'intensely green'—'the same rich green that one sees on forest moss or on the lichen in cases: plants which like these grow in a perpetual twilight'. And it is growing on the south-eastern faces of the rocks. This touch of sharp scientific precision, pinning the fantasy to fact, is typical of Wells. It is a technique also used in his description of plants spectacularly burgeoning in the lunar dawn in *The First Men in the Moon*: 'Compared with such a growth the terrestrial puff-ball, which will sometimes swell a foot in diameter in a single night, would be a hopeless laggard. But then the puff-ball grows against a gravitational pull six times that of the moon.' And it is responsible for a superb moment of vertiginous loneliness in *The Time Machine* when the Traveller, feeling increasingly disoriented in the world of 802,701, looks up to the stars for 'friendly comfort', only to find 'All the old constellations had gone from the sky . . . that slow movement which is imperceptible in a hundred human lifetimes, had long since rearranged them in unfamiliar groupings.' The Traveller's last leap forward in time takes him to a point where life has virtually disappeared from earth: all that remains is the green slime of liverwort and lichen, and something with tentacles flopping around in the blood-red sea. And the idea of obliteration is intensified by a total eclipse, rendering 'absolutely black' this world in which there is no sound of life.

Extinction is a frequent topic in Wells's early writings, and it dominates his final books. There is, however, a considerable shift in his response to it. Looking back at *The Time Machine* and its predictions, he claimed in 1942, in *The Outlook for Homo Sapiens*: 'The possible extinction of humanity appeared to be something so remote that it never gave me a moment's real uneasiness in those days.' Certainly, *The Time Machine* is distinguished not by unease but by imaginative excitement held powerfully under fabular control. And the tone of Wells's early essays on extinction, also, tends to be unperturbed. When he touches on man's vulnerability—as he does in 'The Rate of Change in Species'—his main concern is with the dangers of slow physical adaptation:

> Man . . . is indisputably lord of the world as it is, and especially of the temperate zone; but, face to face with the advance of a fresh glacial epoch, or a sudden accession of terrestrial temperature, or the addition of some new constituent to the atmosphere, or a new and more deadly disease bacillus, he would remain obstinately man, with the instincts, proclivities, weaknesses, and possibilities that he has now. His individual adaptability and the subtlety of his contrivance are no doubt great, but his capacity for change as a species is, compared with that of a harvest mouse or a green-fly, infinitesimal.

Soon, though, the emphasis moves to the need for speeding up man's process of mental evolution. The necessity of achieving, and adapting to, major cultural transformation is what Wells becomes urgently concerned with. 'A complete biological revolution', he says in 1940 in *The Common Sense of War and Peace*, 'has happened to our species. There has, in the past half century, been a complete reversal of the conditions under which human beings have to live.' And in *The New America*, written five years earlier, he warned, 'Man is to-day a challenged animal. He has to respond, he has to respond successfully to the challenge, or he will be overwhelmed like any other insufficiently adaptable animal.' Stumbling into vehement clumsiness, *Science and the World-Mind* puts the matter even more emphatically: 'The question is whether he can adapt himself with sufficient rapidity to become either a progressive super-*Homo*, an ascendant species, or one of a series of degenerating sub-human species, or whether he will fail altogether to adapt himself, and end altogether.' *The Outlook for Homo Sapiens*, published the same year, specifies the solution: 'the wilful and strenuous adaptation by re-education of our species'.

For decades, Wells campaigned for this in various ways. He put together monitory Utopias, model life-support systems for the human species. He depicted in fiction and non-fiction the calamitous results of non-co-operation and outmoded ways of thinking. He produced three massive educational books—*The Outline of History*, *The Science of Life* and *The Work, Wealth and*

Happiness of Mankind—designed to spread accurate knowledge of man's place in the world. And he fired off endless ultimatums, stating, as in the final lines of *'42 to '44*, 'Knowledge or extinction. There is no other choice for man.' Despite all these efforts to create a better climate of opinion, though, conditions deteriorated; and by the end of his life he took bitterly to the idea that circumstances had changed too rapidly for man to be able to adjust to them. 'Without world unification the species would destroy itself by the enlarged powers that had come to it', it is said in *The Holy Terror*.

This was the spectacle Wells felt he was witnessing in his last days. Extinction, so utterly remote in *The Time Machine*, was suddenly close: and, it brought with it odd reminders of that early, distant book. Far in the chilling future, the Traveller found 'The alterations of night and day grew slower and slower, and so did the passage of the sun across the sky.' In his final book, *Mind at the End of Its Tether*, Wells complains of a similar phenomenon, 'the fact of the slowing down of terrestrial vitality. The year, the days, grow longer.' And he adds that 'in this strange new phase of existence into which our universe is passing, it becomes evident that events no longer recur.' This is like a shadowy recall of his tableau of the earth's last stage in *The Time Machine*—the planet 'come to rest with one face to the sun', so that there is no longer seasonal or night-and-day recurrence. Very characteristically, the dying Wells invests the setting of his imminent extinction with the circumstances he had once envisaged for the whole world's *finale*.

4 The Pugnacious Pacifist: Wells and Survival-Mechanisms

A creature has three main ways of self-defence—fighting, escape, and co-operation. Each of these gets copious attention in Wells's books, and was of considerable importance to his life. Fighting, in particular, is something his imagination eagerly throws itself into. Categorising Wells as 'a nineteenth-century liberal whose heart does not leap at the sound of bugles', George Orwell once wrote, 'The thunder of guns, the jingle of spurs, the catch in the throat when the old flag goes by, leave him manifestly cold. He has an invincible hatred of the fighting, hunting, swashbuckling side of life.' Nothing could be further from the truth. Belligerent himself, Wells responded keenly to belligerence in others. 'Man has pranced a soldier in reality and fancy for so many genera-tions', states *What Are We To Do With Our Lives?* 'that few of us can altogether release our imaginations from the brilliant pretensions of flags, empire, patriotism, and aggression.' This last quality completely enthralls Wells, as *The Work, Wealth and Happiness of Mankind* makes clear:

> There is something that stirs our unregenerate natures in the foaming advance of a great battleship and in the emphatic thud of gunfire. . . . Most of us could watch aerial warfare with undiluted pleasure if the promiscuous use of bombs were barred. We should follow with sympathetic delight the nimble dance of the conquering ace flying for position, tapping out the bullets from his exquisite gun with finished skill, sending, amidst our applause, his dead and wounded antagonists spin-ning down, poor rabbits, to their ultimate dramatic smash.

This bellicose gusto may appear somewhat incongruous in one

who spent much of his life proclaiming the need for world peace. But, as Wells explains later in the same book, he thought pacifists insufficiently alert to the glamour of aggression: 'Too much pacifist literature is devoted to the more manifest evils and absurdities of belligerence; too little to the hiatus that would be left in human life if, by a miracle, flags, frontiers, arms and disciplines were suddenly and completely abolished.' A campaign for peace, he argues in *The Anatomy of Frustration*, should array itself in the rousing panoply of war: 'Pacifism will continue to be frustrated until there comes such a dream of peace as will stir men like a trumpet. Peace needs its drum-taps. . . . Peace must provide social orgasms more gratifying than warfare.' This desire to keep a foot in both camps, as it were, can lead to fairly staggering contortions. *The Rights of Man*, for instance, published during the Second World War, vehemently transmits Wells's belief that it was 'a misfortune for all mankind that Berlin was not soundly bombed, as it could have been, in 1918'. Firing off a rhetorical question about the Germans—'Would it not rather conduce to a manly mutual respect if, as people say, we gave it to them hot and good?'—it follows this up with a barrage of rhetorical response: 'vigorous bombing and bombarding, town-wrecking and the like, would be an entirely wholesome chastening experience for the German "soul"'; 'Let them run and cower and like it'; 'Let the Germans have their medicine now.' Then, while these bombinations are still echoing in the reader's ears, Wells placidly explains, 'I make these unusual, these un-Quakerlike, remarks without any feeling of vindictiveness towards Germans. I am a pacifist.'

This switch between hawk and dove keeps occurring in his books. Wells's intellectual commitment to the constructiveness of peace is always liable to be swamped by an upsurge of destructive fervour. From his childhood onwards, as he recounts in his autobiography, he found military fantasies powerfully alluring:

I liked especially to dream that I was a great military dictator. . . . I used to fight battles whenever I went for a walk alone. I used to walk about Bromley, a small rather undernourished boy, meanly clad and whistling detestably between his teeth, and no one suspected that a phantom staff pranced about me and phantom orderlies galloped at my commands, to shift the guns and concentrate fire on those houses below, to launch the final attack upon yonder distant ridge.

Carnage retained its hold on his imagination. 'For many years', he says, his adult life was 'haunted by the fading memories of those early war fantasies'; and in *The Way the World Is Going* he declares, 'If I have never killed and massacred in the waking day, I have known all those bright reliefs and excitements in dreams. And in reveries.' He also gave vent to them in some of his fiction. The bloodthirsty perambulations of his boyhood afforded useful training for the writing of *The War of the Worlds*. When working on this, he recalls in his Atlantic preface, he would cycle round Woking 'of an afternoon and note the houses and cottages and typical inhabitants and passers-by, to be destroyed after tea by Heat-Ray'. Much of the book's shock effect comes from juxtaposing Armageddon and suburbia. As St Loe Strachey pointed out with taking frankness in *The Spectator*, 'He brings the awful creatures of another sphere to Woking Junction, and places them, with all their abhorred dexterity, in the most homely and familiar surroundings. A Martian dropped in the centre of Africa would be comparatively endurable.' To shake complacency by sending tentacles snaking into the pantry while the neighbourhood gets smashed to smithereens was, of course, just what Wells wanted. Cosy names are tossed enthusiastically into lurid contexts: 'fire, earthquake, death! As if it were Sodom and Gomorrah!', shrieks a demented curate, '. . . fire, earthquake, death! . . . what has Weybridge done?' (there is a similar effect of grotesquely charred normality in *The Sleeper Awakes*: 'Streatham is afire and burning wildly, and Roehampton is ours. Ours!'). The book takes the invasion-of-England concept, used in a number of late-nineteenth-century novels, and works striking variations on it. The invaders are not from another country, but another planet: aliens in the extremest sense. Their world is traditionally the planet of war, and technically they turn out to be far in advance of human military equipment (to describe their sophisticated weaponry, the narrator keeps falling back on obsolete-sounding imagery: the death-ray is a 'sword of heat'; the space cylinders stick 'into the skin of our old planet Earth like a poisoned dart'). Indignant objections to the Martians taking unfair advantage are quickly squashed by reminders Wells drops about what humans did to dodos, and Europeans to Tasmanians. And man's *amour propre* takes a further battering in scenes of mass hysteria resulting from the Martian menace:

> people were being trampled and crushed even in Bishopsgate Street; a couple of hundred yards or more from Liverpool Street Station revolvers were fired, people stabbed, and the policemen who had been sent to direct the traffic, exhausted and infuriated, were breaking the heads of the people they were called out to protect. . . the engines of the trains that had loaded in the goods yard . . . *ploughed* through shrieking people.

The standard invasion novel set out to foment national belligerence and pride: Wells's variant on the formula displays the need for international co-operation by subjecting the human species to extra-terrestrial humiliation. Like its models, though, it is designed to drive its readers out of a smug sense of security by bringing danger home to them.

Wells's warlike fancies didn't only find outlet in stories that incinerated the vicinity and pulped the local populace. He also channelled them into elaborate games with toy soldiers. Mathilde Meyer, his sons' governess, describes finding Wells lying on the lino, engrossedly firing at his boys' troops with a miniature cannon. 'Up to 1914', he says in his autobiography, 'I found a lively interest in playing a war game, with toy soldiers and guns'; and in *A Year of Prophesying* he recalls how this enthusiasm spread into 'a great war-game on my barn floor with lead soldiers, realistic scenery and guns that hit'. The pastime became a lengthy and absorbing ritual, and in *Little Wars*, the book which sets out the procedures of this 'game for boys from twelve years of age to one hundred and fifty', Wells recounts the metamorphosis that occurred as he immersed himself in it:

> Suddenly your author changes. He changes into what perhaps he might have been—under different circumstances. His inky fingers become large, manly hands, his drooping scholastic back stiffens, his elbows go out, his etiolated complexion corrugates and darkens, his moustaches increase and grow and spread, and curl up horribly; a large, red scar, a sabre cut, grows lurid over one eye. He expands—all over he expands. . . . Now for a while you listen to General H.G.W. of the Blue Army.

This transformation of penman into bristling militarist is constantly occurring in Wells's books. Besides playing little wars with his sons, he concocts numerous big ones in his novels. As a standard feature in Wells's works, the achieving of Utopia is preceded by global warfare. 'I wish . . . I could smash the world of everyday', he remarks in *A Modern Utopia*; and goes on to do this in book after book. Oddly in one so influenced by evolutionary theory, he does not envisage the move towards the ideal state or World Republic as a gradual process. Breaking, not mutation, is what he foresees. His scenarios of world-wide holocaust followed by paradisal bliss possibly owe something to vestigial religious conditioning. He says in *The Future in America*, 'Like most people of my generation, I was launched into life with millennial assumptions. . . . there would be trumpets and shoutings and celestial phenomena, a battle of Armageddon, and the Judgement.' His writing, with its penchant for the *dies irae*, could be seen as a reflection of this. What is jabbered by a German in *The War in the Air*—'All de vorlt is at war! They haf burn' Berlin; they haf burn' London; they haf burn' Hamburg and Paris. Chapan hass burn' San Francisco', etc.—is a fair enough approximation to what happens in numerous books. War is triggered off by a trivial event (in *The Shape of Things to Come* it is started by a Jew having trouble with his dental plate: the facial contortions caused by his efforts to remove a bit of food from under it are fatally misconstrued as mockery by a young Nazi). Hostilities escalate dramatically; civilisation caves in with alarming speed; and the world reverts to the dark ages. Horrendous diseases often ravage the survivors of the wars: the Purple Death in *The War in the Air*; maculate fever (hitherto restricted to captive baboons) in *The Shape of Things to Come*; the Wandering Sickness ('of which the peculiar horror is that the sufferer, like a sheep stricken with the gid, wanders infectiously until death') in the film-script, *Things to Come*. Pestilence is an optional feature of Wells's disaster scenarios; warfare is compulsory. Global strife precipitates the World State: 'as some super-saturated solution will crystallize out with the mere shaking of its beaker,' he explains in *Anticipations*, 'so must the new order of men come into visibly organized existence through the concussions of war.' *The Common Sense of World Peace* puts the same idea with less science and more trenchancy: 'amidst the thunder of the guns the search for *Pax Mundi* must begin'.

Given this belief, it is not surprising that Wells's initial reaction to the First World War was one of almost proprietary relish. Though he failed to anticipate it—'I will confess I was taken by surprise by the Great War', he says in *The Way the World is Going*, sounding slightly cheated—he made the most of it once it was there. 'I find myself enthusiastic for this war against Prussian militarism', he announced in *The War that Will End War* (a phrase he coined); and the pieces contained in this collection show him entering into the spirit of the thing with considerable zeal. One of them, 'Hands Off the People's Food', modishly describes itself as 'a war-torn article, a convalescent article', and Wells excitably heaps up imagery that transforms his desk into an extension of the Western Front: 'It is characteristic of the cheerful gallantry of the time that after being left for dead on Saturday evening this article should be able, in an only very slightly bandaged condition, to take its place in the firing-line again on Thursday morning.' At other times, his desire to participate in the general mobilisation via his pen gets even more breathless: 'I am just running as hard as I can by the side of the marching facts and pointing to them.' Despite this fervour, though, his war-record was a poor one. He went over the top with chauvinist rhetoric— 'I shouted various newspaper articles of an extremely belligerent type', he admits in his autobiography, as well as confessing, 'some of the things I wrote about conscientious objectors in *War and the Future* were unforgivable' ('belated amends' were offered in *The Bulpington of Blup*). And he surrendered to religious mysticism, becoming a 'theological Quisling', as he puts it in *Exasperations*, a collection he was working on when he died. For a while, Wells avowed a belief in God; and the wartime pressures that had pushed him towards it weirdly shape the kind of God he worships. The deity of his theology, he explains in *God the Invisible King*, is 'as real as a bayonet thrust'. He 'should bear a sword, that clean, discriminating weapon, his eyes should be as bright as swords', and Wells would prefer him to be depicted on crucifixes with one hand wrenched from the cross, ready for action. It is in this martial guise that he appears in *Mr Britling Sees It Through*, where we hear that, through the clashes of the Great War, 'God, the Captain of the World Republic, fought his way to empire'.

This book, recording the reactions and the sacrifices of its little Briton, was part of Wells's contribution to the war-effort: as was

Joan and Peter, in which he 'turned on the pacifists' and 'savaged them to the best of my ability'. The war kept him in a state of constant excitement, talking feverishly of plans for fighting in the hedgerows of England should the enemy invade, or brooding on post-war retributions—such as the exacting of punitive taxes by stamping on German railway tickets messages like 'Extra for Belgian Outrages—Two Marks'. Encountering Wells during this time, Wilfred Owen appropriately saw him as 'a pair of bayonet-coloured eyes, threatening at me from over, as it were, a brown sandbag'. But, though Wells's aggressive stance may have given him the look of objects from the trenches, he would not have fitted in there. 'I hate soldiering', he declares in *War and the Future*; and, while it sounds strange amidst his bellicose shouting, the remark is true. Once he lets his imagination get close enough to see war as something more than a rowdy game, his sympathies go into rapid retreat. In *A Year of Prophesying*, he speaks ruefully of his lingering, boyish eagerness 'to play soldiers with the world'— adding, though, 'large parts of me have gone on growing older. This older section of me can see men as something more than lead soldiers, and realise war in terms of spilled human life and utter waste.' Those who persist, with gleeful immaturity, in seeing war as something not much more than the toppling of toys are indignantly rounded on by Wells. Churchill, for instance, is taken to task in *The Shape of Things to Come* for having 'the insensitiveness of a child of thirteen. His soldiers are toy soldiers and he loves to knock over a whole row of them'; and there is a caricature of him as Catskill, the puerile militarist, in *Men Like Gods*. *Anticipations* comments disapprovingly on 'the gentlemanly old general—the polished drover to the shambles'. Demonstrating this point, the butchery of war is lavishly strewn throughout Wells's books. When Peter incurs war-injuries in *Joan and Peter*, the left upper half of his body is 'changed into a lump of raw and bleeding meat'. Gemini, in *Babes in the Darkling Wood*, sees German atrocities in terms of 'Joints. Choice cuts. . . . Omosternum, exactly like the joint out of a butcher's shop.' The smell of 'burnt meat' wafts sickeningly into *The War of the Worlds* after the Martians have roasted Surrey locals with their heat-rays. Soggy dollops of human decay are slopped into the narratives as nauseous reminders that real war is something very different from the harmless skittling of little metal men: Mr Blettsworthy, on the Western Front, is pushed into an awareness of war's rottenness: 'I fell over a dead body alive with maggots; my knee went into the soft horror.' He also sees 'faces, or rather what had been faces, seething masses of flies'. There is a similar moment in *The Research Magnificent* when Benham, riding through a war-zone, catches sight of a man who 'had no face and the flies had been busy upon him'. This is followed by the discovery of a village whose inhabitants have been slaughtered and badly mutilated; 'fly-blown trophies of devilry' dangle from trees. That night, Benham cries out in his sleep about 'The maggots that eat men's faces'. Injury to the human head is specially recoiled from. Stratton in *The Passionate Friends* has a feverish night like Benham, after he has seen his first dead man in the Boer War: one side of his skull over the ear has 'been knocked away by a nearly spent bullet' and there are 'black flies clustering upon his clotted wound and round his open mouth'. Mr Britling's son, shot through the head in France, shows war's senseless waste of intellectual resource: through a big red hole 'rimmed by blood-stiffened hair', 'the scattered stuff of his exquisite brain' drains into the clay. Aunt Wilshire, 'smashed in some complicated manner' in an air-raid, and Teddy, coming back from the war with only one arm, bear further witness, in this book, to humankind's fatal fragility. Mr Blettsworthy, who loses a leg amidst the horrors of 'Britain's putrefying patriotism', asks himself, 'My God! did these pink-faced, intriguing generals of ours never dream of nights?'

Contempt for the military is often voiced by Wells. *The Desert Daisy*, a story he wrote early in his teens, features a General Edieotte, and his later books show little change in his assessment of chiefs-of-staff. Gerson in *The Autocracy of Mr Parham* is like a throwback to the apes; Ardam in *Mr Blettsworthy on Rampole Island*, a malevolently thuggish savage. *The Outline of History* lingers indignantly over the vicious pugnacity of Cato the Elder, from his days as 'a small but probably very disagreeable child of two' to an acrid old age spent 'croaking out "Delenda est Carthago" ("Carthage must be destroyed")'. But, though Wells's hostility towards the military is often made to sound high-mindedly pacific, much of it derives from his aggressive impulses. The humanitarian, poring sadly over the 'red pulp' of war (as *What Is Coming?* has it), is always liable to be shoved aside by the would-be chief-of-staff. Wells both deplores and imitates those who treat warfare as a game. The voice of the barn-floor strategist clamours for attention: 'I detest and fear these thick, slow, essentially defensive methods, either for land or sea fighting', he declares in *Anticipations*. 'I believe invincibly that the side that can go fastest and hit hardest will always win.' And, when real wars break out, he complains fractiously that the military will not let him play his part. During the First World War, as his autobiography recalls, he felt it 'absurd that my imagination was not mobilized in scheming the structure and the use' of tanks: since he had written of machines like these in 'The Land Ironclads' in 1903, he considered that he had invented them. When the armed forces failed to call on him in the next war, as well, he was even more enraged. *'42 to '44* furiously recounts how, on approaching the authorities with a scheme to put a stop to U-boats by the use of helicopters, he found himself 'being snubbed and insulted by a Mr Birmingham or Bulpington or some such name, a man so far as I can ascertain of no scientific attainments whatever'. An appeal to the First Lord of the Admiralty got little further. In the same book, Wells speaks of 'The inability of the human animal, either to keep out of war or to wage it competently'. Both provoke his irritation, but the second far more fiercely than the first.

Periods of war whipped Wells into especial truculence, but he was belligerent throughout his life. 'Baby so cross and tiresome', 'Baby very cross', Mrs Wells wearily records in her diary, sighing as she contrasts him with her earlier, more placid children. Marks of his growing pugnacity were to be found in 'three little scars' left in his brother's forehead by a fork he threw at him, and a hole in the rear fetlock of a horse in a painting at Up Park he discharged an air-pistol at. His 'childish relations' with his brothers, Wells says in his autobiography, 'varied between vindictive resentment and clamorous aggression'. In *The Holy Terror* he presents a luridly unflattering portrait of such aspects of himself in Rud Whitlow, whose 'imagination was fired particularly by the history of wars' and who develops through a harshly caricatured picture of Wells's early life into a nightmare version of his Utopian commanders. Wells once explained, 'I think it preferable to be as unpleasant as possible at the time and to heal as quickly as possible.' Witness after witness gives testimony to his ability to live up to at least the first part of this credo. Rebecca West spoke of his 'need to feel rage'. Odette Keun referred to his 'sweepingly hasty and violent nature', his 'outbursts of passionate hostility'. Julian Huxley, chosen to collaborate with him on *The Science of Life* partly because of Wells's veneration for his grandfather, Thomas Huxley, describes the strains of working with him and the tetchy rupture that eventually ensued. There is an early essay by Wells on 'The Pleasure of Quarrelling'— 'the vinegar and pepper of existence', he calls it—which waggishly expounds his belief that 'it is hygienic to quarrel, it disengages floods of nervous energy, the pulse quickens, the breathing is accelerated, the digestion is improved . . . it sets one's stagnant brains astir and quickens the imagination'. The 'present lamentable increase of gentleness', Wells maintains, has led to a *'fin de siècle* unwholesomeness'. The tone here is jocose, but the idea is one which had already been used seriously in *The Time Machine*, where the suicidally unaggressive Eloi were seen as a symptom of mankind's decline. 'In his natural state', Wells says, 'man is always quarrelling—by instinct.' Wells certainly was. Squabbles with his mistresses, a furore with the Fabians, rumpuses with publishers, a cruel clash with Henry James, numerous exasperated feuds all punctuated his career. Missives conveying his disapproval rained down on those who crossed him—Kingsley Martin ('Dear Judas'), George Orwell ('Read my early works, you shit'), David Low ('Who has got *hold* of you? . . . Who is pumping stuff into your brain arteries?'). Easily provoked to fury, he retained his irascibility to the very end. Among the last things he wrote was 'A Hymn of Hate against Sycamores'. One of these 'Bloody' trees next door to his house in Hanover Terrace was sapping the vitality from his garden, he believed; and in a long retaliatory diatribe he turned 'this dirty, ugly, witless, self-protecting tree' into a symbol of the things he loathed in life.

Antipathy to sycamores sprouted late amidst Wells's resentments. Bishops were a perennial thorn in the flesh. Cheerily admitting this in *Kipps*, he speaks of 'bishops, towards whom I bear an atavistic Viking grudge, dreaming not infrequently and with invariable zest of galleys and landings, and well-known living ornaments of the episcopal bench sprinting inland on twinkling gaiters before my thirsty blade'. For most of his writing life, he chases them with dripping nibs. Hostilities open in *The Desert Daisy*. The villain of this is a blackguard bishop whose numerous misdemeanours are gleefully recorded: from pilfering the Crown Jewels to setting up in business as a fake hermit—'Be Confessed & Have Your Photo taken for 1d'. At the end of the book, he is cut in two (a comparatively mild fate, given what happens to other participants in this energetic tale: a king's son-in-law is 'chopped into inconceivably small bits', and a cook 'banged as flat as a pancake in three seconds'). Later books confine themselves to dishing out verbal damage. Mr Lewisham murmurs, 'I was thinking just then that I would like to boil a bishop or so in oil', but nothing comes of it. *Anticipations* grumbles about 'unimaginative bishops, who have never missed a meal in their lives'. *Star Begotten* sneers at 'a leash of babbling bishops'. *The Food of the Gods* includes 'the old Bishop of Frumps' amidst a line-up of whispering Court gossips like Sir Arthur Poodle Bootlick. *The Sleeper Awakes* derisively points to the Anglican Bishop of London in the twenty-second century, enjoying 'subsidiary wives'. *The Soul of a Bishop*, Wells baitingly declares in his Atlantic preface, depicts the rare phenomenon of 'an Anglican bishop . . . stricken suddenly by a living belief in God'; and Bishop Wampack in *Boon* is outraged by a visit from a clergyman showing signs of real religious faith. Bishops are singled out for particular abuse, but the clergy as a whole get rough treatment in Wells's books. A curate is felled with a meat-chopper in *The War of the Worlds*. Satirical blows descend heavily on hapless vicars. They are stuck into sarcastically named parishes—Cross in Slackness, Marsh Havering, Saint Simon Unawares—and their celibate lives are the subject of much disapproving commentary. Mr Polly's error in thinking the phrase 'Portly capon' refers to 'a dignitary in gaiters' is one Wells obviously feels very understandable. *The Outlook for Homo Sapiens* draws back in disgust from the 'epicene garments' of Catholic prelates. *Crux Ansata* states that 'in the priestly mind we deal with something frustrated and secretly resentful, something sexually as well as intellectually malignant'. And there is a full-scale onslaught on clerical dirty-mindedness in Father Amerton in *Men Like Gods*. Though he occasionally professes sympathetic interest in religious matters, Wells is rarely able to sustain a tolerant tone for long. *The Work, Wealth and Happiness of Mankind*, for instance, remarks that 'it is possible to imagine a Museum of Comparative Religion void of all polemical suggestion'—then goes on to envisage one that is packed with this: 'There could be gramophone records of music, of revivalist preaching and chants, working models of genuflexions and prostrations, and all the instruments and methods of purification, mortification and penance.' *The Outline of History* sounds less than neutrally expository as it recounts how at the end of the twelfth century 'Five Popes tottered to the Lateran to die within the space of ten years.'

Wells's most venomous anti-ecclesiastical writing is, in fact, directed against the Roman Catholic Church. In *Mr Belloc Objects*, presenting himself none-too-convincingly as 'the least controversial of men', he declares he is 'conscious of no animus against Catholicism'; and goes on to back this up by the statement, 'I am as little disposed to take sides between a Roman Catholic and a Protestant . . . as I am to define the difference between a pterodactyl and a bird.' Compared with the anti-Catholic onslaughts of his final years, this slily bruising metaphor is quite benign. By the time he wrote *Guide to the New World*, Wells had taken to inveighing stridently against 'the systematic aggression of the Vatican'. Pius XII, he believed, and proclaimed with some invective vigour in *Crux Ansata*, was 'an open ally of the Nazi–Fascist–Shinto axis'. 'It is necessary to insist upon his profound ignorance and mental inferiority'; he is 'a being at once puerile, perverted and malignant . . . as unreal and ignorant as Hitler. Possibly more so.' As a result of the machinations of this 'Berlin–Rome–Tokyo Pontiff', Wells considered, 'There has been a Catholic Blitzkrieg upon Britain during the immense stress of the war'. The faithful represent a fifth column, *Guide to the New World* violently points out: 'You can no more trust a devout Catholic in your household and in your confidence than you can risk frankness or association with a Nazi spy.' *You Can't Be Too Careful* reaches the conclusion, 'To-day the most evil thing in the whole world is the Roman Catholic Church.' Considering the militarised environment in which he came to think this, it's not surprising that the notion of pounding the Vatican with hardware rose to the forefront of Wells's anti-Papal broodings. 'Why Do We Not Bomb Rome?' is the title of the first chapter of *Crux Ansata*. And in fact the idea of bombing the Pope had earlier been conceived and perpetrated in *The Shape of Things to Come*. Here, Wells's peace-enforcing aviators drop cannisters of knock-out gas on to His Holiness Alban III as he blesses aeroplanes at Ostia: 'it seemed incredible that any human being would dare to gas the Pope', Wells chuckles, revelling in his own audacity. The Pontiff is only temporarily immobilised by the gas tipped out upon him. But one of the cannisters hits a young priest on the head, making him the last martyr in the Latin hagiography, as not long afterwards all religions are wound up.

Besides waging a war against religion, Wells recurrently takes on other foes in his fiction. Prominent amongst them are aesthetes and classicists. In his novels these are often doused with heavy bucketfuls of scorn—as when we are told in *Men Like Gods* that 'The Princess de Modena-Frascati (née Higgisbottom) Prize for English Literature had been given away to nobody in particular by Mr Graceful Gloss owing to "the unavoidable absence of Mr Freddy Mush"' (Eddie Marsh made soppier). Wet literary charlatans keep making fatuous appearances. *The Wheels of Chance* guffaws over 'Thomas Plantagenet', sturdily outspoken author of *A Soul Untrammelled*: in reality, a conservative widow from Surbiton with a limply bookish hanger-on called Mr Dangle. *The Wife of Sir Isaac Harman* shows another inanely literary lady, Susan Sharsper, who preeningly pouts, 'I didn't notice. . . . I was busy observing things'. In *Joan and Peter*, there is Phoebe Stubland, straying affectedly around her home, The Ingle Nook, in a long djibbah-like garment, clutching a gold-mounted fountain pen. *Brynhild* has a novelist called Rowland Palace as one of its main characters. The book has hardly started before he is scornfully pushed into view at a May Day festival, decked in a scarlet robe that's too big for him, a fillet of gold-braid, a bay wreath and a daisy-chain, and carrying a symbolic lyre made of wood and cardboard glued together. Just in case the point has not been taken, we are informed that a picture of this tawdry spectacle appears in a newspaper along with the caption, 'Modern Classicist dresses the Part'.

Classicists, for Wells, are dangerous as well as derisory. Enamoured of the past, they must, he thinks, be inimical to progress. In his books, they side deplorably with the forces of reaction. In *The Camford Visitation*, the mentally mouldering denizens of Holy Innocents College, querulously opposed to the teaching of science and snobbishly sneering at education 'for shop-boys', are reprovingly harangued by a 'steely' voice from out of space. Unable to parry its verbal thrusts, they still cling to their outmoded ways; and are shown fawning to Establishment dodos like Dr Dedlock, Lord Fauntleroy, and Princess Susan Magenta (who, 'smirking like anything', is given an honorary degree). The road to war, some of the books suggest, is paved by a classical education. *In the Days of the Comet* depicts war being declared by 'an undersized Oxford prig with a tenoring voice and a garbage of Greek'. In *The Autocracy of Mr Parham*, a don translates Mussolini's rhetoric into Latin—'it was even more splendid'—and then, in a state of megalomaniac delusion, plunges the world into carnage. He is staunchly opposed in this by Camelford, an industrial chemist, who works on the manufacture of peace gas. This last device is one that Wells has resort to on several occasions. In *The Shape of Things to Come*, the Pope is put to sleep by a dose of 'Pacificin' administered by a man who found 'the sight of the cassocks, the birettas, the canopies and ornaments and robes, the sound of chanting and the general ecclesiastical atmosphere' too much for his prejudices. The film-script *Things to Come* affords Wells further opportunity of being a belligerent pacifist. After a great catastrophe, much of the world falls under the control of thuggish local chieftains. The film shows them being reduced to submission by heavy bombardment with 'the Gas of Peace'. Since this brings about world-wide harmony, the strategy satisfies both Wells's intellectual commitment to pacifism and his emotional propensity towards aggression. Near the end of this scenario, world peace is put in jeopardy again by a revolt instigated by an artist, Theotocopulos, who whips people up into a frenzy with his anti-scientific rantings. Clashes of this kind, between backward-looking exemplars of the humanities and forward-looking scientists, are not infrequent in Wells. *Men Like Gods*, for instance, presents a bunch of reactionaries pitifully arrayed against the near-omnipotent scientific citizenry of Utopia. 'They may trifle with our ductless glands', rants Catskill, the bellicosely speechifying nationalist; and with a motley assemblage of other anti-progressives—they include an unhinged priest, a Tory MP, a food-profiteer, and 'an unintelligent beauty-cow' from the music-hall—goes into paltry action. Disdainfully, the Utopians pitch them all out of their world—'Like a cageful of mice thrown over the side of a ship', the book remarks with a satisfied wiping of its hands.

Ford Madox Ford, caricatured as the Bulpington of Blup and very much aware that he faced Wells from the other side of the lines—'in the kingdom of letters Mr Wells and I have been leaders of opposing forces for nearly the whole of this century', he said—felt Wells resembled 'one of those rather small British generals who were unlimitedly loved by their men', and re-marked, 'what struck one most was his tough, as it were Cockney, gallantry of attack—upon anything'. Certainly, verbal shrapnel whizzes through the books in all directions, picking off targets from Gladstone ('that resonant torrent of pompous emptiness', in *Travels of a Republican Radical*) to Karl Marx ('the maggot, so to speak, at the core of my decayed Socialism', says William Clissold), and winging lesser causes of offence such as 'the gallant and pious but seriously ossified Lord Gort' in *Guide to the New World*. 'A man who is not a fighting man', Wells wrote in *The Anatomy of Frustration*, 'is not much good to world civilization at the present time. The tolerant man, the gentle man, is as bad as a policeman who walks away.'

Wells likes to compare his writings to acts of aggression. *Anticipations* is 'my first line of battleships'; *The Outline of History*, 'a Hussar-ride round the unprotected rear of the academic world'. In *The Outlook for Homo Sapiens*, he claims, like some intellectual Guy Fawkes, to be bringing together facts that 'might form an explosive mixture'. A campaign to publicise a book could also be viewed in terms of military manoeuvres: Macmillan were told it was 'time to push the attack' with *Kipps* by sending out 'a volley of short quotes' about it. Wells often conveys approval through combative imagery. 'Aggressive' was a favourite word. His son Gip and Julian Huxley were, he said, 'very sound and aggressive teachers of biology'; in *The Passionate Friends*, admiring attention is drawn to Lady Mary's 'aggressive lean legs'; Kentlake in *Babes in the Darkling Wood* is praised because 'He writes, he talks, he lectures, aggressively and destructively.' Steele in *The Anatomy of Frustration* likewise wins encomiums because he 'never ceases to be combative'. Wells directs our notice to 'the clear, sharp slash of his mind', and says that, where other polemicists hacked, 'He slashed anatomically.' What this also alerts us to, of course, is the symbolic nature of Steele's name. Blades keenly attract Wells. They often flash into view in his books at moments of particular enthusiasm. After Trafford has proposed to Marjorie, for instance, he rapturously informs his mother that he has plighted his troth to a piece of cutlery: 'She's such a beautiful thing—with something about her—You know those steel blades you can bend back to the hilt—and they're steel!' Cecily in *Mr Britling Sees It Through* is another girl of fine mettle—she stands up 'straight as a spear' (the spirit of youth, in the same book, is 'like a bright new spear . . . like a finely tempered sword' that can, regrettably, 'get dented and wrinkled and tarnished'). Amanda in *The Research Magnificent* doesn't actually resemble such glittering blades, but strongly admires them: after she has read Plato's *Republic*, she says the Guardians 'had a spirit—like sharp knives cutting through life'. This, we hear, 'was her best bit of phrasing and it pleased Benham very much'. Sustaining the aggressive note, he himself has contemplated 'Bushido' as an appropriate title for his elite group. Wells's own crack corps of citizenry in *A Modern Utopia* are called the Samurai: bearing 'a name that recalls the swordsmen of Japan', they 'look like Knights Templars'. Benham is devoted to the concept of a 'new aristocracy'. The Samurai represent a 'voluntary nobility'. Upper-class *sang-froid* is an essential component in the armoury of Wells's warriors for peace. John Cabal in *Things to Come*, for instance, keeps provoking gasps of frightened admiration as he masterfully snubs the thuggish ruffians who try to thwart his world-unifying purposes. 'The rabble is astonished', we are told, 'at Cabal's cavalier treatment of the guard.' Hot-faced lower-class pugnacity is amply on display as well. Mr Waddy, sent into empurpled frenzy by his breakfast, is one instance of this: 'Bacon! Bacon! Bacon! Bacon! Bacon on the brain!' Wells's fiction keeps disconcertingly unleashing near-murderously choleric characters. There are clenched growlers such as Sir Isaac Harman or the rabidly belligerent sea-dogs that Prendick and Mr Blettsworthy are harried by. Some of *Bealby*'s liveliest moments come from the convulsive lashings-out of maddened Moggeridge, about whom a savaged butler complains, ''e sprang on me like a leppard. . . . 'Ere's where 'e bit my 'and.' The Invisible Man actually becomes homicidal with rage: when frustrated, he progresses through the punching of noses and breaking of teeth to smashing a man's head to jelly. Before this, even his mannerisms have implied a murderous malevolence: he has 'a bark of a laugh that he seemed to bite and kill in his mouth'. Uncle Jim in *Mr Polly* is another uncontrollable bruiser: '"I'll make a mess of you," he said, in hoarse whisper. "I'll do you—injuries. I'll 'urt you. I'll kick you ugly, see? I'll 'urt you in 'orrible ways—'orrible ugly ways."' His snarling onslaughts make the Potwell Inn a 'threat-marred Paradise', so that Mr Polly 'knew he had to fight or perish'.

Described by Wells in the Atlantic preface as his 'happiest book', *Mr Polly* is, in fact, bursting with bellicosity. So, indeed, is its hero. Indigestion has turned his inside into 'a battle-ground of fermenting foods and warring juices'. He is 'not so much a human being as a civil war'. His post-prandial turbulences call to mind 'agitators, acts of violence, strikes, the forces of law and order doing their best, rushings to and fro, upheavals, the *Marseillaise*, tumbrils, the rumble and thunder of the tumbrils'. And this imagery is appropriate, since his internal turmoil tends to be given vent in external aggression. Miriam's cooking leads to bilious overflowings of Mr Polly's spleen. But he is far from alone in his resentful squarings-up to life. The book is packed with fighters and unusual fights. Early on, battle is waged in the window of a drapery with a roll of huckaback, a blanket, and an armful of silesia. Later, ironware comes into play after Mr Polly has crashed into a sanitary dustbin and wrestles with his neighbour amongst a pile of pails. The Potwell Inn sees a variety of resounding encounters and eccentric weaponry. At one point, Mr Polly is shown 'considering the militant possibilities of pacific things—pokers, copper-sticks, garden implements, kitchen knives, garden nets, barbed wire, oars, clothes-lines, blankets, pewter pots, stockings, and broken bottles'. And, when it comes to the crucial clash with Uncle Jim, anything gets thrown into the fray, from steak to parasols. Wells is obviously entranced by unusual modes of administering assault and battery. His books are not only constantly awakening what 'A Story of the Days to Come' calls 'that strange delight of combat that slumbers still in the blood of even the most civilised man' and absorbedly pushing even the most pacific of creatures, like Hoopdriver, into bouts of fisticuffs; they also pounce delightedly on peculiar weapons. *The Food of the Gods* depicts threatened humans lining up against enormous predators, with 'a remarkable assortment of flappish and whangable articles in hand'. Implements used to ward off the massive monsters include a croquet mallet, a watering-can, shears, billhooks, and big-game guns. The most inventive improvisation in the weaponry line, however, is found in *The Desert Daisy*: there, a beleaguered king snatches up 'two of the chubbiest infants' he can lay his hands on and 'Using the little innocents like snowballs . . . dashed at his foes.'

Novel methods of attack always interest Wells. They satisfy his taste for speculation as well as his propensity towards aggression. As we have seen, he felt he had given the military imagination a lead by dreaming up the tank as far back as 1903: he complains in a preface that the concept only 'fought its way at last into the British military mind in 1916'. 'The Land Ironclads' also

wheeled forward another bright idea—that of bicycling soldiers—
which Wells had earlier unveiled in *Anticipations*. 'Small bodies
of cyclist riflemen' are excitedly visualised in this book as they
pedal forth on their deadly sorties: 'Under the moonlight and
the watching balloons there will be swift noiseless rushes of
cycles, precipitate dismounts, and the never-to-be-quite-
abandoned bayonet will play its part.'

Using the bicycle for fighting is unusual in Wells, though.
Generally, he associated it with what he calls in his essay on
'Zoological Retrogression' 'the second great road of preserva-
tion—flight'. Getting away from danger is something Wells's
characters often have to do; and, regularly, bicycles sweep them
out to freedom from restrictions that are damaging and stultifying. Wells was himself an eager and proselytising cyclist (he
introduced Gissing to the activity). In his autobiography, he
recalls the days when 'the bicycle was the swiftest thing upon
the roads' and 'the cyclist had a lordliness, a sense of masterful
adventure, that has gone from him altogether now'. *The Wheels
of Chance* takingly reconstructs those times. Documenting a
drapery assistant's cycling tour of the southern counties, it is full
of the bicycle expertise Wells had recently and painfully acquired
(the account of Hoopdriver's contusions, at the opening, is the
transcript of a record he made of his own mishaps as a cycling
novice). Euphoric at having been 'let out for a ten-days' holiday',
Hoopdriver bowls happily along the open road until he bumps up
against grating reminders of his lack of freedom. Lower-class
speech and mannerisms bar his attempts to pass as a gentleman.
His subservient shop-assistant habits, as he is uneasily aware,
contrast with the peremptory and assured behaviour of Jessica
Milton, the girl he meets. There is another contrast, too, which
he does not comment on. Jessica, playing truant from an irritating home-life, talks self-consciously about making a bid for
freedom. 'I wanted to come out into the world, to be a human
being—not a thing in a hutch', she says, bemoaning 'how custom
hung on people like chains'. Both the imprisonment she claims
to be fleeing and the emancipation she prides herself on displaying turn out to be fanciful affectations. At the novel's end, she
returns, amidst a posse of outraged, theoretical progressives, to
an affluent and leisured existence. Hoopdriver, on the other
hand, is going back to real drudgery, a life like that of 'slaves' or
'convicts'. Images of imprisonment are present near the opening

and closing of the book. In between, Wells beautifully conveys the sense of release Hoopdriver feels as he enjoys fresh air, variety of scene, and even some respect.

Wells's most exotic cyclist is Bert Smallways in *The War in the Air*—'almost a trick rider—he could ride bicycles for miles that would have come to pieces instantly under you or me'. Thoroughly exploiting the machine's nomadic possibilities, he makes up with his friend, Grubb, a duo called The Desert Dervishes who ride around beaches on bicycles with crimson wheels, wearing sheets and singing numbers like 'What Price Hairpins Now?' Mr Polly uses a bike for less gaudy but still intensely satisfying excursions. After a legacy gets him out of the drapery, he takes a cycling holiday, 'with a dazzling sense of limitless freedom upon him', we are told. Even during this period of liberty, however, he is struck by the ominous fact that the roads are 'bordered by inflexible palings or iron fences or severely disciplined hedges'. And, soon enough, other restrictions pen him in, so that he becomes one of the most trapped of Wells's characters. 'Hole' is the book's first word, followed by Mr Polly's bitter lament that this is what he is in. After years of servitude in draperies with their 'endless days of interminable hours', he blunders into that Wellsian jail, the little shop, and is trapped as well into a cramping marriage. Images of confinement wrap themselves round him. He is 'netted in greyness and discomfort'; 'It was as if his soul had been cramped and his eyes bandaged from the hour of his birth.' His bicycle enables him to escape into a brief, idyllic holiday—and later gets him out of a tight spot in another way: when Minnie is trying to manoeuvre him into a proposal, he dodges by claiming that a dog is eating his bicycle tyre and he needs to chase it away. For the most part, though, he is kept in a state of physical stagnancy. Only his imagination manages to roam. Travel books transport his mind far away from Fishbourne. Sharing a taste for these with Wells—whose autobiography records his delighted response to a work that 'took me to Tibet, China, the Rocky Mountains, the forests of Brazil, Siam and a score of other lands'—he enthusiastically embarks on readings such as 'the voyages of La Perouse', 'a piece of a book about the lost palaces of Yucatan', *The Island Nights' Entertainments*, 'the second volume of the travels of the Abbés Huc and Gabet', Fenimore Cooper, Conrad, *Tom Cringle's Log*, *A Sailor Tramp*, and *Wanderings in South America*. These mental peregrinations ventilate his cooped-up life (the young George Ponderevo finds similar relief in poring over 'a broad eighteenth-century atlas with huge wandering maps' and tracing voyages on it 'with a blunted pin': young Remington plays the same game in *The New Machiavelli* with a map of the Crimea). But they don't constitute a real escape route and, eventually, cramped beyond endurance, Mr Polly has to take more decisive steps. Breaking through 'the paper walls of everyday circumstance, those insubstantial walls that hold so many of us securely prisoned from the cradle to the grave', he first sets fire to the hated shop, then walks away from Fishbourne and slips out of wedlock. Flight is the survival-mechanism that transports him to his ideal home in the Potwell Inn; fighting is the means by which he asserts his territorial rights to it.

Kipps is another erstwhile drapery-slave set free by a legacy— a far bigger one than Mr Polly's. Disgorged from the drapery, however, he blunders into another trap, his engagement to Helen Walshingham—from which he runs away twice: once temporarily and alone, then permanently with Ann. The book was originally intended to have a long final section too, Wells reveals in the Atlantic preface, dealing with the adventures of young Mr Walshingham, the loser of Kipps's money, 'as a fugitive in France'. It's surprising he didn't get round to writing this, as the concept of the fugitive regularly fascinates him. Again and again, his books show characters trapped and needing to break out. And his autobiography abundantly displays how much this was a personal preoccupation. 'I need freedom of mind' is the opening statement of the book, followed by a plethora of words such as 'encumbered', 'release' and 'Entanglement'. In this prefatory section, Wells speaks of his 'craving for flight', 'This feeling of being intolerably hampered by irrelevant necessities, this powerful desire for disentanglement'; and declares, 'All my life I have been pushing aside intrusive tendrils, shirking discursive consequences, bilking unhelpful obligations.' The ensuing pages amply support this, as well as suggesting that it was a family trait. His father—who had once been on the point of emigrating: he still possessed the oak-chests he had bought in readiness—'lived from the shop outward'. 'No one to help. Joe out', Mrs Wells despondently confides to her diary. He and Mrs Wells 'both knew they were caught by Atlas House'; but, whereas she could only let her thoughts stray away to brighter prospects in escapist reverie, he physically absented himself as much as possible. Engagements as a cricket coach and player often took him away from home. And, left to his own devices when Atlas House disbanded and Mrs Wells returned as housekeeper to Up Park, he subsided happily into a much laxer existence: 'that hoary Pagan, old Silenus', Wells calls him in a letter, speaking of his 'brigand-like establishment'. Wells's brother Frank, who shared this for a while, also had a nomad streak. Like Wells, he found drapery life intolerable, and walked out of it. 'There is a touch of my brother about Mr Polly', Wells says in his auto-biography, explaining that he 'wandered about the country repairing clocks, peddling watches, appreciating character and talking nonsense. . . . it was amusing—and free'.

Wells himself was always wriggling out of circumstances that he found restricting. Determinedly tugging at his mother's sympathies and clutching at flimsy chances, he pulled himself from the 'dismal trap' of the drapery, and worked his way to a science grant and London. His autobiography records his 'vivid' memory of the song and dance of triumph that he gleefully gave vent to when alone in the railway carriage that was taking him away from the hated Emporium:

> Damn-the-boy has got away, *got* away, *got* away
> Damn-the-boy has got away, got away for ever.

Other threats soon loomed around him: the 'immense luminous coop' of religion; limitations imposed by conventional morality— 'the nets of restraint about me that threatened that I should die a virgin'; the 'entangling preoccupations' of sex (that 'man-trap amongst the flowers', as it's called in *Love and Mr Lewisham*); 'the fear of being caught in a household'. Inexorably, some of these started to wall him in. And, as a result, the 'desperate get-away' from the drapery turned out to be only the first of numerous escape bids. He writes,

> I realise the importance of fugitive impulses throughout my own story. At phase after phase I find myself saying in effect: 'I must get out of this. I must get clear. I must get away from all this and think and then begin again. These daily routines are wrapping about me, embedding me in a mass of trite and habitual responses. I must have the refreshment of new sights, sounds, colours or I shall die away.'

My revolt against the draper's shop was the first appearance
of this mood. It was a flight.

A Houdini impulse to get out of things pervades Wells's life, and
especially his sexual relationships. 'I was trying to undo the knot
I had tied and release myself from the strong, unsatisfying bond
of habit and affection between us', he declares of his first wife. 'Is
there a strain of evasion in my composition?' he wonders. 'Does
the thought of being bound and settling down, in itself, so soon
as it is definitely presented, arouse a recalcitrant stress in me?'
The events of his life suggest it did. He had scarcely married
before he found himself backsliding into infidelity. He eloped
from Isabel with Jane, and later briefly from Jane with
Amber Reeves. For a while, he lived a triangular existence
between Jane in Essex, Rebecca West in various obscure dwellings, and his own flat in London: 'he went to Essex on Saturday,
reappeared on Monday, left for the flat on Tuesday, and came
back to me on Thursday', Rebecca West said, recalling his
prowling restlessness. 'I have shifted from town to country and
from country to town, from England to abroad and from friend to
friend', Wells writes in his autobiography. Remaining married
to Jane, he set up for some years 'a life in duplicate' with Odette
Keun in the South of France. After Jane's death, he multiplied
his dwellings even more, writing to Shaw from St Ermin's that
he intended 'to lead a quadrilateral life—here, Paris, Grasse, &
Easton'. Avidity for experience kept him on the move: so did
dissatisfaction—pushing him away from home after Gip was
born, provoking him to move from house to house and irritably
switch from publisher to publisher.

His writings chart similar patterns of restlessness. 'Is there
potential flight as well as attraction in every love affair?' he asks in
his autobiography. His writings about sex with their heavy stress
on jealousy and possessiveness (even to the point of physical
imprisonment—Lady Harman, Lady Mary) show that there is,
and with good reason. Prospects of polygamous latitude are
wistfully contemplated in some books. Others push against the
straitlaced nature of the *status quo*. Mr Polly penned into the
marriage bed by Miriam's bony back is only one of the casualties
of monogamy Wells shakes his head over. 'Domestic claustrophobia', the autobiography reveals, was an influential factor in
the genesis of *Love and Mr Lewisham*. *Travels of a Republican Radical*

makes the claim that all Wells's novels are 'studies in frustration'. Certainly, very many of them are studies in escape, either from immediate danger or from the more insidious menace of stultifying circumstances. *The Time Machine*, with its hero constantly on the move from physical attack, is a good example of the first. It is followed by numerous books in which Wells makes his main characters run for their lives. Prendick has to do this; so does the narrator of *The War of the Worlds*; Nunez scrambles away in flight from the Country of the Blind. Haring away from danger figures prominently in *The First Men in the Moon* as well. All Bedford does on the moon, in fact, is eat, fight, and run away— first from the Selenites; and then from the deadly shadow of the lunar night, which spills horrifically towards him as he races for the safety of the space-ship, in one of the most exciting passages Wells ever wrote. Graham in *The Sleeper Awakes* is also subjected to a scary escape. Fleeing the Trustees' murderous designs, he has to clamber high up the outside of a dome that covers London until 'he gave way to vertigo and lay spread-eagled on the glass, sick and paralysed. . . . It was like peering into a gigantic glass hive, and it lay vertically below him with only a tough glass of unknown thickness to save him from a fall.'

The other type of escape is introduced in *The Wonderful Visit*: after being brought down to earth by a shot from a vicar, an angel finds his wings start to shrivel as 'The prison walls of this narrow passionate life seemed creeping in upon him.' An unwillingness to have their wings clipped distinguishes quite a few of Wells's characters. In 'The Door in the Wall', Wallace makes frequent escapes from tarnished reality into a glittering paradise that he enters through a mysterious green door—until, one night, he topples out of life altogether by walking through the doorway in a hoarding over railway excavations. 'By our daylight standard he walked out of security into darkness, danger, and death', Wells ends the story. 'But did he see like that?' If he did, he would be unusual amongst Wells's fugitives, most of whom don't count the cost when it comes to the need to break away. The Invisible Man, a 'hemmed in demonstrator' of 'cramped means', is the most alarming instance of this. Theft, assault, murder, and arson result from his flailing efforts to give elbow-room to his swollen egotism. And, for all this, he is still thwarted—unable to disappear totally from view: half-digested meals and flecks of dirt keep him hazily in sight. In *The New Machiavelli*—'essentially a dramatized wish', Wells said in his autobiography, about 'the idea of going off somewhere'—Remington smashes his political career by eloping with Isabel (her taste for reckless mobility has earlier been emphasised by the fact that she is first seen perched on a bicycle with her feet on the fork of the frame). Trafford and Marjorie elope as well; so do Ann Veronica and Capes. Various kinds of flight and imprisonment in fact dominate the book in which the last two appear. The early part demonstrates Ann Veronica's 'desire for free initiative, for a life unhampered by others'. She first frets verbally against the hobbled nature of a young unmarried woman's life in Morningside Park: 'we've long strings to tether us, but we are bound all the same'. Then, making overt the fact that she is a virtual prisoner, there is a scene where her father forcibly bars her way when she tries to go to a fancy-dress ball: 'Ann Veronica and her father began an absurdly desperate struggle, the one to open the door, the other to keep it fastened. She seized the key, and he grasped her hand and squeezed it roughly and painfully between the handle and the ward as she tried to turn it.' Her first escape bid fails when, having climbed out on to the bathroom roof in her outfit as a corsair's bride, she is caught in the fascinated stare of a neighbour working up an appetite by mowing his lawn before dinner. Eventually, though, she gets away to London—only to discover that flight brings menace as well as opportunity: abandoning restriction, she sacrifices security. The next section shows her blundering into various pitfalls, even though she has escaped her father's stuffy repressiveness. Manning's 'inaggressive persistence' and Ramage's *chambre privée* are two traps that lie in wait. But the worst threat is that of the suffragettes. 'The Women's Bond of Freedom', Wells scathingly points out, limits her freedom more drastically than anyone by dispatching her to jail. His irate belief that their activities amount to not much more than perverse antics is exasperatedly epitomised in the line he thrusts upon Miss Klegg, another student: 'I mean to go to prison directly the session is over.' Once Ann Veronica has sloughed off her suffragette entanglements, she is able to move towards a kindred spirit. 'I want to get away. I feel at moments as though I could bolt for it', Capes says to this seasoned fugitive; and, minutes later, she snaps the dainty bonds of etiquette to tell him that she loves him. As a biologist, it turns out, he has been quick to note the meaning of Ann Veronica's behaviour. 'You came out

like an ant for your nuptial flight', he explains, quashing her belief
that she was really pursuing her education. Seeing herself in
slightly more glamorous entomological terms, she cries, 'Never
a new-born dragon-fly that spread its wings in the morning has
felt as glad as I!' and suggests that her past was a kind of cocoon:
'I felt—wrapped in thick cobwebs. They blinded me. They got
in my mouth.' Now, Capes exults, they have both escaped from
'That wrappered life . . . we've burnt the confounded rags!
Danced out of it! We're stark!' 'Stark!' echoes Ann Veronica,
lining them up with the naked libertarians who will later populate
Wells's Utopias.

   Unhampered enjoyment is also on view in *Tono-Bungay*. George,
the son of a runaway—his father 'fled my mother's virtues'—recalls with delight the 'free, wild life' of childhood holiday after-
noons: bathing naked, trespassing in woods, cheeking people,
wandering the countryside, and letting the mind roam agreeably
beyond the bounds of possibility so that local streams seem to come
from the sources of the Nile. Sent off for a bout of penal servitude
with the Frapps—after he has gone beyond the limit by brawling
with his betters—he is inspired to make a break for it by the
sight of a map of Kent 'that set me thinking of one form of
release'. Another is brought to mind by the spectacle of the ships
bobbing around at Chatham. George decides not to run away
to sea, however—fortunately in view of the appalling results of
most sea voyages in Wells: Prendick's marooning, Blettsworthy's
humiliation and near-murder, George's own later nightmarish
experiences on the Mordet Island trip. Instead, he opts to tramp
back to Bladesover House, whose distance from Chatham, he
reckons, is 'almost exactly seventeen miles'. This makes his exodus
a calculated re-enactment of Wells's own departure from the
drapery at Southsea, when, as he recounts in his autobiography,
he 'started off without breakfast to walk the seventeen miles to
Up Park and proclaim to my mother that things had become
intolerable'. As with Wells's walk-out, George's mutinous march
improves his life. He is transferred to the liberating atmosphere
of Uncle Teddy's house. Buoyantly uncompressed by convention
or religious fanaticism, he feels exhilarated there. But Uncle
Teddy does not share the feeling. Wanting to 'escape from the
slumber of Wimblehurst', he sees life there as congealed rather
than congenial: it is like 'Cold Mutton Fat!—dead and stiff! And
I'm buried in it up to the arm-pits.' Moreover, his eagerness to

shrug off mundane responsibilities paradoxically restricts the scope of others. His easy way with money, we are told, has 'clipped' George's chance of getting an education and 'imprisoned' Aunt Susan in a dingy apartment. Sex, described by Ewart as 'a net', is another tangling lure in this book. George is frustratingly impeded by his relationship with Marion until his affections 'wandered'. Then, waiting in his office for the response of a girl he has made overtures to, he 'fretted about that dingy little den like a beast in a cage' before she agrees to go off with him. Infidelity, it transpires, offers no permanent escape from the irksomeness of life. Flying does, however. An absorption in the manufacture and control of aircraft, George discovers, lifts his mind above his troubles. And it also has a practical use. When the crash comes and Uncle Teddy is in danger of arrest, George is able to air-lift him out of the 'sort of hole' he's in. Speaking of their 'flight' from the law, George draws attention to the dual meaning of the word.

It is also used in this double sense in *The Sleeper Awakes*, at the end of which there is a reference to 'Ostrog in flight': he is both in an aircraft and escaping. This novel features, too, an aviation *aficionado* every bit as keen as George. Graham's greatest pleasure in the twenty-second century has been to encounter 'the glorious entertainment of flying':

> His exhilaration increased rapidly, became a sort of intoxication. He found himself drawing deep breaths of air, laughing aloud, desiring to shout. . . . These ascents gave Graham a glorious sense of successful effort; the descents through the rarefied air were beyond all experience. He wanted never to leave the upper air again.

He revels in joy-rides over the Alps, and circles over London, crowing 'Here—or a hundred feet below here . . . I used to eat my midday cutlets during my London University days.' The later sections of the book are suffused by the thrill of flying, and it ends with an aerial battle of a kind to become common in Wells.

The enthusiasm shown by George and Graham is very much Wells's own. He had an insatiable appetite for flying, and increasingly lets his taste for the experience flood into his books. Initially, in fact, he had been sceptical about the possibility of flight. Though flying-machines are glimpsed in an episode, later cut, from *The Time Machine*, *Anticipations* makes it clear that he doesn't think it 'at all probable' that flying will ever be of any importance as regards transport and communications. When news came through that a plane had crossed the Channel, Wells confessed in 'The Coming of Blériot', 'It . . . means that I have under-estimated the possible stability of aeroplanes. I did not expect anything of the sort so soon.' Nor was he only dubious about the likelihood of planes before they arrived. Once they had done so, he was chary of venturing into them. This was because of his vertigo—a disability he shared with Graham and Benham (who forced himself, in *The Research Magnificent*, to walk the vertiginous path around the Bisse of Leysin to establish that he was free from 'Fear, the First Limitation': the crumbling track and giddy drop are reproduced as frontispiece to the Atlantic edition). By the time he wrote *The Research Magnificent*, however, Wells had already flown, so he could state with confidence in that novel that, though there may be 'fear about aeroplanes', there is 'little or no fear in an aeroplane'. He flew over Eastbourne in a seaplane with the aviator Grahame-White in August 1912. The episode is described in 'My First Flight' (collected, along with the Blériot piece, in *An Englishman Looks at the World*) and it shows Wells happily declaring that—unlike the queasy tremors he had felt when going up a skyscraper in Rotterdam—'as for the giddiness of looking down, one does not feel it at all'. 'Hitherto', he announces euphorically, 'my only flights have been flights of imagination, but this morning I flew.' From this point onward, he got in all the real and imaginary flights he could. In an essay on 'The Beauty of Flying' in *A Year of Prophesying*, he writes ecstatically of hanging 'in the crystalline air above the mountains of Slovakia', commenting, 'I was as near the summit of felicity as I have been in all my very pleasant life.' *The Way the World Is Going* refers to 'the happiness and wonder of flying'. It is something that satisfies various aspects of Wells's personality: his liking for being in transit, his fondness for taking panoramic views, his excitement about man's technical achievements. Aviators are heroes to him, and frequently appear so in his books. In addition to George and Graham, there is Leadford, who eagerly joins experimental fliers in the second part of *In the Days of the Comet*. Peter, in *Joan and Peter*, enlists in the Royal Flying Corps, with great authorial approval (Job Huss's son in *The Undying Fire* also belongs to it). For a culminating moment in his scenario, *The King*

Who Was a King, Wells envisages a plane filmed flying towards the audience: it is to be piloted by Paul Zelinka, 'Man the Maker', with Princess Helen, 'Woman the Protector and Sustainer', standing nobly behind him as 'The music throbs up to a climax.'

Aviation, Wells believes, is of particular importance in that it can contribute to world unity in two ways. First, it facilitates geographical links—'Aviation tightens the fabric daily', he says in *A Short History of the World*. Secondly, accessibility by air reduces national autonomy—'The Air Terror', he writes during the Second World War in *Guide to the New World*, 'has taught all reasonable men the urgent need of World Federation.' As a result, aviators are frequently the harbingers and preservers of world peace in Wells's books. 'I have remarked', he says in *The Outlook for Homo Sapiens*, 'in the course of such air travel as I have done, that the airmen of all nations have a common resemblance to each other and that the patriotic virus in their blood is largely corrected by a wider professionalism.' Quite a number of his books are designed to confirm this diagnosis. *The Shape of Things to Come* declares, 'it was in the air at last and along the air routes that the sword of a new order reappeared', and goes on to depict 'world order based on air power'. In *The Holy Terror*, Bellacourt, 'a good airman', wants International Air Control. He is thwarted for a while by vicious Reedly, who detests the *'prig-ridden* air'; but, eventually, his bombers strafe all opposition and, under his aegis as Air Master, world unification is assured.

Wells's most extravagant paean to flying, though, is his film-script *Things to Come*. In this, John Cabal, a pioneer aviator, 'passes unscathed through both war and epidemic and becomes the stalwart grey-haired leader and inspiration of the airmen'. He is first encountered, like so many of Wells's decent researchers, surrounded by the insignia of his calling. There is a model plane on his mantelpiece, a propeller hanging over it, and engineering drawings are strewn around the table. Not long after this, war breaks out and Cabal is seen in an elevating tableau with an enemy airman who has crashed after dropping poison gas. The pluck and *esprit de corps* that Wells expects of his fliers draw the men together across national boundaries. Humanely, Cabal offers help; and gallantly, the alien ace brushes it aside, believing he must expiate his crime against humanity: 'Good fellow—but I'll take my dose.' The Dark Ages then descend and the world reverts to semi-feudal barbarism, with local robber-chiefs gaining control by their malevolence and muscle. All seems grim, until an unusual noise is heard, heralding the arrival of 'the first *novel* aeroplane seen in the film'. This dramatically disgorges John Cabal, wearing a mask 'that makes him over seven feet high', so that 'He stands out against the sky, a tall portent.' 'You have the manner of one who commands', gasps the Boss, thuggish despot of the district, as Cabal loftily explains that airmen 'are the natural trustees of civilisation when everything else has failed' and are, at that very moment, restoring law and order to the Mediterranean basin from their headquarters in Basra. 'The new world of the united airmen will *get* you', he warns the Boss, who none the less claps him into prison. Here, he is approached by the Boss's moll, who fawns invitingly upon him, 'I'm yours. You big strong thing, all steel and dignity.' Cabal steels himself against her, though, and prepares to meet his fate. Luckily, however, the neighbourhood contains another aviator, a local who has been tinkering with planes for years and finally gets one off the ground. Terrifying his guard into acquiescence by looping the loop and doing the falling-leaf trick, he flies out with the news of Cabal's capture to Basra, where planes buzz about like hornets. Soon, 'flying with a sort of remorselessness', the airmen of peace are zooming purposefully towards the Boss. The sky is 'dotted with the new aeroplanes. Hundreds of men drop from the sky with parachutes.' The message 'SURRENDER' is threateningly blazoned in sky-writing, until the Boss and his brigands do so, and the world is safely unified under the hovering canopy of pacifying planes. Aviation and its spin-off, space travel, dominate the film's final moments. An artist eager to restore the past incites a mob of latter-day Luddites to march against technology. But the symbolic couple they are trying to detain first escape by plane, then get away on board a rocket that shoots them out on a voyage round the moon.

Wells's fliers enforce what he regards as the most crucial of survival-strategies—co-operation. That human beings should rise above the barriers of self, religion, race and nation and, through dedicated team-work, rapidly establish a World State was the doctrine that he spent most of his writing-life transmitting. Ultimately, his incessant clamour about peaceful co-operation came to seem a personal foible. 'The usual rigmarole about a World State', sighed George Orwell, examining Wells's proposals on how to deal with Hitler, '. . . the same gospel as he has been preaching almost without interruption for the past forty years, always with an air of angry surprise at the human beings who can fail to grasp anything so obvious'. He wrote this in 1941, and was, in fact, underestimating the amount of time Wells had been nurturing the concept. As far back as 1892, it had taken strong root in his mind, as an essay on 'Ancient Experiments in Co-operation' makes clear. It is 'altogether false', 'a horrible conception, as false as it is evil', he states here, 'to find the nexus of life, and its changes, in competition alone': in actuality, 'a thing essentially different from competition, the co-operative union of individuals to form higher unities, underlies the whole living creation as it appears to our unaided eyes'. As evidence for this, he adduces the lichens, which 'are not simple vegetables at all, but co-operative unions of various fungi with green algae; the fungus doing much the same work as the root of a higher plant, and the algae discharging the duty of a leaf'. These lowly instances of vegetable mutual aid are, moreover, not so far removed from man as he may like to think. Nowadays, Wells declares, 'no zoologist or botanist of repute appears to have any doubt that the higher animals and the higher plants are alike descended from such forms, and are, in fact, *colonies* of imper-fectly-separated amoeboid cells'. The essay then goes on to suggest that nature has even more in store for us in the merger line: 'The village commune of the future will be an organism; it will rejoice and sorrow like a man. Men will be limbs—even nowadays in our public organisations men are but members.' Nor is this to be seen in a merely metaphorical way. It is not just a question of being one in spirit. What Wells has in mind are biological alloys of a more striking kind. 'There can be no doubt', he believes, 'that such phenomena as the now almost forgotten Siamese twins and double-headed monstrosities are tentative experiments on the part of Nature towards a "colonial" group-ing.' Such lumpings-together may be taken even further in the future: mankind must realise that 'its extensive modification into even such strange forms as we have hinted at, human trees with individuals as their branches and so forth, is as imperatively admissible in science as it is repugnant to the imagination'. Not that it seems all that repugnant to Wells's imagination. Even after he has abandoned (as he soon does), his theory that the human race may literally coalesce, his imagery wistfully returns to linger round the discarded concept. We hear at the end of *The War of the*

Worlds of 'the innumerable hosts of lives that had gone to build this human reef'; we are told in *The Shape of Things to Come* that 'the whole race is now confluent; it is becoming as much a colonial organism as any branching coral or polyp'. 'The body of mankind', Wells says here, 'is now one single organism of nearly two thousand five hundred million persons'. This super-amalgamation is what he continually campaigns for. And he feels he has a valuable ally—writing in *The Work, Wealth and Happiness of Mankind* that 'Nature is a great friend of co-operation. . . . she has something like a passion for making living things interdependent.'

Wells shares this passion. 'I shall make the World State my mistress and love that', he once wrote to Rebecca West. With insatiable excitement, his writings explore 'the possibilities of co-operation leading to scarce dreamt-of collective powers', as *First and Last Things* has it. This book, Wells's 'Confession Of Faith And Rule Of Life', sees combination everywhere. 'Synthesis' and 'synthetic'—always favourite words of his—shuttle hectically across his prose, weaving everything together: life is a 'great synthesis'; history, 'the slow unfolding . . . of a synthesis of the species'; religion comes from the need for 'some synthetic idea and belief'; Christ is 'a synthesis of emotions, experiences and inspirations'; concepts such as Good and Beauty 'are in their nature synthetic things'; Socialism 'is one of those . . . synthetic ideas'; love, 'a synthetic force in human affairs'; and so on. From such synthetic fibres, the artificial fabric of the World State is manufactured in Wells's theories and novels. Accordingly, he likes to see his own works as synthesising ventures. *The Anatomy of Frustration* is 'an attempt to . . . make a synthesis of life to-day'. *The Outline of History* is described in his autobiography as a 'broad but compact historical synthesis'; *The Work, Wealth and Happiness of Mankind*, as 'an experiment in synthetic, descriptive economics and politics'. *The Science of Life*, the other book in Wells's educational trilogy, also constitutes a 'synthesis', he makes clear in his introduction to *The Work, Wealth and Happiness of Mankind*, expatiating here, too, on the problems and the triumphs of collaboration the three works gave rise to. Those called upon to co-operate with him in these undertakings soon found where the emphasis had to fall. Julian Huxley, for instance, writes in his *Memories* that Wells demanded he use 'a gift I had never fully exerted before—that of synthesising a multitude of facts into a manageable whole, aware of the trees yet seeing the pattern of the forest'. Arthur Bliss, writing the music for *Things to Come*, was instructed by Wells, 'I want the audience at the end not to sever what it sees from what it hears. I want to end on a complete sensuous and emotional synthesis.'

'My particular line of country', Wells states in *World Brain*, 'has always been generalization and synthesis.' The thought of men banding together in this area delights him. Intellectual endeavour of a collaborative kind is continually being smiled upon, especially in the later books. *Men Like Gods* records approvingly that 'a hundred million good brains have been put like grapes into the wine-press of science', while, in *The Outlook for Homo Sapiens*, Wells declares, 'The achievement of the French Encyclopaedists has always appealed very strongly to my imagination.' He wanted, in fact, to emulate their work and extend it even further. In the same book, he explains that he would like the establishment of a 'permanent World Encyclopaedia . . . a permanent institution, a mighty super-university'. 'There exist already scattered about the world', he says, 'all the knowledge and imaginative material required to turn the whole world into one incessantly progressive and happily interested world community. All that is needed is to assemble that scattered knowledge and these constructive ideas in an effective form.' This form is outlined in *World Brain*, a book whose ideas stem from Wells's eagerness to see not merely human beings but also human institutions in biological terms. What we need, it is insisted here, is 'a World Brain which will replace our multitude of unco-ordinated ganglia, our powerless miscellany of universities, research institutions, literatures with a purpose, national educational systems and the like'. Giving a new twist to the concept of the head of state, Wells sees this as the governing force of his Utopias.

Many of his books are designed to channel influential data into such a think-tank. *The Outline of History*, for instance, was conceived as propaganda—as his autobiography makes clear: 'I proposed . . . the writing and publication of a history of mankind which should show plainly to the general intelligence, how inevitable, if civilization was to continue, was the growth of political, social and economic organizations into a world federation.' As 'an essay on the growth of association since the dawn of animal communities', it seizes hopefully on any embryonic instance of human co-operation. The Crusades are used to illustrate not the divisive warrings of religion but the unifying powers of belief in a cause: 'Never before in the whole history of the world had there been such a spectacle as these masses of practically leaderless people moved by an idea.' The convulsions of the French Revolution are 'but the opening outbreak of a great cycle of political and social storms that still continue, that will perhaps continue until every vestige of nationalist monarchy has been swept out of the world and the skies clear again for the great peace of the federation of mankind'. And, as a sort of whistling in the dark ages, Wells sporadically emits cheery bursts of reassurance: 'The idea of the world state, the universal kingdom of righteousness of which every living soul shall be a citizen, was already in the world two thousand years ago never to leave it.'

His fiction, too, often sets out to show the inevitable advent of world unity. The scenario outlined for *Things to Come*—'The film moves swiftly through opening scenes of warfare, destruction and deepening misery, and broadens out to display the grandiose spectacle of a reconstructed world'—summarises the pattern of book after book. As pressures mount in a hopelessly fragmented world, civilisation bursts apart; plunged into didactic chaos, human beings learn to think in global terms. This demonstration-lesson is invariably accompanied by a vigorous, board-rapping commentary. And, just in case the point is still being missed, Wells fills his books with monitory figures reciting his doctrines. Stratton and Gidding in *The Passionate Friends*—'secessionists from all contemporary nationalities and loyalties'—are typical examples of these model mouthpieces. As one of them pon-derously enunciates,

We found ourselves rather than arrived at the conception of ourselves as the citizens neither of the United States nor of England, but of a state that had still to come into being, a World State, a great unity behind and embracing the ostensible political fabrics of to-day—a unity to be reached by weakening antagonisms, by developing understandings and toleration, by fostering the sense of brotherhood across the ancient bounds.

In pursuance of this ideal, they become publishers, with branches from China to Peru; disseminate classics of world literature; and plan a World Encyclopaedia. Similar propagandists, in Wells, are legion. Together, they constitute what he calls in *What Are We To Do With Our Lives?* 'The Open Conspiracy, the world movement for the supersession or enlargement or fusion of existing political, economic, and social institutions'. Honorary group-membership of this is bestowed, from time to time, on whole categories of people Wells considers promising material, from imperialists to multi-national industrialists. But, when their potential for co-operation turns out to have been overestimated, the affiliation is rapidly cancelled.

Co-operation fascinated and eluded Wells. His film scenario *The King Who Was a King* brings this out clearly. Near the opening, we are told, 'The hero, Paul Zelinka, is discovered in workman's overalls at work. . . . He is gravely intent upon his work. It is team work. He has to take a part from a fellow worker, manipulate it and hand it on. He is obviously chief of the group and is directing the group task.' This last sentence points to an important fact. Despite the heavy stress on team work, and Wells's claim that Paul 'is really a concentration of hundreds of committees, thousands of leaders and millions of mute followers', it is the man's individual pre-eminence that keeps being spot-lit. Wells finds the thought of personal celebrity irresistible. His script preaches sober co-operation, but keeps singling out charismatic figures and throwing them into romantic relief. Paul's lonely, nobly brooding presence dominates the opening and the close of scenes. Likewise, Harting, the film's theorist for the World State, is to be 'photographed with the camera turned somewhat upward in such a way as to make Dr Harting slenderly dominant, like the prow of a ship'. The film's story-line, too, makes it a star-vehicle rather than a panoramic study of a cast of thousands labouring self-effacingly for international peace. The climax occurs at the crest of a pass when Paul first freezes the enemy into submission by his statuesque confidence, and then shoots down his personal rival, Prince Michael. This odd way of demonstrating the necessity for joint endeavour is of a piece with the use of a matinée idol to represent collectivism. The same kind of thing is seen in *Things to Come*, where, although the aviators as a body receive fulsome praise and there is verbal patting on the back for 'workers doing responsible co-operative team-work', Cabal hogs the limelight as a very individual hero.

There was a split in Wells between a theoretical commitment

to co-operation and a real ambition for pre-eminence. This caused problems in his life as surely as it gave rise to inconsistencies in his fiction. Man, he writes in 'The Past and the Great State', 'has attained nothing of that frictionless fitting to the needs of association one finds in the bee or the ant'; and, declaring a more personal interest in 'The Problem of the Troublesome Collaborator', he says, 'Collaboration is not a very easy business.' He found it particularly difficult since his considerable self-esteem not only generated a belief that his fellow-workers should be of exceptionally high calibre—'Berlioz is badly needed to co-operate in the development of this Music-Spectacle Film,' he grumbles in *The King Who Was a King*, 'and it is a great pity we cannot recall him from the silences'—but also convinced him that he must take the leading role. In 'The Problem of the Troublesome Collaborator', after complaining bitterly that a Mr Vowles, engaged to help him on *The Work, Wealth and Happiness of Mankind*, turned out to be hopelessly unsatisfactory—'My rash confidence in him may have distended his estimate of himself'— he goes on to say that *The Science of Life* progressed far more smoothly because his son Gip and Julian Huxley, the collaborators there, 'treated me as the captain of the adventure, and the result has fully justified their confidence in my leadership'. Despite Wells's claims about the easier running of that enterprise, however, Julian Huxley—recalling being bombarded with such missives as '*This job is an important job*; your own researches and your professional career are *less important*'—records in his *Memories* that 'Since H. G. demanded an impossible rate of progress, the atmosphere was apt to become stormy.' Later, too, there was permanent estrangement, accompanied with pettily vengeful behaviour on Wells's part after Huxley, chairing a British Association meeting and instructed to limit all speeches to twenty minutes, refused to allow him to speak for forty.

Huxley's experiences would not have surprised Beatrice Webb. Attempting to work with Wells in the Fabian Society, she noted 'this is absolutely the first time he has tried to co-operate with his fellow-men—and he has neither tradition nor training to fit him to do it'. Further experience of his intractability led her to shift her emphasis to his temperamental awkwardness: 'He has neither the patience nor the good manners needed for co-operative effort.' Constantly urging that personal bias be surrendered in favour of group endeavour, Wells was himself strikingly incapable of doing this. With truculent assertion, he continually broke ranks. Consensus is elbowed aside when it gets in the way of his own convictions. Human rights take second place to a waspish touchiness about personal wrongs. As if in some sardonically anti-Utopian parable, even such a high-minded exercise as the drafting of the Sankey Declaration of the Rights of Man was disrupted by his furious rows and vehement persistences. Speaking of this exercise—an attempt to draw up a charter of basic human rights, a section of which was to be published each day in the *Daily Herald* and debated by the public—Wells bitterly remarked in *'42 to '44*,

> It is an interesting sidelight on human behaviour, that the utmost difficulty was experienced in collecting the assent of the drafting committee in order to agree upon the revisions we were finding necessary. . . . These ten people had embarked upon the most important job human beings had ever attempted. . . . Yet, even at our meetings, after an hour or so of discussion, only a novelist could describe how eagerly they adjourned.

What he does not make clear here is how much his own behaviour contributed to that eagerness. The project got off to a disastrous start, with Wells using his opening article for a savage attack on Chamberlain and Lord Halifax and thus causing two members of the Drafting Committee, Lord Sankey and Lord Lytton, to resign. Sankey was eventually persuaded to return, replacing Wells as chairman of the committee, by Ritchie Calder—who later wrote to Vincent Brome that 'Even after this, behind closed doors, H. G. continually tried to force his point of view and on one occasion "stalled" the Drafting Committee which was meeting at his house by refusing to give them lunch' until 3 p.m. Sir Richard Gregory's biographer, W. H. G. Armytage, explains that the cause of the deferred dining was 'a fantastic interlude on the "Right of Work" with a fierce argument between Wells and Margaret Bondfield, as to who had the better right to speak for the shopkeepers—a fully-paid-up member (Margaret Bondfield) or an honorary member of the Shop-Assistants Union (Wells)'. Wells's career as campaigner for human solidarity is full of moments such as these, with the old Adam stubbornly barring the way to the New Jerusalem. Often, he seems the most entrenched embodiment of a way of thinking and responding that his theories castigate.

Pugnacious assertion also sends disruptive tremors through his writing. Prejudice, especially of a racial kind, undercuts his rhetoric about world unity. Jews, for instance, constantly provoke hostile commentary in his books. There is a strange section in *Anticipations*—where, as so often when professing tolerance, Wells oozes dislike—in which he says,

> I really do not understand the exceptional attitude people take up against the Jews. There is something very ugly about many Jewish faces, but there are Gentile faces just as coarse and gross. The Jew asserts himself in relation to his nationality with a singular tactlessness, but it is hardly for the English to blame that. Many Jews are intensely vulgar in dress and bearing, materialistic in thought, and cunning and base in method, but no more so than many Gentiles. The Jew is mentally and physically precocious, and he ages and dies sooner than the average European, but in that and in a certain disingenuousness he is simply on all fours with the short, dark Welsh.

Making Jews a grotesque amalgam of disfigurements individually scattered throughout a few other groups, this piece of wounding advocacy is hardly calculated to dispel anyone's 'exceptional attitude' towards them. Nor are Wells's other writings. Brumley feels 'a peculiar—a eugenic qualm' on catching sight of the noses of Sir Isaac Harman's children, and Harman himself is presented as a nutcracker-faced embodiment of ghetto avidity. *In the Days of the Comet* singles out a Jew called Gurker, with 'a big nose, a coarse mouth with a drooping everted lower lip, eyes peering amidst folds and wrinkles', who, in the new climate of the post-cometary world, makes 'his confession for his race':

> We Jews . . . have gone through the system of this world, creating nothing, consolidating many things, destroying much. Our racial self-conceit has been monstrous. We seem to have used our ample coarse intellectuality for no other purpose than to develop and master and maintain the convention of property, to turn life into a sort of mercantile chess and spend

our winnings grossly. . . . We have had no sense of service to mankind.

Benham in *The Research Magnificent* loftily denounces 'these confounded differences of colour, of eye and brow, of nose or hair' that 'give a foothold and foundation for tremendous fortifications of prejudice and tradition, in which hostilities and hatreds may gather'. 'When I think of a Jew's nose, a Chinaman's eyes, or a negro's colour,' he writes, 'I am reminded of that fatal little pit which nature has left in the vermiform appendix, a thing of no use in itself and of no significance, but a gathering-place for mischief.' This is followed by a scene illustrating the virulence that can result from such vestigial festerings. Coming upon some Jews putting up 'rather a poor and hopeless fight' during a pogrom, Benham goes to their assistance and soon 'found himself the leading figure'. Routed by his presence—'Benham's tallness, his very Gentile face, his good clothes, and an air of tense authority about him had its effect'—the would-be persecutors slink away. Whereupon, the author suddenly succumbs to twinges of prejudice. As the Jews grovel gratefully, Benham lectures them on that notorious cupidity which has made them universally detested, and, by way of an object lesson, throws a handful of their 'beastly mortgages' on to the fire. Gratitude is instantly replaced by near-homicidal outrage; and in the ensuing fracas Benham is badly battered and scratched. *The Shape of Things to Come* comments sharply on the Jews' 'traditional wilful separation from the main body of mankind', their 'racial egotism'. And this is something Wells—who declined to join a committee against anti-semitism on the grounds that it was 'a natural reaction to the intense nationalism of the Jews'—keeps returning to. *The Outlook for Homo Sapiens* speaks of 'these inassimilable aliens' who 'dun Jehovah still, at the Wailing Wall and elsewhere, for a Promise he perpetually evades'. *The Anatomy of Frustration*, referring to 'the essential parasitism of the Jewish mycelium upon the social and cultural organisms in which it lives', declares, 'we are dealing here with *a distinctive tradition of behaviour* that taints, hampers and frustrates much human effort'. *Travels of a Republican Radical*, published in 1939, shows Wells adamantly keeping up his disapproval despite what is happening in Europe:

I met a Jewish friend of mine the other day and he asked me, 'What is going to happen to the Jews?' I told him I had rather he had asked me a different question, 'What is going to happen to mankind?'

'But *my* people—' he began.

'That,' said I, 'is exactly what is the matter with them.'

There is an almost gloating suggestion that the Jews are now receiving a well-earned come-uppance. 'The Zionist movement was a resounding advertisement to all the world of the inassimilable spirit of the more audible Jews'; the Jews, who 'are going to be hit much harder than they have ever been hit before', are paying 'the penalties of a cultivated racial egotism'.

Not, of course, that Wells held any brief for those who were exacting these penalties. His propensity for generalising about races and nations also keeps the Germans at arm's length, as the same book reveals: 'The German people are an orderly, vain, deeply sentimental and rather insensitive people. They seem to feel at their best when they are singing in chorus, saluting or obeying orders. Obeying orders is their ruling passion. The more raucous the voice and the harsher and more irrational the order, the stiffer their salutes and the grimmer their gusto.' *En masse* dismissal of the Teutons was a long-established habit of Wells's. In *War and the Future*, written during the First World War, he triumphantly claimed that 'The ordinary German has neither the flexible quality of body, the quickness of nerve, the temperament, nor the mental habits that make a successful aviator', explaining, 'This idea was first put into my head by considering the way in which Germans walk and carry themselves, and by noting the differences in nimbleness between the cyclists in the streets of German and French towns.' Heinrich in *Mr Britling Sees It Through*—though presented with some sympathy: he has internationalist ideals, as is shown in his enthusiasm for Esperanto and Ido—demonstrates the basically pedestrian nature of the race. He is '*Echt Deutsch*—if anything ever was', a quality that takes the form of a plodding submission to rules: '"But when one talks German one *must* shout," said Herr Heinrich. "It is taught so in the schools."' Generic denigration of Germans even gets into Wells's D.Sc. thesis, with a reference to 'the most gregarious and least original people in Europe, the German community'.

Negroes are another group Wells has reservations about. In

A Modern Utopia, after quite a lengthy section on the absurdity of thinking in racial or ethnic terms, and the need to encourage human intermixing, there is an odd moment when the narrator remarks to his companion, 'There may be—neither of us knows enough to deny—negroes who are handsome, capable, courageous.' 'Ugh!' responds his botanist-companion. Whereupon the narrator first cites Othello; then suddenly—with a candour that throws the preceding exhortations into doubt—owns up to a personal queasiness about miscegenation: 'It is my Utopia, and for a moment I could almost find it in my heart to spite the botanist by creating a modern Desdemona and her lover sooty black to the lips, there before our eyes. But I am not so sure of my case as that.' *The Future in America* reveals even more ambivalence towards negroes. Chuckling amusedly at his own benevolence, Wells discloses that, when visiting the States, he 'took and confirmed a mighty liking to these gentle, human, dark-skinned people'. The give-away inclusion of the adjective 'human' chimes in with another surprised-sounding reference to 'the dear humanity of these people, their slightly exaggerated vanity, their innocent and delightful love of colour and song'. Wells has been favourably impressed, it emerges, by 'the genial carriage of the ordinary coloured man, his beaming face, his kindly eye, his rich, jolly voice, his touching and trustful friendliness, his amiable, unprejudiced readiness to serve and follow a white man who seems to know what he is doing'. Commending the 'marvellous and simple-minded patience' of these ebony pets, Wells doubts if America

> can show anything finer than the quality of the resolve, the steadfast effort hundreds of black and coloured men are making to-day to live blamelessly, honourably, and patiently, getting for themselves what scraps of refinement, learning, and beauty they may. . . . They know they have a handicap, that they are not exceptionally brilliant nor clever people.

This orgy of head-patting actually represents something of an advance since, earlier in the book, Wells had expressed his fear that

> In the 'coloured' population America has already ten million descendants of unassimilated and, perhaps, unassimilable

labour immigrants. The people are not only half civilized and ignorant, but they have infected the white population about them with a kindred ignorance. For there can be no doubt that if an Englishman or Scotchman of the year 1500 were to return to earth and seek his most retrograde and de-civilized descendants, he would find them at last among the white and coloured population of Washington.

The coloured population seem unlikely candidates for the descendants of a sixteenth-century Englishman or Scotsman. But the passage does clearly suggest that negroes and their like are unpromising ingredients for the world mix Wells has in mind. And, in fact, they tend to be markedly absent from his Utopias. Their most memorable incursion into the books of the future is in *The Sleeper Awakes*, where they function as bogymen. The most fearsome forces used to quell the World State citizenry in this book are the negro police—'fine loyal brutes, with no wash of ideas in their heads'. Resolutely, Graham opposes their being sent in as mob-suppressors: 'I do not want any negroes brought to London. It is an archaic prejudice perhaps, but I have peculiar feelings about Europeans and the subject races.' Eventually, however, the Timbuctoo, Senegal, and Niger regiments are given their head. Torturing and mutilating, they put down an uprising in Paris. Then Helen Wotton erupts dramatically from the Council House, crying out the news that the Black Police are coming to London, a disclosure that stampedes the populace— as well it might, considering the way the approaching forces are described: 'craning their black necks and staring to see the filmy city that was rising out of the haze, the rich and splendid city to which "Massa Boss" had brought their obedient muscles. Bright teeth gleamed and the glossy faces shone. . . . They knew they were to have lordly times among the poor white trash.' Perhaps this was the kind of danger Wells had in mind when he urged in his collection *In The Fourth Year*, 'It is absolutely essential to the peace of the world that there should be no arming of the negroes beyond the minimum necessary for the policing of Africa.'

Wells's practice, both in life and literature, continually undermines his preaching. The belief he endlessly proclaims is that the way to a co-operative Utopia is short and smooth. The truth he actually displays is that it is hopelessly blocked by obstacles and pitfalls. What emerges beyond any doubt, however, in his campaign for world unity is a hankering after leadership. In *Christina Alberta's Father*—a book about a man who is 'a sort of emigrant from himself, to find a fantastic universal kingdom'— it is mooted that 'Perhaps all leadership is a kind of flight.' In fact, the situation Wells manoeuvred himself into as belligerent overseer of a movement for world-wide peace and harmony ingeniously satisfied various impulses in him. His aggression could be channelled at those he saw as the opponents of world reconstruction, making it seem justified, part of a holy war. He could escape from the problems of personal commitment into talk about working for the species, with the implication that this was something far more altruistic. And, most importantly of all, his publicity campaign for the World State made him a celebrated figure. He was able to tour the world as a well-known solo performer advocating team-work.

5 The Grand Earthly:
Wells and Self-Image

Individuality, Wells likes to argue, is illusory: each human being is, as *Babes in the Darkling Wood* explains, 'a sort of armoury of selves', a 'collection of different moods, personalities, value-systems which endlessly compete for dominance'. What imposes shaky unity on this diverse bundle is man's self-image, his *persona*—something Wells's thesis defines as the 'wabbling working self we imagine for ourselves . . . what we pretend and intend to be'.

This guiding view of the self, Wells's autobiography points out, 'may be resolutely honest or it may draw some or all of its elements from the realm of reverie'. Wells's mother, cheering herself up amidst the menial drudgery of Atlas House by identifying with Queen Victoria, gave a good instance of the latter case. 'The Queen, also a small woman, was . . . my mother's compensatory personality', Wells states, adding that, in later years, clad in a black bonnet and a black silk dress, Mrs Wells 'became curiously suggestive of the supreme widow'. Extreme examples of this tendency—people weirdly taken over by a phantom personality—appear in some of Wells's novels in the 1920s: *The Dream, Christina Alberta's Father, Mr Blettsworthy on Rampole Island*.

These are all cases of a self-image grotesquely remote from reality. His own *persona*, Wells believes, is in close accord with fact. 'There is, I maintain, a sufficient justification among my thoughts and acts from quite early years,' he insists in his autobiography, 'for that pose of the disinterested thinker and worker, working for a racial rather than a personal achievement.' As with his mother, though, his *persona* paid homage to imposing figures. One of these was Roger Bacon, the thirteenth-century *savant*. 'There is', Wells says in his autobiography, 'a queer little twist in my private vanity, a streak of snobbish imitativeness, which disposes me at times to parallel my lot with Roger Bacon's. I dress up my persona in his fashion.' Descriptions of this monkish *alter ego*—'irritable, hasty, honest and shrewd . . . two centuries ahead of his world' (*The Outline of History*); 'the father of modern experimental science. . . . His writings are one long tirade against ignorance' (*A Short History of the World*)—cast light on the feeling of affinity. When Wells summarises Bacon's life, marked resemblances are heavily underlined—right down to a taste for prophecy that included the prediction of flying-machines. Dissident, far-seeing, keen on science and education, Bacon comes to seem a Wellsian prototype, surreally stranded—as if by some Time Machine—in the Middle Ages.

The man Wells most modelled himself on, however, was from his own day—Thomas Huxley, whose lectures he attended as a first-year student in South Kensington. When he encountered Huxley, Wells was in a highly impressionable state. A new and vastly better way of life was unfolding for him; what had made this possible was scientific education; Huxley was the most celebrated scientific educator of his time. Excitement, gratitude, and awe all combined to render Wells unusually receptive: and, as a result, the impression Huxley made on him left permanent contours. He moulded Wells's interests and shaped the pattern of his career. His course in biology gave Wells a way of looking at the world; his life, showing the prestige that could be won by campaigning on behalf of science, suggested the role that Wells increasingly sought out for himself.

Later, another scientific educator deepened this initial imprint—Sanderson of Oundle. His school (to which Wells sent his sons, Gip and Frank) appears in two of the novels: it is Caxton in *Joan and Peter*, and Woldingstanton in *The Undying Fire*. And in 1924 Wells wrote a book about him, *The Story of a Great Schoolmaster*. Saying of Sanderson, 'I think him beyond question the greatest man I have ever known with any degree of intimacy', Wells soon makes it clear that—as with Roger Bacon—he feels he has found a kindred spirit. Quoting Sanderson as saying that 'work in schools should be permeated by Science and by the scientific method and outlook', recording how he attacked the primacy of the classics, argued for 'the supersession of competition by co-operation', and added to his school 'a temple to the whole human adventure' (called the House of Vision), the biography starts to sound distinctly autobiographical. Wells also admiringly recounts how Sanderson changed, after the First World War, 'from a successful schoolmaster into an amateur statesman': 'He became a propagandist. . . . He tried to find industrial magnates who would take up the methods of Oundle in productive organisation.' It emerges, too, that Sanderson took Wells very seriously—listing him as a writer particularly valuable for use in schools, and quoting approvingly from him in his last lecture (Wells was in the chair on this occasion, which ended dramatically when Sanderson collapsed and died).

Bacon, Huxley, Sanderson were all educators: and this was a role in life Wells valued intensely. Modelling himself on the lines of Huxley in particular, he would have been delighted with the epitaph—'the greatest international scientific educator of modern times'—that Sir Richard Gregory, a close friend from his student days, bestowed on him in his obituary notice in *Nature*. 'At bottom I am grimly and desperately educational', Wells says in his autobiography, recalling how he used to wish he 'had some virus with which one might bite people and make them mad for education'. Failing that, he tried to infect them with his own enthusiasm.

Wells owed a great deal to education. It not only took him from the draperies to South Kensington; it also introduced him to his second wife, who was a student at a crammer where he worked: his memoir *The Book of Catherine Wells* looks back fondly on her in those days, 'with her schoolgirl satchel of books and a very old-fashioned unwieldy microscope someone had lent her'. When this meeting occurred, in the autumn of 1892, Wells had been engaged in various kinds of educational work for over five years. After his somewhat ignominious departure from South Kensington—'as a result of my insubordinations, inattentions, digressions and waste of energy', his autobiography ruefully explains—'it seemed that such prospects in life as remained open to me, lay in school teaching'. Accordingly, he made his way, first, to what turned out to be a quite horrific school in Wales, and then to a pleasant one in Kilburn. He undertook part-time educational work as well—drawing wall-diagrams on canvas for his friend Jennings's biological course at Birkbeck, and enlisting as a tutor for a university correspondence college (a place, 'at once preposterous and necessary', to which he eventually moved as a full-time tutor). During this period—as in his days as pupil-teacher at Midhurst—he was studying as well as teaching. In addition to working hard for his BSc, which he got with first-class honours in zoology in 1890, he was taking exams in educational theory and history for the College of Preceptors. For their first diploma, the LCP, he wrote a short thesis on Froebel; for the second, the FCP, which also earned him their Doreck scholarship, he wrote one on Comenius (an interest which came to the fore again in his later life).

Describing himself as 'an old and seasoned educationist' in *The Salvaging of Civilization*, Wells declares that most of his earliest writings 'are concealed in the anonymity of the London educational papers of a quarter of a century ago'. He is referring here to the *Educational Times* (which belonged to the College of Preceptors) and *The University Correspondent* (which belonged to the man who ran the correspondence college where he worked). Wells's first books are rooted in this background, too. His *Text Book of Biology* consists of a revision and expansion of some of the instruction papers from the college, he explains in his auto-biography. And his next production was also 'a small but useful cram-book', *Honours Physiography*, which he wrote in conjunction with Richard Gregory. It was not until 1893 that Wells, after a breakdown in his health, abandoned the career of teacher: 'I guess class teaching is over for me for good, and that whether I like it or not, I must write for a living now,' he told Catherine Robbins in May of that year. The writing-career that followed often seems an extension of his teaching-work. A didactic note, discernible even in the early books, becomes deafening in the later ones. Wells's last novel, *You Can't Be Too Careful*, loudly advertises the vitally educative nature of some of his wares:

> A few of us who have had the good fortune to get some real education have tried to supplement your possible deficiencies. We made, and we have tried in vain to force into school and college use, a group of encyclopaedic books of which *The Science of Life* is the most relevant here. You can get it now in a single volume brought up to the date of 1938. You ought really to read it all.

In addition to these instructional tomes—*The Outline of History, The Science of Life, The Work, Wealth and Happiness of Mankind*—he wrote novels about education. *Joan and Peter*, according to the Atlantic preface, 'was designed to review the possibilities of a liberal education in contemporary England'; *Babes in the Darkling Wood*, Wells told Richard Gregory, is 'essentially . . . a criticism of contemporary education'. His novels, from *The Wonderful Visit* (1895) to *You Can't Be Too Careful* (1941), are packed with schoolteachers; and one of these books, *The Undying Fire*, is dedicated 'To All Schoolmasters and Schoolmistresses and Every Teacher in the World'. The educational experiences of Wells's characters are often the subject of extensive commentary. In both fiction and non-fiction, he continually mounts attacks on those he sees as impeding educational advance; and there is much satiric battery directed at the gargoyles and mildewed bastions of Oxbridge (or Camford, as he likes to call it).

Scientific education, Wells comes to believe, can save the world. As far back as *The War of the Worlds*, he had been nurturing this idea. There, the Artilleryman the narrator meets on Putney Heath urges 'saving our knowledge and adding to it' as the way in which defeated humanity, hidden away in pockets of resistance, must prepare to assail Martian supremacy: 'Especially', he says, 'we must keep up our science—learn more.' This eventually becomes an obsessive concern of Wells's. *World Brain* speaks of 'the race between education and catastrophe'. In some of his books, grimly dedicated characters are seen trying to stave off global disaster by the circulation of encyclopaedias. A world *in statu pupillari* is a world of peace, Wells's later books keep emphasising. 'We need only a reasonable and possible elevation of the educational level of the world for the "Jewish Question" to vanish altogether', affirms *Travels of a Republican Radical* (published in November 1939). *In the Fourth Year*, written during the First World War, also optimistically declares, 'even now there exists all the knowledge that is needed to make mankind universally free and human life sweet and noble. We need but the faith for it.'

'Knowledge is Power' is the slogan Mr Lewisham has pinned up on the wall to exhort himself to a life of effort. Knowledge should have power, Wells's later books continually proclaim. In order to exercise its beneficial influence, education should be vested with world-wide authority. In *Men Like Gods*, this has been achieved: Utopia, there, 'has no parliament, no politics, no private wealth, no business competition, no police nor prisons, no lunatics, no defectives nor cripples, and it has none of these things because it has schools and teachers who are all that schools and teachers can be'. Exactly how mental and physical deformities are forestalled by the educational system is not made clear. But the Utopians insist, '*Our education is our government.*' It is a social structure Wells would like to see transferred to earth. What he campaigns for is a 'World Brain', which, as he explains in his book of that title, would consist of a massive assemblage of didactic literature and those engaged in the production or revision of it. This cerebral complex would control the body politic, in the World State. In making this proposal, Wells appears to be acting on a hint from his early book *The First Men in the Moon*, where Cavor finds the moon is ruled by a giant brain, the Grand Lunar. In Selenite society, knowledge is stored in brains, not libraries. Those specialised for this function become almost all grey matter, 'wabbling jellies of knowledge'. 'These beings with big heads, on whom the intellectual labours fall, form a sort of aristocracy in this strange society,' we are told, 'and at the head of them, quintessential of the moon, is that marvellous gigantic ganglion the Grand Lunar.' A sort of mental monarch, this 'enhaloed supreme intelligence' with a brain-case 'many yards in diameter' imposingly thinks out every aspect of lunar policy. Wrestling with knotty problems, though, can cause his spectacular cerebrum to get overheated, and necessitates the use of cooling sprays by his attendants. This is called for after Cavor has explained democracy to him: 'When I had done he ordered cooling sprays upon his brow, and then requested me to repeat my explanation conceiving something had miscarried.' 'But who thinks? Who governs?' gasps the baffled brain, and incredulously asks, 'Do you mean . . . that there is no Grand Earthly?'

Cavor is forced to admit that there is not. Wells, as his career develops, seems increasingly to be edging toward this vacancy. The idea of becoming a world-dominating *savant* clearly enthralls him. Probably Atlas House—given its grandiose name because there was a figure of Atlas holding a lamp in one of its windows— first suggested the notion of the Titanic global luminary. Certainly, Wells says in his autobiography, 'It is unavoidable . . . that at times I should write as if I imagined that—like that figure of Atlas which stood in my father's shop-window—I sustained the whole world upon my shoulders.' The statue and the idea are set side by side in *The Sleeper Awakes*. When Graham emerges from his cataleptic trance and finds that, due to the burgeonings of

compound interest, he is now 'King of the Earth', he is taken to a
hall dominated by 'a gigantic white figure of Atlas, strong and
strenuous, the globe upon his shoulders', and informed, '*you* are
the Atlas, Sire. . . . The world is on your shoulders.' Similarly, in
The Holy Terror, Rud Whitlow reflects that, though he is building
up a World Civil Service, 'essentially, the world's still on my
shoulders. On my shoulders. Prometheus-Atlas.'

Towering figures with a crucial hold upon the world fascinate
Wells. His books are full of global potentates and aspirants to the
position. In *The Sleeper Awakes*, Graham, 'The Master', finds
himself up against 'Ostrog the Boss', 'fighting for the whole future
of the world'. Ostrog is a murderous megalomaniac—so is the
Invisible Man, who begins his reign of terror with the
proclamation, 'This is day one of year one of the new epoch. . . . I
am Invisible Man the First.' Benham, in *The Research Magnificent*,
declares, 'what I want is to be king of the world'; while the
significantly named Masterman in *Kipps* thwartedly laments,
'I'm a better man than any ten princes alive. And I'm beaten and
wasted.' Bedford, in *The First Men in the Moon*, dreams of a Cavorite
company that will rule the earth. Teddy Ponderevo, as his Tono-
Bungay empire spreads, muses eagerly on Nietzsche and
Napoleon. In *Christina Alberta's Father*, Mr Preemby graduates
from practising will-power in front of the looking-glass to the
conviction that he is Sargon, King of Kings. Mr Parham swells
into a caricature of the European dictators of the 1930s. *The Holy
Terror* charts the rise and fall of a World State despot.

The idea of the man of destiny has intense appeal for Wells—
despite his continual insistence that history is made by mass-
movements, not individual personalities. As if trying to reconcile
his excitement about the one with his faith in the other, he ensures
that his colossi sooner or later come to grief. Graham, the
Invisible Man, Benham, Rud Whitlow all die in the books in
which they appear: so do benignly depicted comic figures such as
Mr Preemby, or Teddy Ponderevo, who expires after babbling of
'Kingdoms Caesar never knew . . . . Under entirely new manage-
ment.' Ostrog flees in disarray. Mr Parham shrivels back to a
deflated don.

The Holy Terror offers a particularly interesting example of
Wells's setting out to explode his own triumphalist obsessions.
Rud Whitlow, the central character, is given a personality and life
that, in many ways, parallel the author's own. Similarities

include a quarrelsome disposition which in childhood took the form of hurling cutlery at his brothers; a youthful fondness for wandering round the countryside, whistling through his teeth, while fighting imaginary battles; a literary style which began as 'Babu English' and developed into 'good, nervous prose' showing a 'gift for effective phrases'; an enthusiasm for aeroplanes; a dislike of Catholics and Jews; and a growing tendency towards 'gigantically apocalyptic' reverie. Like Wells, Rud believes in the World State. He works for human co-operation, but does so because he wants personal pre-eminence: '"Leadership. Leadership. Leadership." The word sang through his brain.' The later sections of the book show him succumbing to galloping megalomania: 'Two inches taller than Napoleon' (as Wells also was), he becomes a paranoid and homicidal emperor of the world. What has caused this lust for power, it is claimed, is 'a profound, maybe innate dread of the closest of all forms of domination—love'. Rud is very unlike Wells in that he is a neurotic celibate; he is like him, though, in his qualms about close emotional commitment. Rud's capacity for full involvement with another person, we are told, 'has vanished and then returned in a vague, cloudy desire to be appreciated, admired, obeyed—loved by all the world'. His career represents an enormous compensation for deficiency. And, since Wells, throughout this virulent book has remorselessly invested Rud with his own worst features, this implies that—at least sometimes—he fears this may also be the case with him.

More usually, he turns to Adler's belief about the inferiority complex to explain hankerings after power. In *The Science of Life*, Adler is praised for 'stressing how the sense of inferiority, from which so many human beings suffer in their early years, produces by over-compensation an exaggerated or even abnormal desire for success, power, and accomplishment'. 'I am in agreement with the psychology of Adler rather than Freud about the essential motives of human beings', Wells declares in *The Common Sense of War and Peace*. 'The desire to feel secure and superior, to command . . . respect and recognition, amounts to a primary hunger; it is far more essential than the intermittent drives of sex.' His thesis congratulates Adler since, of all the psychoanalysts, it is he who has come 'nearest to the primitive disposition of the human self' in pointing to 'an innate desire for mastery'. This 'hormic craving for the sensation of power', *'42 to '44* reveals, has in Wells's own case 'been "sublimated" very largely into constructive and intellectual activities'.

Wells's lowly beginnings strongly influenced his work. Many of his early books delve engrossingly into recollections from his years of under-privilege; his later books, more often, attempt to escape into various kinds of exaltation. In his autobiography, Charlie Chaplin—who was a friend of his—says Wells's humble origin had left its mark . . . in an over-emphasis of personal sensitiveness', adding, 'I remember once he aspired an "h" in the wrong place and blushed to the roots of his hair.' Lower-class shames of this nature are repeatedly, but gently, touched on in the earlier books—rather as a recent bruise may be gingerly fingered to see if it still causes any wincing. Hoopdriver—humbly eager to pass as a gentleman, but continually betrayed by his accent and obsequious drapery mannerisms—is a case in point. So is Kipps, embarrassedly and embarrassingly trying to explain why he has no handkerchief: 'I dunno 'ow I managed *not* to bring one. . . . I— Not 'aving a cold, I suppose some 'ow I didn't think. . . .' Remembered ignominies from Wells's student days—such as a celluloid collar which could be cleaned with a toothbrush, saving on laundry bills—are wryly attached to Mr Lewisham.

Engagingly cheerful chronicles of under-privilege, *The Wheels of Chance*, *Love and Mr Lewisham*, *Kipps* and *Mr Polly* all display the kind of jaunty resilience Wells needed to weather the humiliations, deprivations, and servilities of his early years. What his books more often show, however, is a rebound from this world into aspirations towards celebrity. His blueprints for world reconstruction, it is noticeable, regularly postulate the existence of a prestige group, at the heart of which he would be conspicuously situated. The creation of a World State, *Phoenix* declares, 'must begin, and can only begin, as the work of a small and devoted elite'. The Open Conspiracy, a far-sighted band of believers in global co-operation, represents such an elite. Committed, in theory, to the fellowship of mankind, they must be, in practice, sedulously segregated—as *What Are We To Do With Our Lives?* points out: 'Necessarily for a time, but we may hope unconsciously, the Open Conspiracy children will become a social elite . . . it will be a waste and loss to put them back for the scholastic stage among their mentally indistinct and morally muddled contemporaries.' Even after the ideal state has been achieved, to judge from *A Modern Utopia*, a caste-system will obtain. There, people are divided into four descending classes, the Poietic, the Kinetic, the Dull, and the Base. And there is a controlling elite of moral grandees, called the Samurai, who are the 'voluntary nobility' and constitute 'something of an hereditary class'. They wear distinctive clothing—white robes with a purple edge—and are required to lead a life of ostentatious gravity. Though 'they may lecture authoritatively or debate', they are not allowed to act, sing, or recite. Nor may they take part in competitive sports. Cricket, for instance, is out of bounds as 'It was undignified and unpleasant for the Samurai to play conspicuously ill, and impossible for them to play so constantly as to keep hand and eye in training against the man who was fool enough and cheap enough to become an expert' ('Negroes', the book adds, 'are often very clever at cricket'). Certain jobs—like those of barber, waiter, or boot-cleaner—are also proscribed.

The notion of the elect features prominently in Wells's schemes for world improvement. In *After Democracy* he unequivocally declares, 'I am asking for a Liberal Fascisti, for enlightened Nazis.' He is fully in accord with William Clissold, who speaks of the need for 'an aristocratic and not a democratic revolution'. Wells's books constantly write off democracy. Benham, riding through scenes of Balkan carnage in *The Research Magnificent*, knows exactly what moral to draw: 'This is a masterless world. This is pure democracy.' Putting his faith in the 'aristocratic life', he believes that global harmony can only be accomplished by 'the new aristocracy, the disguised rulers of the world'. Who these are is resoundingly revealed in *Travels of a Republican Radical*: 'the authentic writer and artist and scientific worker are the aristocrats of the human community. There is nothing above them under heaven. They are masters.' *'42 to '44* makes it plain that Wells sees himself as one of them. 'I am a scientific aristocrat,' he says, 'but I am no gentleman.' Below-stairs in the old world social system, he becomes a patrician in the new one. An oblique kind of social climbing has occurred. At times, in fact, his reconstruction theories seem like an elaborate attempt to annex the upper quarters of Up Park. 'The place had a great effect upon me', he says in his autobiography. This partly shows itself in a belief that the movement towards the World State was put under way by a social as well as an intellectual aristocracy:

Out of such houses came the Royal Society, the *Century of*

Inventions, the first museums and laboratories and picture galleries, gentle manners, good writing, and nearly all that is worth while in our civilization to-day. . . . It is the country house that has opened the way to human equality, not in the form of a democracy of insurgent proletarians, but as a world of universal gentlefolk no longer in need of a servile substratum.

Wells has a marked taste for homing in on people in high places. His prose often preeningly puffs out with self-important cooings about his ability to do this—'most of the people in the world in key positions are more or less accessible to me' (*Experiment in Autobiography*); 'I have been living these last few months in close contact with the political life of Westminster' (*Travels of a Republican Radical*); 'I have had plentiful opportunity of sounding the minds of socially well-placed people' (*The Outlook for Homo Sapiens*). The role of hobnobber with the celebrated very much appeals to him. Some eluded him: *The Rights of Man* exasperatedly records, 'I went to Stockholm last September mainly to get hold of Mr Thomas Mann and work out some common statement with him about world affairs. . . . But I could get nothing out of him.' He did, however, achieve some notable coups. One of them was an interview with Stalin in 1934 ('I have come to you to ask you what you are doing to change the world', Wells dramatically begins: modestly, Stalin replies, 'Not so very much'). 'At the present time there are in the world only two persons to whose opinion, to whose every word, millions are listening', Wells exclaims to Stalin; 'you and Roosevelt.' He had already cornered the American president. For all his self-important bustlings round the Northern Hemisphere, however, Wells has nothing of note to show—apart from a tendency to jump to comically wrong conclusions about the dignitaries he has tracked down. His assessments of Stalin—'essentially self-critical and modest' (*Guide to the New World*), 'no one is afraid of him and everybody trusts him' (*Experiment in Autobiography*)—fall particularly wide of the mark.

Rebecca West's recollections of Wells in the 1920s show him priding himself on having 'really changed British policy about Russia' and talking vaingloriously about his influence upon 'the Franco-British situation'. On a number of occasions, he tried to convert this urge to be politically influential into direct action. But these efforts failed depressingly. His attempt to take over the

Fabian Society was decisively scotched by Shaw. Standing twice as Labour candidate for London University, he came bottom of the poll on both occasions.

His big ambitions encountered far less impediment in his writing. Here, they take various forms. One of them is a propensity towards vast undertakings and large-scale pronouncements. Perhaps in keeping with Wells's memories of Atlas, the word 'world' features in the title of eleven of his books. Many others are given heavily portentous names—*Mankind in the Making, First and Last Things, The Fate of Homo Sapiens*, and so on. And a cartoon Wells drew of himself in 1886, surrounded by tomes with titles like *Secret of the Kosmos* and *Wells's Design for a New Framework for Society*, shows that the impulse to take a panoramic view of things was present from the beginning of his literary career. In *The Way the World Is Going*, he says he thinks 'with less detail and in longer stretches' than most people. Many of his books show this—especially *The Outline of History*, which tackles the daunting feat of offering 'the whole story of life and mankind'. *The Work, Wealth and Happiness of Mankind* takes on another formidable task: 'This book is intended to be a picture of all mankind to-day', its opening line proclaims. In pursuance of this mammoth aim, it indefatigably generalises about an enormous range of matters, with nothing too humble to be heaped into the survey: 'the present underclothing of the world', the book authoritatively declares, 'is disgustingly dirty, ragged and defective' (a state of affairs rectified in *The Shape of Things to Come*, where 'such light underclothes as we wear last about three days').

Besides a *penchant* for global perspective, Wells's works favour cosmically open endings. *An Englishman Looks at the World* fades out with the picture of 'Man on his planet, flying swiftly to unmeasured destinies through the starry stillness of space'. The afflatus *finale* to *The Outline of History* elaborates the picture with a lift-off into rhetoric: 'Life, for ever dying to be born afresh, for ever young and eager, will presently stand upon this earth as upon a footstool, and stretch out its realm amidst the stars.' In the last scene of *Things to Come*, with a space-craft shown as 'a very small speck against a starry background', man has started on this process of astronomical expansion.

The process of broadening out is both praised and practised in Wells's books. *The Food of the Gods*, with its giant paragons, lumberingly equates quantity with quality: gigantic works like *Joan and Peter*, *The World of William Clissold*, *The Shape of Things to Come* seem to have been written in this belief. Many of Wells's books are very long; and he sometimes gives the appearance of working to some Brobdingnagian scale of his own—describing *New Worlds for Old*, for instance, as 'this little book of explanations': it is 355 pages long. A number of Wells's books bear the marks of both his impatience and his monumentalism in being, as he says of *Joan and Peter* in his Atlantic preface, 'at once truncated and lengthy'. *Love and Mr Lewisham*, he told Elizabeth Healey, was only a plank from the vast scaffold he initially envisaged. *Kipps*, the Atlantic preface reveals, is 'only a fragment of a much larger and more ambitious design', while *Ann Veronica* was 'planned originally, as *Kipps* was planned, to be much larger and fuller'.

Wells not only went for bulk; he also produced his books with extreme rapidity. 'It is magnificent, of course; but it can't be literature', gasped W. E. Henley, registering that in 1895, the year of *The Time Machine*, Wells had four books published. Arnold Bennett, hardly a literary dawdler himself, frequently appealed to Wells to spend at least a little time tidying up the slapdash errors that his hasty progress left behind: 'There were sundry examples of bad grammar,' he noted of *Mankind in the Making*, 'scores of bad punctuation, hundreds of striking inelegance, and not a few of an obscurity that might easily have been avoided.' Blunders can, in fact, be found everywhere in Wells. He has a continuing belief, for instance, that 'euphuism' means 'euphemism'. His geographical sense can go awry—ironically enough, in *An Englishman Looks at the World*, where he remarks on 'Canada . . . looking eastward to Japan and China, westward to all Europe'. Literary references are a particularly shaky area. *The Secret Places of the Heart* mentions Joyce's *Portrait of the Author as a Young Man*. *Brynhild* switches Hardy's Little Father Time from *Jude the Obscure* to *Tess of the d'Urbervilles*. *You Can't Be Too Careful* carelessly misattributes Mr F.'s aunt to *David Copperfield* (earlier, *The New Machiavelli* had correctly placed her in *Little Dorrit*).

A lack of attentiveness to detail can be spotted everywhere in Wells, and sometimes causes unintentional comedy. Words and phrases are sloppily flung into contexts where they take on farcically inappropriate connotations. In *The War in the Air*, for instance, we are solemnly informed that, after one of their number has been hanged, 'The men are all getting strung up.' *The Undying Fire* takes this tendency to a baroque extreme. Here, one of the main ordeals endured by Job Huss is the accidental burning down of his school, Woldingstanton; two boys die in this horrific incident, and Huss himself has to carry out the charred corpse of one of them. Spectacularly disregarding this, Wells sets him praising the intellectual achievements of his school with lines like 'Woldingstanton has become a torch at which lives are set aflame.' And the book is packed with fiery imagery, often of a curiously arsonist nature: 'I have lit a candle . . . the winds of fate may yet blow it into a world-wide blaze', 'The life of man must be like the perpetual spreading of a fire.' Nowhere does Wells show any sign of noticing that his real conflagration casts a lurid light on these metaphoric kindlings. Sometimes, too, his handling of narrative is startlingly perfunctory. For most of *The War of the Worlds*, for instance, the narrator is separated from his wife, and assumes—which the book presents as highly likely—that she has been killed by Martians. In the novel's final pages, she suddenly reappears: calmly offering no explanation for this near-miracle, Wells goes out of his way to lay stress on its unlikelihood, with the book's concluding line—'And strangest of all is it to hold my wife's hand again, and to think that I have counted her . . . among the dead.'

Even more damaging to Wells's writings than carelessness is repetition. In *The Way the World Is Going*, he refers laughingly to 'my voluminous and—I am told—correctly I think—reiterative works'; and *Phoenix* attempts to excuse his procedure on the grounds that 'Repetition is a necessary feature of propaganda in a world that reads inattentively.' It is not only Wells's opinions that are reiterated, though. Much of his fiction—dusting down the same themes, techniques, and situations—can be very second-hand. 'Just as *The New Machiavelli* repeats *The Sea Lady*,' he remarks in an Atlantic preface, 'so *Marriage* repeats *Love and Mr Lewisham*.' There are numerous other instances of recycling of this kind. Sometimes, it extends to a whole book—*Babes in the Darkling Wood* seems a virtual rewrite of *Joan and Peter*. At other times, it takes the form of a reduplicated character—Christina Alberta is really Ann Veronica reincarnated—or a carbon-copied incident—an unexpected legacy is the device that unshackles both Kipps and Mr Polly from their draperies; the Time Traveller and Mr Barnstaple both return from their interdimensional journeyings clutching an exotic flower. The books about sexual relationships show a particularly listless tendency to fall back on the same formulae.

Their narrative perfunctoriness was one of the things that convinced Henry James that Wells was abandoning imaginative writing. 'He has cut loose from literature clearly—practically altogether', he wrote to Gosse in 1912; 'he will still do a lot of writing probably—but it won't be *that*.' Originally, he had been very much taken with Wells's work. Hyperbole regularly fluttered out from Rye—'You reduce me to mere gelatinous grovel', 'I live for your agglomerated lucubrations.' Then, as the books became more polemical, James's approval withdrew. In 1914, in *The Times Literary Supplement*, he deplored Wells's 'quite gratuitous sacrifice to the casual' and 'well-nigh heart-breaking miscarriage of "effect"' in *Marriage*. Wells's response was twofold: first, he savagely lampooned James in *Boon*; and, secondly, he took to parading an ostentatious indifference to literary merit. His commitment to this had never been whole-hearted. Bennett shrewdly noted in 1905, 'Art, really, you hate. It means to you what "arty" means to me.' And Wells says in his autobiography, 'I have never been able to find the artistic attitude fundamentally justifiable.' For about fifteen fruitful years, however, he often behaved as though he did. 'I came off artistically from the beginning and got slovenly later', he once told Rebecca West. The far higher quality of the writings he produced between 1895 and 1910 amply bears this out. Their superiority is not fortuitous. They were generally worked at more meticulously. The Atlantic prefaces, for instance, testify that 'Some of the earlier books were very carefully written': *Love and Mr Lewisham* and *The First Men in the Moon* were 'sedulously polished'; *Tono-Bungay* was 'planned . . . with elaborate care'. Wells had worked hard, too, he discloses in his autobiography, to improve his style. Originally, he wrote a comically pompous 'Babu English': the title of the first version of *The Time Machine*— *The Chronic Argonauts*—is a sample of such fustian. It was reading Swift, he claimed, that showed him the kind of prose to aim for. It influenced some of his works in other ways as well. *The Island of Doctor Moreau* often brings to mind, especially in its conclusion, the last book of *Gulliver's Travels*; and the Laputa episode has been pillaged for some of the satire in *The First Men in the Moon*. Interestingly, too, Wells returned to Swift as a partial model for the one really well-written novel of his later years, *Mr Blettsworthy on Rampole Island*—which was, as he told Julian Huxley, 'my *Candide*, my *Peer Gynt*, my *Gulliver*'.

Later in life—when his books were increasingly becoming dropsical assemblages of rhetoric, locally enlivened by the gift for trenchant phrasing and inventive metaphor he never entirely lost—Wells tended to dismiss those years when he was primarily a novelist as a temporary aberration. Attempting to explain why he swung towards literature and then away again, he says of the literary luminaries—such as James and Conrad—into whose sphere of influence his life had taken him, 'I felt their gravitational attraction', but 'The scientific pull was earlier and stronger.'

In fact, Wells's writings, even when they are most consciously striving for literary effect, never break away from the scientific background of his earlier years. As we have been seeing, a biologist's way of looking at the world pervades all his work. And in various other ways his books show the imprint of impressions from his student days. A nostalgia for South Kensington, for instance, suffuses some of his earlier writings. *Love and Mr Lewisham* offers an affectionately detailed reconstruction of the Science School, and—as with *Tono-Bungay*—gives a romanticised account of Wells's progress as a student there. Lewisham and George Ponderevo are seduced away from science by a passionate infatuation: contrary to what this might suggest, Wells played truant because he was bored with the poorer teaching in his second and third years. A more acrid version of South Kensington appears in one of Wells's best short stories, 'A Slip Under the Microscope'. Here, the laboratory is pungently evoked—'bleached dissections in spirits', green gas-lamps on the tables, fog against the windows—and Wells expertly records a number of reactions generated by the social mix inside the place, ending with a bitter residue of waste caused by failure to detect dishonesty and recognise integrity. 'The Argonauts of the Air' subjects Wells's *alma mater* to even harsher treatment, sending a flying-machine crashing into 'the solid mass of masonry that was formerly the Royal College of Science'. Usually, though, his handling of South Kensington is more benign. It is there, for instance, that the narrator of *The War of the Worlds* first hears the howling which signifies that the Martians are dying and the earth is saved (a pickled Martian is donated at the book's conclusion to the Natural History Museum). In *Ann Veronica*, the college represents the centre of an unflinchingly candid quest for knowledge, with Huxley coming briefly into view as Russell, a 'great figure' from the days of Darwinian controversy, and Wells slipped onto the staff under the disguise of Capes ('I recognise in him . . . many parts of yourself', wrote Richard Gregory).

At times, Wells's fiction can resemble a reunion of Huxley's old *alumni*. Prendick has studied under him; so have Oswald Sydenham and William Clissold. Sir Rupert York, a grand old man of science in *The World of William Clissold*, has been in contact with him from a particularly early age: we are told that 'Professor Huxley was a frequent visitor to his home' when he was a child, 'and Charles Darwin patted his head'. Previously hard to find in English fiction, scientists populate Wells's books in sizable numbers. Some are scattered to esoteric settings: the Time Traveller goes scudding through the centuries; Cavor is propelled to the bottom of the lunar craters; in 'The Plattner Story', a chemistry-teacher gets blown into the fourth dimension. Most of them, however, are located in laboratories, working on research. Prendick refers to 'the overmastering spell' of this: it is one under which many of Wells's characters profitably fall. Parload's 'work upon intersecting radiations' in *In the Days of the Comet* 'has broadened the intellectual horizon of mankind for ever'. Trafford and William Clissold both engage in valuable research until their wives sabotage it. In *The Invisible Man*, Dr Kemp is working on material for his FRS when Griffin, 'the most gifted physicist the world has ever seen' (now invisible) breaks in on him. Rivalling Griffin in the field of biology is Foxfield of *Star Begotten* and *Apropos of Dolores*, who, according to the narrator of the latter book, 'knows everything there is to be known about biology'. In the later novels, psychotherapists and nerve-specialists suddenly proliferate: Martineau in *The Secret Places of the Heart*, Devizes in *Christina Alberta's Father*, Minchett in *Mr Blettsworthy on Rampole Island*, Finchatton and Norbert in *The Croquet Player*, Keppel in *Star Begotten*, Kentlake in *Babes in the Darkling Wood*. Doctors are often in attendance, too, such as the Carstalls in *The Holy Terror* or Margaret Broxted and Laverstock in *The Bulpington of Blup*.

The latter couple assist in a book-long diagnosis of what is wrong with the artistic mentality, and dole out bitter medicine to the booby aesthete suffering from it. The arty and the anti-scientific frequently lose out to scientists in Wells's novels. In *Ann Veronica*, the heroine, eager to devote herself to biology, is harassed by three men. Her father, who wants to immure her in domesticity, is addicted to escapist literature with colourful titles, '*The Red Sword, The Black Helmet, The Purple Robe*'; Manning, who is trying to manoeuvre her into a sentimental relationship, enthuses over Ruskin and pens verses with lines like 'Green and dewy is Nellie-bud fairy'; Ramage who hopes to seduce her, takes her to the opera to soak in *Tristan and Isolde* as part of the softening-up process. Opposed to these is Capes, who not only puts their arty deviousness to shame with his biological directness, but also beats them at their own game by becoming a literary celebrity. Literature is outclassed by science in *Marriage* as well. Marjorie breaks away from Mr Magnet, author of plays like *Our Owd Woman*, after Trafford crashes into her existence and challenges her father with the cry, 'why can't I fall in love with your daughter? I'm a Doctor of Science' (his pedigree is excellent, too, since his father died as a martyr to research, having picked up a fatal infection 'in an investigation upon ulcerative processes').

Wells bestows scientific honours lavishly upon his characters. One of the most glitteringly bedecked is Teddy Broxted in *The Bulpington of Blup*. He not only writes an acclaimed, Wellsian-sounding book, *Human Association from the Point of View of General Biology*, but is 'a Professor of the new most fashionable branch of biology, Social Biology, the youngest Fellow of the Royal Society and all sorts of brilliant things'. Another prodigy is George in *Tono-Bungay*, who 'had my FRS by the time I was thirty-seven'. Capes is even more precocious: he has an FRS 'and he can't be much over thirty'. William Clissold is a Fellow, too, but Trafford is not. Though Marjorie feels he is 'an FRS in the sight of God' and he affects contemptuous indifference—'Confound the silly little FRS'—bitterness seeps through as we hear that, despite his brilliance, 'He was still outside the Royal Society, of course.' Wells himself greatly wanted to be inside it. Sometimes, he suggested that his books were equivalent, or superior, to the work required for membership: saying in a letter, for instance, that *Love and Mr Lewisham* represented 'really more work . . . than there is in many a first-class FRS research'. Late in life, he nudgingly urged Sir Richard Gregory, who was a Fellow, 'why not increase the numbers of the RSoc so as to take a new group of fellows representing the more social sciences? Even apart from that the

RSoc needs expansion.' And he prepared a thesis for the London DSc, in the hope that this would also bring the FRS he coveted—though, to his chagrin, it didn't.

Wells's scientists are not only distinguished by letters behind their name; they also like to have *recherché* items dotted round their rooms. In *The New Machiavelli*, Remington's father, a science-teacher, has big fossil bones and a large lump of white coral on his mantelpiece; hanging above them is 'the portrait of a brainy gentleman, sliced in half'. Ann Veronica keeps a pig's skull and a dissected frog on her bookcase. Sir Rupert York has a plaster-cast of a gorilla's foot on his desk. And Professor Broxted's emblematic decor includes 'miniature restorations of some extinct reptiles in bronze' and 'a big silver model of a cuttle-fish'. Usually, these exotic objects merely serve as tokens of a character's scientific bias. In 'The Reconciliation', though, one is used more purposefully: in a room littered with the skulls of hedgehogs and shrew-mice, a scientist is battered to death with a whale's ear-bone.

Even more than bony bits and pieces, technical vocabulary is strewn around by Wells in a rather ostentatiously initiated way. In *The Wonderful Visit*, an angel's injuries give rise to talk of the 'second glenoid' and the '*ala spuria*'. In *The Invisible Man*, 'Tapetum', 'Nauplii and tornarias' get discussed. Crucial moments in some of the narratives are accompanied by outbursts of knowledgeable phraseology. In *Marriage*, Trafford woos Marjorie with questions like 'Do you know anything of the effects of polarised light, the sight of a slice of olivine-gabbro . . . between crossed Nicols?' 'A Slip under the Microscope' shows a girl using chat about 'the alisphenoid of a rabbit's skull' to arouse the hero's interest: as a result of her knowing distractions, his attention badly wanders from 'the fate of the mesoblastic somites or the probable meaning of the blastopore'. In *Love and Mr Lewisham*, Miss Heydinger's breakdown is seen to be imminent when a student confides, 'I asked her yesterday what were the bones in the parietal segment, and she didn't know one.' Lewisham's academic collapse is also made apparent as we watch him in the examination-room, vainly 'struggling to keep cool and to mount the ciliated funnel of an earthworm's nephridium'. Sometimes, scientific disquisitions are slipped into the novels. Griffin gives Kemp a lecture on refraction and reflection; Teddy Broxted explains evolution to Theodore Bulpington. The later books reverberate with biological harangue: the narratives of the earlier ones often bounce off from a basis of stretched scientific theory. *The Time Machine* is launched by talk about the fourth dimension; gravity-blocking Cavorite sends *The First Men in the Moon* out into space (apart from this imaginary substance, Wells boasted in a preface, the book contains 'nothing that a properly informed science student could contradict flatly').

Early writers on Wells were struck by the way his work derived its character from the interaction of two different worlds: reviewing *The Island of Doctor Moreau* in 1896, Chalmers Mitchell, a zoologist, described him as 'an author with the emotions of an artist and the intellectual imagination of a scientific investigator'. Some—such as Clement Shorter in 1897—applauded Wells's move to literature from science: 'We probably lost a quite indifferent man of science to gain the really able author of *The Time Machine* and *The Invisible Man*.' Others saw it as an irresponsible emigration into frivolity. Gosse, for instance, also in 1897, haughtily deplored Wells's slide away from science: 'Mr Wells might have risen in it to the highest consideration, but he prefers to tell little horrible stories about monsters.' This latter view was the one Wells subsequently favoured, liking to suggest that his later abandoning of the literary constituted a responsible return to the more exacting realm of science. This is not quite accurate, though. His allegiance did not waver between the life of an artist and that of a scientist. By the time he took to proclaiming his indifference to fiction, his scientific attainments were rusted and out-of-date: 'he had forgotten much of his biology', says Julian Huxley of Wells in 1926, 'and what he remembered was by now old-fashioned—pre-Mendelian, with little study of animal behaviour or ecology'. The journalistic jottings he submitted as a thesis, towards the end of his life, show the distance that he had, by then, travelled away from scientific rigour. Wells forked off from his career as a novelist to become a propagandist for science, not a scientist.

It was publicity whose attraction he found irresistible. In his autobiography, he refers to 'the pleasures, the very real pleasures, of vanity', and declares, 'My very obstinate self-conceit was . . . an important factor in my survival. . . . Occasionally I make inelegant gestures of self-effacement but they deceive nobody and they do not suit me.' Gestures of self-aggrandisement were what Wells's associates would have been more familiar with. In 1920,

Beatrice Webb found him 'fat and prosperous and immensely self-congratulatory'. Rebecca West remembered him as being 'enormously vain, irascible, and in a fantasy world' by 1922. Letters that he wrote around this time confirm it: 'The Outline Of History is going to change History. I've done good things and big things.' Though Wells once said, 'humility in the artist is what charity is in the saint', he showed little of it. To Arnold Bennett, in particular, he revealed an intense desire for celebrity. Claiming, in 1901, to be 'an absolutely unique figure in contemporary literature . . . relevant to the criticism of prose writing and prose reading in more directions than any other man who writes', he stated, 'With the people in an omnibus it would be convenient to pretend I didn't care a damn for my public reputation and acceptance but it would be silly not to admit to you that these things are primary values in my life.' While Bennett joked, 'You will have to see a doctor about that modesty of yours', Wells's letters kept up the bombast: 'There is no illusion. I *am* great', 'I do honestly regard myself as a First Class Man.' Opportunities of bringing the public round to this opinion were cannily pounced on—as instructions to Bennett, who was writing an article about him, make clear: 'If so be there is a chance of a casual allusion to . . . my first class BSc Lond. or to my translated editions in French, German, Italian, Spanish, Norwegian, Hungarian, Czech and Danish, there's no need to be secretive.'

The advertising of his books was always of considerable concern to Wells. Macmillan's gentlemanly modes of sales-promotion, for instance, constantly goaded him to exasperated protest: 'I don't think you advertise well. . . . I don't think you have any idea of what could be done for me.' Contemptuous of their advertising manager—originally 'Dear Fame Maker' but soon 'Macmillan's advertisement imbecile'—Wells bombarded Frederick Macmillan with unusual suggestions for arousing public interest. Bundles of favourable press-cuttings, gleaned by Mr Wells, arrived at the publishers with the recommendation that they be made up into a pamphlet to be 'used . . . *copiously* for advertisements'. Sandwich-board men patrolling Oxford Street, and the City at lunch-time, were an especially favoured project: 'I wish I could make you think differently about those sandwich men. . . Try sandwich men the second week in December—good simple boards—and you'll put up the sales 2,000 a week.' The publication of *Kipps*, and his desire 'to shove the thing into a sale

of five figures', put Wells into a state of particular excitability. He
showered plaudits on the novel in his frequent letters to Frederick
Macmillan—'It is not as if I were asking you to push rubbish',
'It's an infernally good book as a matter of fact. I have had it
praised tonight by Barrie, Arthur Morrison, Jeremy Jacobs, and
Sidney Lee. . . . I refuse absolutely to be modest about it'—and he
tirelessly concocted advertising ploys with a vulgar ingenuity
worthy of Teddy Ponderevo (he was, in fact, working on *Tono-
Bungay* at the time).

Wells not only wants to 'push' his books; he also uses them to
push himself: increasingly, they become display-cases for his
egotism. In *Certain Personal Matters*, there is an essay criticising
what he calls 'The Pose Novel', fiction in which the author
presents an idealised picture of himself; *Mankind in the Making*
warns 'The way of self-advertisement . . . has brought many a
man of indisputable gifts to absolute vulgarity of thought and
work'; 'None so poor that cannot swagger at a writing-desk', we
are reminded in *Brynhild*. Despite these strictures, though, much
of Wells's writing is in the pose-novel genre. His fiction is a great
theatre of self-dramatisation. Sometimes, he has himself discussed
by name—as when William Clissold talks about his 'distant
cousin Wells'. At other times, he grinningly lets a character
disparage him on social grounds—this happens in *Joan and Peter*
and *Brynhild*. Usually, however, he likes to appear in the book,
lurking blatantly behind some cellophane disguise. Doubles,
stand-ins, *alter egos* populate Wells's fiction to a startling degree.
There are some characters who look like him—Barnet, say, in *The
World Set Free*, or the narrator of *A Modern Utopia*—and there are
dozens who sound like him, chorusing his doctrines. Often, there
are two or even three self-presentations in one book. *The World Set
Free* has a trio of mouthpieces—Barnet, Karenin, and King
Egbert of England—reciting the Wellsian credo. In *Mr Britling
Sees It Through*, Wells treats himself to a flattering self-portrayal in
the hero—'the fountains of Mr Britling's active and encyclo-
paedic mind played steadily', etc.—and throws in another
version of himself as Wilkins the novelist. 'Mr Britling found a
kindred spirit in Wilkins', we are told: as well he might,
considering they are both near-clonings of the author. Wilkins
keeps getting into Wells's books. In *The Wife of Sir Isaac Harman* he
holds forth on 'the natural and necessary disreputableness of
everyone who produces reputable writing'. In *The New Machiavelli*,

the Wells-figure, Remington, complains of 'a foul-mouthed attack on poor little Wilkins the novelist—who was being baited by the moralists . . . for making one of his women characters, not being in holy wedlock, desire a baby and say so'. In *Ann Veronica*, where this situation occurred—and about which a Grundyish fuss arose—the man the heroine wants to be impregnated by is another Wellsian stand-in, Capes (who later, in a tribute to Wells's Utopian interests, gives himself the *nom de plume* of Thomas More). There is also reference in that book to Wilkins's 'daring essays'. *Boon* reintroduces Wilkins in person—giving him scope to expound his ideas and indulge in a difference of opinion over the use of food-metaphor with the hero, a further Wellsian self-portrait (who has written a book, from which extracts are given, containing yet another).

This profusion of self-images reflects Wells's vanity. By packing his books with characters who represent him, he also ensures a consensus for his opinions. His later books, he sometimes claims, are dialogue novels—and he blames their unpopularity on his readers' aversion to intellectual debate. But ideas are not really debated in these novels: there is far more diatribe than dialogue. Varying opinions are allowed on minor points, but Wells's World State doctrines and their like are never exposed to testing criticism. Their opponents are let into the books only to be castigated or derided. 'I don't believe in tolerance,' Beatrice Webb reports Wells as saying, 'you have got to fight against anything being taught anybody which seems to you harmful, you have got to struggle to get your own creed taught.'

Education, for Wells, becomes indoctrination. For all his emphasis on the value of science, it is anti-scientific—the implanting of fixed ideas, not a training in conjecture, analysis, and criticism. What it amounts to, in fact, is social conditioning. 'Education is the preparation of the individual for the community', says *The Outline of History* (itself written to facilitate this); and in his autobiography Wells refers to 'the primary function of the school in human society, which is to correlate the intelligence, will and conscience of the individual to the social process'. This scheme of things invests a teacher with considerable powers of domination. In his autobiography, Wells recalls 'the nice authoritative feeling of dictating knowledge to a class'. 'Authoritative' and 'dictating' touch the prose with a totalitarian stamp and there are other passages that suggest Wells saw the step from dictater to dictator as a fairly short one. In his book on Sanderson, he writes, 'He filled me, a mere writer, with envious admiration when I saw how he could control and shape things to his will . . . how he could use his boys, his govenors, his staff, to try out and shape his creative dreams.' This makes the classroom seem a small-scale version of the Wellsian Utopia, a place where education is government and the World State is the answer to all problems.

One of the most striking features of these ideal states is their air of uncanny accord. *The Shape of Things to Come* affirms that 'there can be only one right way of looking at the world for a normal human being'. The citizenry of Utopia assemble in obedient phalanxes behind this belief. This regimentation, Wells likes to imply, has evolved quite naturally. But, from time to time, remarks are dropped which show that a fairly fearsome weeding-process has occurred. Pointing out that the New Republicans 'will naturally regard the modest suicide of incurably melancholy, or diseased or helpless persons as a high and courageous act of duty rather than a crime', *Anticipations* loftily urges inferior types to do the decent thing: 'So far as they fail to develop sane, vigorous and distinctive personalities for the great world of the future, it is their portion to die out and disappear.' By the time we get to *Men Like Gods*, high and courageous acts of duty have become compulsory: 'the melancholic type has taken its dismissal and gone; spiteful and malignant characters are disappearing'— not of their own altruistic volition but as the result of 'a certain deliberate elimination of ugly, malignant, narrow, stupid and gloomy types'. 'The world and its future is not for feeble folk any more than it is for selfish folk', Wells gloatingly warns in *After Democracy*. 'It is not for the multitude, but for the best.' Criminals can expect especially short shrift in such communities, as *Anticipations* makes clear. Those not kept in line by 'good scientifically caused pain' will come up against the New Republicans' bias towards execution rather than incarceration: 'To kill under the seemly conditions science will afford is a far less offensive thing. The rulers of the future will grudge making good people into jailers, warders, punishment-dealers, nurses, and attendants on the bad.' They will, Wells explains, 'have an ideal that will make killing worth the while; like Abraham, they will have the faith to kill'.

That the New Republicans should find elevating parallels for their righteous slaughterings in the Old Testament is not so unusual as it might appear. Traces of the religion he was steeped in as a child often permeate Wells's prose. In his earlier books, they are used to give satiric colouring. *The Island of Doctor Moreau*—'an exercise in youthful blasphemy', as he called it in his preface to *Seven Famous Novels* in 1934—was partly written, as a contemporary reviewer worriedly noted in the *Guardian*, 'to parody the work of the Creator of the human race, and cast contempt upon the dealings of God with his creatures'. To this end, travesty—what Wells termed, in his Atlantic preface, 'theological grotesque'—is derisively daubed around the book. A megalomaniac crazily attempts to make other creatures into his image and likeness. Threatening them with 'the House of Pain', he imposes absurd rules alien to their natures. Cowering and backsliding, they chant placatory litanies 'about *Him*, whoever he might be'. After Moreau's death, Prendick—'That Other who walked in the Sea'—uses memories of the Ascension as a means of policing the island: '"He has changed his shape. . . . For a time you will not see him. He is there"—I pointed upward—"where he can watch you."' *The Sleeper Awakes*, a book about a miraculous resurrection, also has its moments of religious burlesque. Graham, Master of the World, finds his interests being administered by dubious disciples, the Twelve Trustees; and, as with *The Island of Doctor Moreau*, speech sometimes becomes a sort of tongue-in-cheek plainchant: 'Verily it is the Sleeper.' Other parody-versions of the Divinity are the Martians of *The War of the Worlds*—who create, near Chobham, a pillar of fire by night that becomes a pillar of smoke by day—and the Invisible Man—placed, at one point, in the midst of a crowd who are singing, 'When shall we see His face?'

Despite the gaudy caricature in these early works, however, Wells increasingly makes use of religious tones to highlight the gravity and grandeur of his purposes. Talking of his faith in the ideal of human co-operation, he explains in *First and Last Things*, 'I write in phrases that the evangelical Christianity of my childhood made familiar to me, because they are the most expressive phrases I have ever met for the psychological facts with which I am dealing.' In accordance with this, he testifies, of his progress towards acquiescence in the creed of the World State, 'I have been through the distress of despair and the conviction of sin, and

. . . I have found salvation.' The 'scheme of conversion and salvation, as . . . presented by many Christian sects' is, he declares, 'a very exact statement of the mental processes I am trying to express'. This casts a revealing light on the way the New Jerusalem, in his books, seems to be largely achieved by fervent professions of belief. 'Give yourself to World Communications', urges a proselytising zealot of this secular religion in the film-script *Things to Come*. *In the Days of the Comet*, recounting the change to a regenerate society, is heavy with imagery of the 'last days', and 'Conversion'. 'The idea of human brotherhood struggles now to possess the human soul' just as Christianity once did, claims *A Short History of the World*; and 'if you choose . . . to declare that the world-state is God's church, you may have it so', says *God the Invisible King*. Wells does try to have it so. In his books, hallowed parallels work busily everywhere, converting his enthusiasms into an alternative religion. Teachers, in *The Dream*, are 'holy saints'. 'Scientific research', we learn from *The Work, Wealth and Happiness of Mankind*, 'is the modern form of the religious life.' In *Boon*—where reading is described as 'sacramental'—writers and painters are apostrophised with the words, 'all you are priests, you do a priestly office, and every bookstall and hoarding is a wayside shrine'.

Returning to the notions of Comenius, about whom he wrote the dissertation for his FCP, Wells speaks, in *The Salvaging of Civilization*, of the need for 'a common book of Necessary Knowledge', a 'Bible of Civilization'. This book, affording guidance and sustenance to every citizen in the community, would apparently be a compendium of holy writ and World Encyclopaedia. Much of it, it transpires, has already been written by Wells himself. What he calls 'our New Genesis and our new historical books' would be found in *The Outline of History*, which had appeared the previous year. 'Books of Conduct and Wisdom'—equivalents to Deuteronomy and Leviticus—could be taken by the bushel from his later writings. There is an abundance of prophecy, and the flailing exhortation that traditionally accompanies this in the Old Testament. *The Shape of Things to Come* offers a kind of Apocalypse. And there are specific reworkings of biblical stories. *The Undying Fire* is 'the Book of Job frankly modernized', as Wells's autobiography has it: with Bildad appearing as William Dad, Zophar as Joseph Farr, and so on. *Star Begotten*, featuring Joseph and Mary Davis, is a Wellsian version of the Incarnation. *All Aboard for Ararat* is an updating of the Noah legend.

Equipped with its encyclopaedia-bible, bookstall-shrines, teacher-saints, and researcher-hermits, the World State becomes a kind of scientific theocracy. 'In effect', we are told in *The Holy Terror*, 'the scientific body was deliberately taking upon itself the role of the Church in the theory of Medieval Christendom, it was becoming the repository of knowledge, the directive power in education, and the criterion of all social organisations and readjustment.' The office Wells envisaged for himself, in relation to this scientific priest-state, varied. Sometimes, he is an evangelist or missionary, spreading the good news: Richard Gregory saw him rather like this, saying of his letters, 'The word "epistle" seems appropriate . . . because you are the apostle of a philosophy of human and social biology, which in the course of time, must determine the conduct of individuals and of nations.' On other occasions, Wells presents himself as 'a prophet by use and wont', as *What Is Coming?* has it—gazing vatically at apocalyptic preludes to the coming of the kingdom, or assailing the blindness of his contemporaries with vigorous jeremiads. 'I can't be Aaron to my own Moses', he told Joad in 1932. The preference for the more celebrated role is typical. In fact, there are moments when he seems to have his eye on an even loftier position. 'I would rather be after God's pattern,' he informed Beatrice Webb in 1904, 'gross, various, fecund and comprehensive, inexact and continually unexpected.' By 1932, she noted, he had 'become a sort of "little God" demanding payment in flattery as well as in gold'. In later years 'God Wells' was one of his ways of referring to himself (Odette Keun, it may be remembered, called him *Le Petit Dieu*). There is a strange episode in *All Aboard for Ararat* where God announces he is the true author of a number of Wells's books.

More and more inflated, Wells's self-image lifted him ever upwards. But, as it swelled, it squashed his creativity. His imagination was never entirely stifled: to the very end, it could make its voice heard. But, from about 1910 or so, it was up against formidable—and ultimately all-but-overwhelming—opposition. As Wells settled, with a kind of disgruntled complacency, into the role of prophet-messiah of mankind, his attention swivelled inwards. He fantasised more and more about himself: and, in keeping with the grandiose *persona* he was building up, even his novels changed their nature. In his later books, life is not so much portrayed as theorised about; inventiveness yields to the doctrinaire. The early works are constantly enriched with unexpected detail scooped from life by deftly imaginative phrases. In the later ones, predictable generalisations are ponderously laid down across pages of prosy *longueurs*. Wells's imagination is increasingly tethered by his sense of self-importance. In his early books, it was not hampered in this way. Given proper scope, it zestfully exercised itself, translating his excitement over scientific facts into powerfully memorable scientific fiction, seizing on the dreary actualities of his early life and investing them with an engaging freshness. In those days, even something as humble as a cough in *Kipps* could detonate vivid absurdities of metaphor: 'a sound rather more like a very, very old sheep a quarter of a mile away being blown to pieces by a small charge of gunpowder than anything else in the world'. Wells had no need, at that time, for images of celebrity: he was displaying real distinction.

Bibliography

A. WORKS BY WELLS

1893   *A Text Book of Biology* (Clive).
       Honours Physiography, with R. A. Gregory (Hughes).
1895   *Select Conversations with an Uncle* (John Lane).
       The Time Machine (Heinemann).
       The Wonderful Visit (Dent).
       The Stolen Bacillus and Other Incidents (Methuen).
1896   *The Island of Doctor Moreau* (Heinemann).
       The Wheels of Chance (Dent).
1897   *The Plattner Story and Others* (Methuen).
       The Invisible Man (Pearson).
       Certain Personal Matters (Lawrence and Bullen).
1898   *The War of the Worlds* (Heinemann).
1899   *When the Sleeper Wakes* (Harper).
       Tales of Space and Time (Harper).
1900   *Love and Mr Lewisham* (Harper).
1901   *The First Men in the Moon* (Newnes).
       Anticipations (Chapman and Hall).
1902   *The Discovery of the Future* (Fisher Unwin).
       The Sea Lady (Methuen).
1903   *Mankind in the Making* (Chapman and Hall).
       Twelve Stories and a Dream (Macmillan).
1904   *The Food of the Gods* (Macmillan).
1905   *A Modern Utopia* (Chapman and Hall).
       Kipps (Macmillan).
1906   *The Faults of the Fabian* (Fabian Society).
       In the Days of the Comet (Macmillan).
       The Future in America (Chapman and Hall).
       Socialism and the Family (Fifield).
1907   *This Misery of Boots* (Fabian Society).
1908   *New Worlds for Old* (Constable).
       The War in the Air (Bell).
       First and Last Things (Constable).

1909   *Tono-Bungay* (Macmillan).
        Ann Veronica (Fisher Unwin).
1910   *The History of Mr Polly* (Nelson).
1911   *The New Machiavelli* (John Lane).
        The Country of the Blind and Other Stories (Nelson).
        Floor Games (Palmer).
1912   *Marriage* (Macmillan).
        'The Past and the Great State', in the anthology *The Great State* (Harper).
1913   *Little Wars* (Palmer).
        The Passionate Friends (Macmillan).
1914   *An Englishman Looks at the World* (Cassell).
        The World Set Free (Macmillan).
        The Wife of Sir Isaac Harman (Macmillan).
        The War that Will End War (Palmer).
1915   *Boon* (Fisher Unwin).
        Bealby (Methuen).
        The Research Magnificent (Macmillan).
1916   *What Is Coming?* (Cassell).
        Mr Britling Sees It Through (Cassell).
1917   *War and the Future* (Cassell).
        God the Invisible King (Cassell).
        The Soul of a Bishop (Cassell).
1918   *In the Fourth Year* (Chatto and Windus).
        Joan and Peter (Cassell).
1919   *The Undying Fire* (Cassell).
1920   *The Outline of History* (Newnes).
        Russia in the Shadows (Hodder and Stoughton).
1921   *The Salvaging of Civilization* (Cassell).
1922   *Washington and the Hope of Peace* (Collins).
        The Secret Places of the Heart (Cassell).
        A Short History of the World (Cassell).
        The World, its Debts and the Rich Men, speech to the University of London Labour Party (Finer).
1923   *Men Like Gods* (Cassell).
1924   *The Story of a Great Schoolmaster* (Chatto and Windus).
        The Dream (Jonathan Cape).
        A Year of Prophesying (Fisher Unwin).
1924–8 *The Atlantic Edition of the Works of H. G. Wells*, 28 vols (Fisher Unwin).
1925   *Christina Alberta's Father* (Jonathan Cape).

1926   *The World of William Clissold* (Benn).
            Mr Belloc Objects (C. A. Watts).
1927   *Meanwhile* (Benn).
            Democracy under Revision (Hogarth Press).
            The Short Stories of H. G. Wells (Benn).
1928   *The Way the World Is Going* (Benn).
            The Open Conspiracy (Gollancz).
            The Book of Catherine Wells (Chatto and Windus).
            Mr Blettsworthy on Rampole Island (Benn).
1929   *The King Who Was a King* (Benn).
            The Common Sense of World Peace (Hogarth Press).
            The Adventures of Tommy (Harrap).
1930   *The Autocracy of Mr Parham* (Heinemann).
            The Science of Life, with Julian Huxley and G. P. Wells (Amalgamated Press).
            'The Problem of the Troublesome Collaborator' (privately circulated).
            'Settlement of the Trouble Between Mr Thring and Mr Wells' (privately circulated).
1931   *What Are We To Do With Our Lives?* (Heinemann).
1932   *The Work, Wealth and Happiness of Mankind* (Heinemann).
            After Democracy (C. A. Watts).
            The Bulpington of Blup (Hutchinson).
1933   *The Shape of Things to Come* (Hutchinson).
1934   *Experiment in Autobiography* (Gollancz and Cresset Press).
            Stalin: Wells Talk, the Verbatim Record (New Statesman).
1935   *The New America: The New World* (Cresset Press).
            Things to Come (Cresset Press).
1936   *The Anatomy of Frustration* (Cresset Press).
            The Croquet Player (Chatto and Windus).
            The Idea of a World Encyclopaedia (Hogarth Press).
1937   *Star Begotten* (Chatto and Windus).
            Brynhild (Methuen).
            The Camford Visitation (Methuen).
1938   *The Brothers* (Chatto and Windus).
            World Brain (Methuen).
            Apropos of Dolores (Jonathan Cape).
1939   *The Holy Terror* (Michael Joseph).
            Travels of a Republican Radical in Search of Hot Water (Penguin).
            The Fate of Homo Sapiens (Secker and Warburg).

1940   *The New World Order* (Secker and Warburg).
        The Rights of Man (Penguin).
        Babes in the Darkling Wood (Secker and Warburg).
        The Common Sense of War and Peace (Penguin).
        All Aboard for Ararat (Secker and Warburg).
1941   *Guide to the New World* (Gollancz).
        You Can't Be Too Careful (Secker and Warburg).
1942   *The Outlook for Homo Sapiens* (Secker and Warburg).
        Science and the World-Mind (New Europe Publishing Co.).
        Phoenix (Secker and Warburg).
        The Conquest of Time (C. A. Watts).
        *A Thesis on the Quality of Illusion in the Continuity of the
        Individual Life in the Higher Metazoa, with Particular
        Reference to the Species Homo Sapiens* (privately printed).
1943   *Crux Ansata* (Penguin).
1944   *'42 to '44* (Secker and Warburg).
1945   *The Happy Turning* (Heinemann).
        Mind at the End of its Tether (Heinemann).
1957   *The Desert Daisy*, written 1878–80, ed. G. N. Ray (Beta
        Phi Mu, Urbana, Illinois).
1969   *The Wealth of Mr Waddy*, written 1898–9, ed. H. Wilson
        (Southern Illinois University Press).
1975   *Early Writings in Science and Science Fiction by H. G. Wells,*
        ed. R. Philmus and D. Y. Hughes (University of
        California Press).

B. BIOGRAPHICAL AND CRITICAL MATERIAL

Place of publication is London unless otherwise stated.

Armytage, W. H. G., *Sir Richard Gregory* (Macmillan, 1957).
Bennett, A., *Journals* (Penguin, 1954).
Brome, V., *H. G. Wells: A Biography* (Longmans, 1951).
——, *Six Studies in Quarrelling* (Cresset Press, 1958).
Chaplin, C., *My Autobiography* (Bodley Head, 1964).
Dickson, L., *H. G. Wells: His Turbulent Life and Times* (Macmillan,
    1969).
Doughty, F. H., *H. G. Wells: Educationist* (Jonathan Cape, 1926).
Edel, L., and Ray, G. N. (eds), *Henry James and H. G. Wells: A
    Record of their Friendship, their Debate on the Art of Fiction, and their
    Quarrel* (Rupert Hart-Davis, 1958).

Ford, F. M., *Mightier than the Sword* (Allen and Unwin, 1938).

Gettman, R. A. (ed.), *George Gissing and H. G. Wells* (Urbana, University of Illinois Press, 1961).

Huxley, J. S., *Memories I* (Allen and Unwin, 1970).

Keun, O., 'H. G. Wells—the Player', *Time and Tide*, XV (13, 20 and 27 Oct 1934), pp. 1249–51; 1307–9; 1346–8.

Korg, J., *George Gissing* (Methuen, 1965).

Mackenzie, N. and J., *The Time Traveller: The Life of H. G. Wells* (Weidenfeld and Nicolson, 1973).

Meyer, M. M., *H. G. Wells and his Family* (International Publishing Co., 1956).

Nowell-Smith, S. (ed.), *Letters to Macmillan* (Macmillan, 1967).

Orwell, G., 'Wells, Hitler and the World State', in S. Orwell and I. Angus (eds), *Collected Essays, Journalism and Letters of George Orwell* (Secker and Warburg, 1968).

Owen, W., *Collected Letters*, ed. H. Owen and J. Bell (Oxford University Press, 1967).

Parrinder, P. (ed.), *H. G. Wells: The Critical Heritage* (Routledge and Kegan Paul, 1972).

Raknem, I., *H. G. Wells and his Critics* (Allen and Unwin, 1962).

Ray, G. N. (ed.), *H. G. Wells and Rebecca West* (Macmillan, 1974).

Richardson, D., *Pilgrimage* (Dent, 1938).

Roberts, M., *The Private Life of Henry Maitland* (Eveleigh Nash, 1912).

Webb, B., *Diaries 1912–1932*, ed. M. Cole, 2 vols (Longmans, 1952, 1956).

——, *Our Partnership* (Longmans, 1948).

West, G., *H. G. Wells: A Sketch for a Portrait* (Howe, 1930).

Wilson, H. (ed.), *Arnold Bennett and H. G. Wells* (Rupert Hart-Davis, 1960)

Index

823.912   Kemp, Peter
K32h   H.G. WELLS AND THE
1982   CULMINATING APE

MAR 5 88   1459

823.912
K32h
1982

DEMCO

Library
Western Wyoming Community College